Milton, the Bible,
and Misogyny

Milton, the Bible, and Misogyny

by Philip J. Gallagher

Edited by Eugene R. Cunnar
and Gail L. Mortimer

University of Missouri Press
Columbia and London

Library of Congress Cataloging-in-Publication Data

Gallagher, Philip J., d. 1987
   Milton, the Bible, and misogyny / by Philip J. Gallagher ; edited
by Eugene R. Cunnar and Gail L. Mortimer.
      p.   cm.
   Includes bibliographical references.
   ISBN 0–8262–0735–9 (alk. paper)
   1. Milton, John, 1608–1674—Religion. 2. Milton, John, 1608–1674—
Political and social views. 3. Christian poetry, English—History
and criticism. 4. Epic poetry, English—History and criticism.
5. Misogyny in literature. 6. Women in literature. 7. Bible in
literature. I. Cunnar, Eugene R. II. Mortimer, Gail L. (Gail
Linda), 1943–. III. Title.
PR3592.R4G35   1990
821′.4—dc20   90–10702
                                                                    CIP

Designer: Liz Fett
Typesetter: Connell-Zeko Type & Graphics
Printer: Thomson-Shore, Inc.
Binder: Thomson-Shore, Inc.
Type face: Palatino

Dedicated with love
to *Noreen, Adam, Nathaniel,*
Catherine, and *Jonathan*
—sine qua non.

Contents

Editors' Preface

Philip Gallagher died on July 1, 1987, as the tragic result of a road accident. Recipient of the Distinguished Achievement Award for Teaching Excellence at the University of Texas at El Paso and of the Milton Society's James Holly Hanford Award for the most distinguished article on Milton in 1980, Phil was widely respected for his precise and insightful reading of literary texts. He had a special interest in and talent for close syntactic readings of texts that included an attempt to recreate as closely as possible the author's perception of his sources and of his own artistic endeavor. The present book, completed a few months before his death, is an especially vivid expression of Phil's concern with the precision of our encounters with literary texts.

This study is based upon the idea that John Milton, far from accepting the concept of biblical inerrancy, had devoted much attention—particularly in *Paradise Lost*—to reconciling biblical discrepancies and working out his own rational theology. In the course of his work, Phil concluded that Milton has been wrongly assumed to be perpetuating the biblically derived misogyny that has characterized interpretations of Eve and that his careful recasting of the stories of the creation and fall constitutes, in fact, a defense of Eve. The present book develops this argument through scrupulous attention to the texts themselves. Phil's plan had been to publish this, his main argument, and in subsequent work to explore and elaborate upon some of its historical contexts. In part, he planned to do this in a later book focusing on the Promethean myth in Milton and other literary texts.

Because Phil's writing of this book was complete, our tasks as editors have been relatively minor ones. We have made a few corrections and implemented changes required by the publication process, we have followed the advice and suggestions of the manuscript's readers where we believed Phil would have found them congenial and beneficial, and we have attempted in all our decisions to retain the special verve and unique style of Phil's writing. This book embodies the meticulous reading, attention to nuance, and zeal for understanding that were characteristic of all of his scholarship, his teaching, and his writing.

Phil's sense of appreciation of his literary and critical forebears was profound. We are unable to express its true scope and depth as he would have done had he had the opportunity to do so, apart from hinting at the contributions of such scholars as John James Teunissen, about whom he wrote in one of his articles, "[He] taught me much of what I know about Milton." His gratitude for the support of William Kerrigan, Stanley Fish, Robert West, Arthur Kinney, Georgia Christopher, and Joseph Wittreich was deep and of long standing, and we know there are numerous others in the community of Milton scholars—we simply don't know their names.

Our own work has been aided by a number of individuals who offered time, information, and assistance as we proceeded with final work on the book. Among them, three helped in especially notable ways: Sandra Blystone, who worked with Phil as his research assistant, was invaluable in helping us locate materials and information in his papers. Phyllis Strauss worked energetically and carefully in retyping needed portions of the manuscript. And we have benefited from the sound advice and practical support of Larry Johnson, who has helped us resolve various snags—complicated diskette conversions, and the like—that had to be dealt with in bringing the book to this worthwhile conclusion. To the editors and readers at the University of Missouri Press, we offer our thanks, as well, for helping to insure the excellence of this endeavor.

Milton, the Bible,
and Misogyny

Introduction

Ye shall not add unto the word which I commanded you, neither shall ye diminish *ought* from it, that ye may keep the commandments of the LORD your God which I command you.

—*Deuteronomy 4:2*

Christ hath pronounc't that no tittle of his word shall fall to the ground, and if one jot be alterable it is as possible that all should perish.

—*Of Prelatical Episcopacy*

. . . the external scripture, particularly the New Testament, has often been liable to corruption and is, in fact, corrupt.

—*Christian Doctrine*

Shortly before the Restoration, Milton wrote, apropos of the translation of the Bible into various vernacular languages, "Therefor are the Scriptures translated into every vulgar tongue, as being held in main matters of belief and salvation, plane and easie to the poorest."[1] The author of *Paradise Lost* and *Samson Agonistes,* however, knew also that the plain and perspicuous in all things needful to salvation may not be self-evident in all things: what is dark in God's Word must be illumined, as witness (for example) the tortuous process by which Milton's Adam comes to divine the import of the protevangelium (Gen. 3:14–15).[2] Adam's exegetical struggle is for Milton paradigmatic of fallen man's relationship to Holy Writ: biblical hermeneutics is a difficult and tricky business, replete with pits into which lame faith, leading understanding blind, is all too likely to fall. Nevertheless, in his major poetry Milton plunges unhesitatingly into the arena of biblical commentary, anticipating many of the discoveries of modern exegesis— and this, necessarily, without availing himself of the extraordinary

1. *Considerations touching the Likeliest Means to remove Hirelings out of the Church,* in *The Complete Prose Works of John Milton,* ed. Don M. Wolfe et al. (cited hereafter as *YP*), 7:303.

2. The process begins explicitly at *Paradise Lost* 10.1028–40 and continues throughout the remainder of the epic.

explanatory power of the documentary hypothesis.[3] Consistent with his intention to "justify the ways of God"[4] down to their last recorded syllable, the poet habitually clarifies vexing scriptural passages, especially from Genesis 1–3, I Timothy 2:11–15, and Judges 13–16. In the process he often divagates from what appear to be more or less self-evident biblical implications, seeking always to accommodate the details of the received narrative to a pious interpretation. Moreover, as Irene Samuel has observed, and as I shall be attempting to demonstrate, "the direction of Milton's [biblical] nonconformities was never toward greater mystery, greater miracle, but rather always toward greater rationality, greater availability as a guide in living."[5]

The following chapters essay detailed exegesis of the most powerful of Milton's scriptural nonconformities. I take it as axiomatic that the poet did not endorse the conservative view of biblical inerrancy expressed in the Westminster Confession of Faith I, viii, namely, that "the Old Testament in Hebrew . . . and the New Testament in Greek . . . being immediately inspired by God, [are] by his singular care and providence kept pure in all ages."[6] In the *Christian Doctrine* Milton argues that "the external scripture, particularly the New Testament, has often been liable to corruption and is, in fact, corrupt. This has come about because it has been committed to the care of various untrustworthy authorities, has been collected together from an assortment of divergent manuscripts, and has survived in a medley of transcripts and editions." Although Milton is much more circumspect with respect to the status of the Old Testament, believing that "the law of Moses" has been preserved "uncorrupted" due to the assiduous "care of its pledged protectors,"[7] he honors this distinction more in the breach than in the observance in *Paradise Lost* and *Samson Agonistes:* the poet in him found the texts of Genesis and Judges no less imperfect than the New Testament deutero-Pauline First Epistle to Timothy. If God "Left" "the truth" untainted "in those written Records pure," their verbal traces are nonetheless most emphatically "not but by the Spirit understood" (*PL* 12.511–14), a libertarian hermeneutic that justifies, for Milton, an extreme latitudinarianism with respect to interpreting both Testaments.

3. According to the documentary hypothesis, to some form of which most modern biblical scholars subscribe, the Pentateuch comprises four or more disparate sources woven together into a more or less organic whole by a final redactor or redactors. Among many excellent accounts, the work of E. A. Speiser is brief, lucid, and accessible to the nonspecialist; see his *Genesis: Introduction, Translation, and Notes*, xx-lii.

4. *Paradise Lost* 1.26, in *John Milton: Complete Poems and Major Prose*, ed. Merritt Y. Hughes. This edition is cited throughout the Introduction.

5. "The Regaining of Paradise," 116.

6. Cited in A. A. Hodge, *A Commentary on the Confession of Faith*, 64.

7. *YP* 6:587–88.

The operational ramifications of Milton's conviction that "the Spirit which is given to us is a more certain guide than scripture" itself have been analyzed in principle by Mary Ann Radzinowicz, and I will not pause to repeat her conclusions. Nor will I attempt to adjudicate the contradiction between Radzinowicz's modest assertion that for Milton the "progressive discernment of the truth does not imply that human beings may add to the meaning of Scripture but simply that they may progressively discover the truths always latent in the text" and William Kerrigan's more radical opinion that the author of *Paradise Lost*, "writing with prophetic inspiration higher than 'those Hebrews of old,' . . . assumes divine authority for every word, every event in the epic that does not appear in Scripture."[8] Although I incline to agree with Kerrigan, his thesis cannot be proven; nor is it essential, given the sort of analysis I envision, to believe that Milton was (or thought he was) divinely commissioned to "add to the meaning of Scripture." My position is that he in fact does so, with or without supernal authorization. This poet was "Smit" not only "with the love of sacred Song" (*PL* 3.29), but also with an unshakable zeal to rationalize the perplexing discontinuities of the received biblical text. Whether "prophetic" or not, his "song fills in the paratactic transitions" of Holy Writ with circumstantial hypotaxes, "representing the conceptual logic of events missing" or confusedly represented in the inspired Word of God.[9] Invoking the "Heav'nly Muse" who "didst inspire / That Shepherd, who first taught . . . / . . . how the Heav'ns and Earth / Rose out of *Chaos*" (1.6–10), Milton declares his intention to continue— and perhaps to surpass—the Mosaic tradition itself. He will provide detailed elaborations of events (such as the rebellion of Lucifer) only hinted at in the Bible; and not seldom he will alter obscure, elliptical, and especially misogynistic scriptural passages almost beyond recognition, effecting massive metamorphoses for theodicy's sake.

The bulk of this book is concerned with Milton's radical transformation of his sources rather than with the sometimes "weak" biblical allusiveness of *Paradise Lost,* though of course both his epics and his tragedy of regeneration are suffused root and branch with significant scriptural references. When, for example, Satan enjoins his fallen troops to "Awake, arise, or be for ever fall'n" (1.330), he is inadvertently echoing Ephesians 5:14 ("Awake, O sleeper, and arise from the dead, and Christ shall give you light") and Revelation 20:10 ("the devil . . . was thrown into the lake of fire and sulphur . . . and . . . will be tormented day and night for ever and ever"). Milton's allusions are

8. *YP* 6:589; Radzinowicz, *Toward "Samson Agonistes": The Growth of Milton's Mind,* 273–82; Kerrigan, *The Prophetic Milton,* 264.
9. Kerrigan, *Prophetic Milton,* 264.

here designed neither to clarify nor to transform the Bible but to suggest the absurdity of Satan's command: unlike those addressed by Saint Paul, whom the apostle enjoins to take heart because they live in hope of final resurrection, the damned angels will be "forever fallen" even *if* they resurrect themselves "from . . . slumber, on [their] fiery Couch" (1.377). Satan should have advised them to "Awake, arise, *and* be for ever fall'n,'" and that, rather than an attempt to clarify the meaning of the New Testament, is the point of Milton's references to Ephesians and Revelation.

Similarly, in another "weak" allusion Milton mentions "four main Streams" of Paradise at 4.233. He has in mind the rivers Pishon, Gihon, Tigris, and Euphrates inventoried at Genesis 2:10–14. But beyond merely confirming the Bible's geography with respect to these streams (and implying their quantitative symmetry with the four rivers of Hell [2.570–81]), Milton's reference seems devoid of exegetical import, as indeed he himself confirms by decreeing that the cartography of these Assyrian bodies of water "here [i.e., in *Paradise Lost*] needs no account" (4.235). He means either that Genesis 2:10–14 is so plain and perspicuous as to require no further commentary, or (more likely) that the varied meanderings of the four rivers are irrelevant to the prelapsarian concerns of Book 4.

More arresting exegetically are allusions whose biblical resonances serve primarily to clarify the eschatology of one or another creature in *Paradise Lost*, but whose aftershocks also imply at least modest adjustment of the text of Scripture. To characterize the fallen angel Belial, who surfaces reductively at II Corinthians 6:15 ("What accord has Christ with Belial?") as an abstract noun personifying moral iniquity, Milton mobilizes a startling range of apposite Old Testament references. He attributes the impiety and fornication of the sons of the priest Eli (they "fill'd / With lust and violence the house of God" [*PL* 1.495–96 = I Samuel 2:12–25]) to the seductive suggestions of this devil: Eli's children are indeed more "the Sons / Of *Belial*" (501–2) than of their biological father.[10] So are (Milton insists) the abusers of the ancient code of hospitality at Genesis 19:1–11 and Judges 19:16–30. The former passage describes the attempted homosexual rape of two angelic guests at the home of Lot, a sojourner in Canaanite Sodom (Genesis 19:9). To prevent this outrage the desperate host offers to substitute his "two daughters who have not known man; let me bring them out to you, and do to them as you please; only do nothing to these men, for they have come under the shelter of my roof" (19:8). This bizarre vignette is repeated in more detail at Judges

10. Throughout this study I use the = sign to indicate parallels between biblical texts and Milton's treatment of those texts in his poetry.

19, where a Levite returning with his concubine to his home in Ephraim is offered protective custody for the night (in the Israelite town of Gibeah) at the home of an aged fellow-countryman sojourning there (19:16). Host and guests alike are subsequently accosted by lustful Benjaminites (within whose jurisdiction Gibeah lies) who, like their Sodomite forebears, wish to "know" the Levite guest sexually (22–23). The harried host proposes to substitute as victims his own "virgin daughter" and his guest's "concubine" (24) in order to protect his Levite guest. In the event, the concubine alone is ravaged and murdered by these insolent Israelites (25–28), a crime the more horrible because perpetrated not by pagan Canaanites but by confederates from one of the twelve tribes.

Milton recapitulates these two biblical pericopes in a brilliant three-line epitome deployed to give persuasive heft and a cult history to Belial. Do you require proof that this devil is more than a poetic fiction, Milton implicitly asks? Although Genesis and Judges do not say so, the outrages against consensual heterosexuality and the oriental code of hospitality recorded in Genesis and Judges comprise a depth of depravity explicable only as the work of Belial himself:

> Witness the streets of *Sodom,* and that night
> In *Gibeah,* when the hospitable door
> Expos'd a Matron to avoid worse rape.
> (1.503–5)

These three verses from *Paradise Lost* arrest, immortalize, and rationalize a nightmarish biblical world. The poet can dispose of Sodom in a mere half-line, for since the crime against Lot's angel-guests is (or will be) a twice-told tale, the details of this abortive rape can be inferred retrospectively from the mnemonic suggestiveness of Milton's more leisurely exfoliation of its analogue at Judges 19. Focusing on Gibeah, the bard distills the ethical core of the Benjaminite transgression from its surrounding circumstances. Under the inept leadership of its judges, Israelite life has so degenerated that one must evaluate rape hierarchically (as, say, Dante might) as comprising simple and compound variants. This casuistical distinction requires the Levite's host to enact a true Solomonic choice, sacrificing his guest's "Matron" (not his biblical "concubine") to heterosexual violation and death "to avoid worse [i.e., homosexual] rape." Milton is sensitive both to the agonizing moral dilemma posited in Judges and to the overarching biblical concern to observe the protocols of hospitality whatever the costs. Thus he insists (in a brilliant metonymic substitution) that not the Ephraimite sojourner (who is blameless under the circumstances) but "the *hospitable* door" of his house "Expos'd" the victim of Benjaminite lust to her hideous fate.

Milton's commentary on Genesis 19 and Judges 19 thus corroborates two biblical pericopes in what is for the most part a work of straightforward (if compressed) recapitulation. To this extent it comprises a "weak" allusion. But his strategy also hints at the sort of transcendent metamorphoses that will be the major focus of the present inquiry. By affiliating the crimes of Sodom and Gibeah with the fallen angel Belial, Milton demystifies the biblical narratives of whatever residue of unmotivated innate human depravity occasions them. Such enormities as Genesis and Judges depict make more sense if they can be attributed to the industrious viciousness of a lustful demon. And as I shall argue, "making sense" of the Bible is what *Paradise Lost* and *Samson Agonistes* are all about.

There is nothing eccentric about the plan of this book: I discuss creation, fall, and regeneration consecutively in three chapters. The argument was not *composed* seriatim, however. I began work on Chapter Three in 1978, when it occurred to me that the Woman of Timna in *Samson Agonistes* occupies a prevenient regenerative slot in that tragedy analogous to the role of Raphael in *Paradise Lost.* This kernel insight prompted me to explore in its entirety Milton's recasting of the biblical Samson saga and to investigate the Hesiodic, Homeric, and Virgilian prototypes of the celestial descent of Raphael. The bulk of the chapter was written during the summer of 1980, while I was in residence at Yeshiva University as a National Endowment for the Humanities fellow studying Hellenistic Judaism under the expert tutelage of Louis Feldman. The essay was subsequently revised at the instancing of Lawrence J. Johnson, Mary Ann Radzinowicz, Irene Samuel, James Simmonds, Camille Slights, Robert West, and Joseph Wittreich. It appeared in essentially its present form in *Milton Studies* 18 (1983): 255–94.

Chapter One came second. It was occasioned by a special session on Milton and the Bible at the 1980 Modern Language Association Convention. During that session, I discovered that the recovery of Milton's intentions in recasting these ancient tales of origination could be facilitated by dispensing with the so-called Genesis tradition and by instead immediately juxtaposing the relevant biblical data with their reincarnations in *Paradise Lost.* The eventual outcome was a lengthy study in comparative literature revised under the wise guidance of James Simmonds and published, in essentially its present form, in *Milton Studies* 20 (1984): 163–204.

Chapter Two was written last. I had for years thought Book 9 of *Paradise Lost* to be the most enigmatic portion of the epic and the least patient of rational exegesis. Moreover, what could I hope to add to the exemplary findings of such pioneers in the field as Arnold Williams,

J. M. Evans, Joseph Summers, and (most recently) Diane McColley? Then, in late 1983, Jean Gagen sought to prove, in a *Milton Quarterly* essay,[11] that Milton's Adam is unaware, prior to his own fall, that Satan is the foe who has somehow defrauded Eve into believing that the forbidden fruit can make her godlike. Gagen's thesis struck me as challenging, but requiring a rebuttal that soon issued in an extended meditation on the tropes of deception in *Paradise Lost*. I came to believe that the seminal commentary on Genesis 3 at I Timothy 2:11–15 is the generative axis about which Milton's epic spins, and that the falls of both angels and men are structured so as to repudiate the institutional misogyny implied in Genesis and certified in the New Testament under the auspices of the deceived/undeceived dichotomy postulated by deutero-Paul.

Chapter Two is the centerpiece—I hope the vital centerpiece—of my argument. Unlike Chapters One and Three, it not infrequently relies on the corroboratory potential of medieval and Renaissance scriptural commentary. My goal, however, is less to elucidate the permutations of an exegetical tradition than to dragoon those commentators—including Augustine, Aquinas, Calvin, and Thomas Browne, among others—whose misogyny Milton seeks so assiduously to extirpate from his text. It is a strange irony that, as our culture evolves unremittingly toward male-female equality, the author of *Paradise Lost* should continue to be regarded as misogynist. The evidence mobilized throughout this book suggests—I hope beyond reasonable doubt—that, far from being an advocate of the subjection of woman, this good and great poet set out with Abdelian zeal to divest both the Bible and the Judaeo-Christian tradition of virtually *every* vestige of antifeminism. Against the preponderating inclinations of the exegetical tradition, Milton demonstrates, thanks to certain pivotal casuistical niceties, that Eve's sinless fall into deception renders her far less culpable for original sin than her undeceived husband. His decidedly majority opinion is the foundation of Milton's profoundly feminist justification of the ways of God to women.

I have been anticipated in part by J. M. Evans, Barbara Lewalski, Diane McColley, Mary Ann Radzinowicz, Irene Samuel, Joseph Summers, and Joan Webber.[12] Evans and McColley will recognize my silent indebtedness to the exegetical data they have compiled. I remain convinced, however, that even Milton's most passionate apologists have failed to grasp how relentlessly he attacks the misogynistic tradi-

11. "Adam, the Serpent, and Satan: Recognition and Restoration."
12. [Editors' Note: Professor Gallagher would want to note that he had read Joseph Wittreich's *Feminist Milton* in manuscript before its publication and that Professor Wittreich had read the manuscript of this book, as well.]

tion. Weighted down by the very massiveness of the materials they mobilize, or by their zeal to rehabilitate Eve, the poet's friendliest critics have unwittingly perpetuated the very misogyny they would exorcise—usually by imposing hermeneutic and ethical imperatives on prelapsarian woman that no unfallen creature, angelic or human, could hope to enact. There is no need, however, to overstate one's defense of Milton, whose magnanimity transcends cultural prejudices; the blind bard is a noble exponent of human equality, and I hope that my efforts will contribute, however partially, to the progressive demonstration that he is among the most powerful allies the modern feminist movement can hope to find in Western culture. The demonstration begins where it must—in the beginning in Eden Garden before the fall, the biblical narrative of which Milton boldly presumes to rewrite in the service of the zealously rational theodicy of *Paradise Lost*.

1

Creation
Genesis and *Paradise Lost*

And for all this, nature is never spent;
   There lives the dearest freshness deep down things;
And though the last lights off the black West went
   Oh, morning, at the brown brink eastward, springs—
Because the Holy Ghost over the bent
   World broods with warm breast and with ah! bright wings.
           —G. M. Hopkins, "God's Grandeur"

I. GENESIS 1:1–5 AND 14–19

"In the beginning," the King James Bible solemnly begins, "God created the heaven and the earth."[1] This translation is, however, problematical in at least three ways: (1) it implies creation *ex nihilo,* a common but illogical interpretation (for nothing comes from nothing—nothing ever could) nowhere supported by the Hebrew Scriptures; (2) it involves the Creator in apparently shoddy workmanship, for what ensued after verse 1 was chaos (1:2a), which consequently demanded his immediate attention; and (3) it implies that the original creative gesture (1:1) was anomalous, the God of Genesis 1 having created everything *except* the heaven and the earth by the power of the Word ("Let there be light," 1:3, "Let there be a firmament," 1:6, "Let the waters," 1:9, and so forth). These difficulties are nowhere present in *Paradise Lost,* however. Milton eliminates the first two by relying on the doctrine of creation *ex Deo.*[2] Contrary to the Authorized Version, the poet believes that Moses taught the ancient Jews "In the Beginning

---

1. Genesis 1:1. I cite the Authorized Version throughout Chapter One. Although Milton read Hebrew and Greek and had access to other versions, *Paradise Lost* 7 and 8 echo chiefly the A.V. See Harris F. Fletcher, *The Use of the Bible in Milton's Prose;* and James H. Sims, *The Bible in Milton's Epics.*
2. See *The Christian Doctrine* in *YP* 7:303. All citations of Milton's poetry in Chapter One will be to *John Milton: Complete Poems and Major Prose,* ed. Merritt Y. Hughes, whose interpretations I address.

how the Heav'ns and Earth / Rose," not out of nothing, but "out of *Chaos*" (*PL* 1.9–10), a portion of whose contents "th' Almighty Maker . . . ordain[s] / His dark materials" (2.915–16) to shape into the visible universe.[3] Unfallen Adam seems intuitively to recognize this state of affairs and to dismiss *ex nihilo* creation as unthinkable. His curiosity aroused perhaps by a reminiscence of Raphael's allusion to the "one first matter all" (5.472) whence all nature proceeds,[4] Adam wants to know "When" our world began, "whereof created, [and] for what cause" (7.64). He thus affirms in a single stroke his belief in a world made in time, of preexistent matter, and teleologically. Whence did the matter of Chaos derive? From God, clearly, *ex Deo* (7.168–73). Who differentiated part of the chaotic mass "Of neither Sea, nor Shore, nor Air, nor Fire" (2.912) into the elemental heaven and earth of Genesis? Although Satan assigns such creative efficacy to Chaos itself ("*Space* may produce new Worlds," he heretically alleges [1.650; emphasis mine]), Milton attributes the world's beginning to the Word of God, which he hypostatizes, on the analogy of John 1:1–18, as the instrumental cause: "As by his Word the mighty Father made / All things" (5.836–37).

So committed is Milton to a logos-cosmogony that, boldly extrapolating from the opening chapters of Genesis and John, he traces to an originative verbal gesture even Hell itself, "which God by curse / Created evil" (2.622–23).[5] Consequently, it should come as no surprise that, even before Raphael has illuminated their darkness, unfallen Adam and Eve can intuit that God "out of Darkness *call'd up* Light" (5.179; emphasis mine); nor should the reader be perplexed to find Milton eliminating the anomaly of Genesis 1:1 by asserting that *all* God's creative acts, including the making of heaven and earth, are effected by the spoken Word: "ride forth," the Father tells the Son, "and bid the Deep / Within appointed bounds be Heav'n and Earth" (7.166–67). According to the Archangel Uriel, God's Word became flesh

> when at his Word the formless Mass,
> This world's material mould, came to a heap:
> Confusion heard his voice, and wild uproar
> Stood rul'd, stood vast infinitude confin'd.
> (3.708–11)

Rather than being *ex nihilo*, then, creation in *Paradise Lost* entails the

3. Milton writes "the Heav'ns" for Genesis's "the heaven" to distinguish the visible sky and its inhabitants from the Empyrean, the home of God that the poet elsewhere identifies as the "Heav'n of Heavens" (*PL* 3.390).
4. Echoing the concept of primary matter elaborated by Aristotle, *Physics* 1, esp. chaps. 5–7.
5. The same point is implied at the end of the War in Heaven when Raphael remarks that "strict Fate had cast too deep / [Hell's] dark foundations" (*PL* 7.173).

verbal imposition of form upon an already-present material matrix. The making of heaven and earth proceeds in three well-defined stages, two of which are divine speech acts. Before riding into Chaos, Messiah, by the power of his Word, prepares the region to receive him: "Silence, ye troubl'd waves, and thou Deep, peace, / Said then th' Omnific Word, your discord end" (7.216–17). Whereupon he enters the abyss, takes in hand compasses that Milton found in Proverbs 8:27, and with them circumscribes a spherical universe (218–29), saying the while: "Thus far extend, thus far thy bounds, / This be thy just Circumference, O World" (230–31). Where, therefore, the Authorized Version can assert simply (but problematically) *that* "God created the heaven and the earth," Milton can investigate "*how* this World / Of Heav'n and Earth conspicuous first began" (62–63; emphasis mine). Raphael, aided by the witness of the eye, can characterize the *how* and conclude definitively, "Thus God the Heav'n created, thus the Earth" (232). So much is required in *Paradise Lost* to make Genesis 1:1 safe for Miltonic rational orthodoxy.

Next, whereas Genesis 1:2a ("And the earth was without form, and void; and darkness *was* upon the face of the deep") appears to describe a newfound chaotic situation brought into being *ex nihilo,* for Milton the verse merely records the consequence of God's bounding what was previously chaotically unbounded (233–34); and whereas Genesis continues, "And the Spirit of God moved upon the face of the waters" (2b), Milton greatly expands this cryptic half-verse to assure the purposefulness of the Deity's so moving and to render explicitly the biblical implication that God is hovering over the new-made world much as a bird would brood over an egg.[6] Although the opening invocation of *Paradise Lost,* like Genesis, makes it appear that God is impregnating the Chaos that has resulted from the supposedly creative activity of 1:1 ("with mighty wings outspread" the Spirit "Dove-like satst brooding on the vast Abyss / And mad'st it pregnant" [1.20–22]), Raphael's more extended narrative confirms that we are involved rather with the further differentiating of an already-made heaven and earth:

> but on the wat'ry calm
> His brooding wings the Spirit of God outspread,
> And vital virtue infus'd, and vital warmth
> Throughout the fluid Mass, but downward purg'd
> The black tartareous cold Infernal dregs
> Adverse to life; then founded, then conglob'd

---

6. In the *Christian Doctrine* Milton translates as *incubabat* (brooded) the Hebrew word that the King James Version translates as *moved* (perhaps on the precedent of Jerome's Vulgate, which has *ferebatur*). See *YP* 6:304.

> Like things to like, the rest to several place
> Disparted, and between spun out the Air,
> And Earth self-balanc't on her Centre hung.
> (7.234b–42)

These lines have no warrant in Genesis, though the notion of an earth self-suspended centrally within the circumference of the world's great circle derives from Job 26:7, where it is said that God "hangeth the earth upon nothing." If we may regard Uriel's brief account as an anticipatory gloss upon Raphael's, Milton is probably describing the creation of the five elements and the separation of the four earthly from one another and from their heavenly counterpart:

> Swift to thir several Quarters hasted then
> The cumbrous Elements, Earth, Flood, Air, Fire,
> And this Ethereal quintessence of Heav'n
> Flew upward.
> (3.714–17a)[7]

The "Ethereal quintessence" or fifth element to which Uriel refers is the *aether,* which emerges from Chaos to form the indestructible substance of the supralunary world, most notably the sun. It therefore implies the creation of light, which returns Milton at last to Genesis 1:3 ("And God said, Let there be light: and there was light"), which he paraphrases as follows:

> Let there be Light, said God, and forthwith Light
> Ethereal, first of things, quintessence pure
> Sprung from the Deep, and from her Native East
> To journey through the airy gloom began.
> (7.243–46)[8]

The poet's nonbiblical reference to the birthplace of light explains why, between verses 2 and 3 of Genesis 1, he describes the differentiating of

7. According to Uriel, however, the separation of elements occurred after God created light; Raphael reverses Uriel's chronology.

8. In *Paradise Lost* many phenomena lay claim to being the "first of things": the Greek god "*Titan*" is said to be "Heav'n's first born" (1.510), a lie exploded when Milton, confirming Raphael's opinion, invokes "holy Light, offspring of Heav'n first-born" (3.1). But elsewhere Milton calls Night the "eldest of things" (2.962), and Adam and Eve speak of "Air, and ye Elements the eldest birth / Of Nature's Womb" (5.180–81). Milton's Samson, on the other hand (who has read Genesis), believes with Raphael that "Light is the prime work of God," his "prime decree" (*SA* 70–85). I am not sure how to adjudicate these apparently conflicting claims. According to the translation of Genesis 1:1–3 favored by Speiser (*Genesis,* 3, 11–13), the Bible indeed declares light to be the first creature produced in the six days' work; but Milton, as we have already seen, describes heaven and earth as antedating light. Perhaps he regarded the unlighted universe as a container and light as the first fully differentiated "thing" called forth from the "Matter unform'd and void" (7.233) of the just-circumscribed world.

the world's chaotic contents into the several elements that hasten to occupy their proper places therein: Chaos being a region "Without dimension, where length, breadth, and highth, / And time and place are lost" (2.893–94), God's aboriginal circumscription of part of the region into a "hollow Universal Orb" (7.257), and his separation of earth, water, air, fire, and the *aether* from one another, comprise the creation of dimensionality and place, enabling Milton to posit "her Native East" as light's point of origin. Moreover he importantly describes light as *moving* from its indigenous abode to traverse the "airy gloom" of the new world as a discrete parcel of radiance. This unbiblical detail effectively registers the creation of time, which Aristotle defines as the measure of motion according to the spatially prior and posterior.[9] Genesis merely assumes time's existence by mysteriously asserting that God somehow "divided the light from the darkness. And God called the light Day, and the Darkness he called Night" (1:4b–5a). Unlike the Bible, however, Milton can tell us *how* God separated these antipodes into temporal categories: "light from darkness *by the Hemisphere* [he] / Divided" (7.250–51; emphasis mine) into day and night—that is (on the analogy with the apparent diurnal movement of our sun across the firmament), by specifying the half of Milton's spherical world that moving light illuminates as it circumnavigates it. Consequently, whereas Genesis concludes simply *that* "the evening and morning were the first day" (1:5b), the poet of *Paradise Lost* can again aver that "*Thus* was the first Day Ev'n and Morn" (7.252; emphasis mine), by which he implies not only how God spent the first creating day, but also how he created day one itself.

At the same time Milton eliminates a final biblical crux issuing from the fact that in Genesis God creates light on day one (1:3) but the sun on the fourth day (1:14–19): this paradox is deftly resolved by having light sojourn "in a cloudy Tabernacle" (7.247–49) until, on day four, the "greater" portion God "Transplanted from her cloudy Shrine" into "the Sun's Orb," which hitherto was "unlightsome . . . , / Though of Ethereal Mould" (355–61).[10]

The reconciliation of this biblical crux concludes Raphael's elegant elaboration of Genesis 1:1–5 and 14–19. Eleven richly suggestive but problematic biblical verses have prompted from Milton a poetic recension including such spectacular modifications of the Authorized Version as creation *ex Deo*, a tripling of the *inquit* formula of Genesis 1:3, and a disquisition on how light could "as with a Mantle . . . invest / The rising world of waters dark and deep" "Before the Sun" existed

9. *Physics* 4.10–14, esp. chap. 11.
10. See Arnold Williams, *The Common Expositor: An Account of the Commentaries on Genesis, 1527–1633*, 52–53.

(3.8–11). As we shall now see, similar (but increasingly complex) hypotactic strategies are characteristic of Milton's retelling of the biblical narratives of creation.

II. GENESIS 1:11–13 AND 2:5–6; GENESIS 1:20–25A AND 2:19A

The two passages from *Paradise Lost* that I am about to discuss reconcile certain chronological inconsistencies between the creation accounts of Genesis 1 and 2.[11] Milton's treatment of Genesis 1:11–13 and 2:5–6 may be schematized as follows: Genesis 1:11–12a = *PL* 7.309b–28a; 2:5b = 331b–33a; 2:6 = 333b–34a; 2:5a = 334b–37a; 1:12b–13 = 337b–38. First, at 1:11–13 all vegetation is said to have been created on the third day—that is, fully three days prior to the making of man (1:26–28); at Genesis 2:4–9a, on the other hand, God forms Adam first and only then creates the plant kingdom, when there is a man to care for it. The biblical contradiction is explicable as such if one accepts the hypothesis of separate and independent composition for the narratives; but Milton, ignorant of the conclusions of biblical higher criticism, found it necessary to reconcile the two versions.[12] He accepts the formulation of Genesis 1:11–12a, which he repeats almost verbatim (with appropriate expansions) at 7.309b–28a: in both the Bible and in *Paradise Lost,* on day three "th' Earth / Put[s] forth the verdant Grass, Herb yielding Seed, / and Fruit Tree yielding Fruit" (309–11) in the sequence "grass . . . herb . . . tree" (1:11–12a). But whereas the scriptural version concludes with the formulaic utterance "God saw that *it was good.* And the evening and the morning were the third day" (1:12b–13), Milton, in the interest of harmonization, at this point interpolates into his narrative selected materials from Genesis 2:4–9a, which reads as follows in the Authorized Version (I have italicized those portions that Milton incorporates):

> [4] These are the generations of the heavens and of the earth when they were created, in the day that the Lord God made the earth and the heavens,
> [5a] *And every plant of the field before it was in the earth, and every herb of the field before it grew*:

11. I omit discussion of Milton's brief but fascinating elaboration of Genesis 1:6–8 (at *PL* 7.261–75). Kester Svendson has definitively analyzed the poet's transformation of the biblical firmament into the entire "expanse of liquid, pure, / Transparent, Elemental Air" that the Ptolemaic cosmology of *Paradise Lost* extends "In circuit to the uttermost convex / Of this great Round" (7.264–67). See *Milton and Science,* 60. I also omit Milton's recension of Genesis 1:9–10 (at *PL* 7.276–309): it is an entirely straightforward elaboration of the biblical verses that the poet found unproblematic.

12. The first creation account is thought to be a redaction edited by the priests of Jerusalem (and hence is referred to as the "P" version), while the second narrative is attributed to an entirely different source (identified as "J," after the tetragrammaton YHWH, vocalized as *Yaweh* or *Jahweh,* which "J" habitually uses to identify God).

[5b] *for the Lord God had not caused it to rain upon the earth, and there was not a man to till the ground.*
[6] *But there went up a mist from the earth, and watered the whole face of the ground.*
[7] And the Lord God formed man of the dust of the ground, and breathed into his nostrils the breath of life; and man became a living soul.
[8] And the Lord God planted a garden eastward in Eden; and there he put the man whom he had formed.
[9a] And out of the ground made the Lord God to grow every tree that is pleasant to the sight.

These details Milton repeats, omitting, however, verse 4 (which in context would imply that God created the heavens and the earth on day three), verses 7–8 (which would imply that God made man on the third day), and verse 9a (which would imply that the trees were formed after Adam):

> Earth now
> Seem'd like to Heav'n, a seat where Gods might dwell,
> Or wander with delight, and love to haunt
> Her sacred shades; [5b] though God had yet not rain'd
> Upon the Earth, and man to till the ground
> None was, [6] but from the Earth a dewy Mist
> Went up and water'd all the ground, [5a] and each
> Plant of the field, which ere it was in the Earth
> God made, and every Herb, before it grew
> On the green stem.
>
> (7.328b–37a)

Having relocated part of the *disjecta membra* of Genesis 2:4–9a immediately after his lengthy paraphrase of 1:11–12a, Milton now completes the transplantation by looping back, in conclusion, to the terminal formulaics of 1:12b–13: "God saw that it was good: / So Ev'n and Morn recorded the Third Day" (7.337–38). The net effect of his omissions (of 2:4, 7, 8, and 9a), interpolations (of 2:5–6 between 1:12a and 12b), and rearrangements (of 2:5–6 into the sequence 5b, 6, 5a) is to make chapter 2 conform to the normative chronology of chapter 1, a goal Milton pursues even to the point of substituting the concessive conjunction *though* (7.331) where King James utilizes the causative *for* (that is, *because*, 2:5b). This apparently minor adjustment is really a major instance of the poet accomplishing great things by small: for whereas Genesis 2 implies that the plants came *after* man *because* there was at first no farmer to till the ground, *Paradise Lost* insists—so determined is Milton to remake chapter 2 in the image of its predecessor—that the vegetation came *before* man *even though* no gardener was yet available.[13]

13. Merritt Hughes, in a note at line 331, repeats the relevant biblical verse but

Turning now to a second chronological inconsistency that Milton takes pains to eliminate, at Genesis 1:20–23 the "fowl *that* may fly above the earth" are said to be born from the sea on day five, and at 1:24–25a all the land animals—"cattle, and creeping thing[s], and beast[s] of the earth"—are said to be born autochthonously during the first portion of day six: both bird and beast therefore antedate man's creation, which occupies God during the second half of the sixth day. At Genesis 2:19a, on the other hand, the nonhuman sentient inhabitants of both air and land are described as earth-born creatures formed after Adam, not before him. Milton mediates these biblical discrepancies artfully and expeditiously, relying once again on a strategy of interpolation and omission. Milton's overall treatment of Genesis 1:20–25a and 2:19a may be summarized as follows: Genesis 1:20–23 = *PL* 7.387–448; 1:24 = 450b–56a; 2:19a = 456b–58; 1:25a = 456b–58; 1:25a = 459–92.

First Milton composes a greatly expanded version (7.387–448) of the three verses (1:20–23) that Genesis devotes to day five, confirming chapter 1's contentions about the aquatic origin of birds on that day. Milton next turns—as does the Bible—to the events of the sixth day. After repeating the autochthonous narrative of 1:24 ("Let the earth bring forth the living creature after his kind"), however, he deftly subjoins to it a similar passage from Genesis 2:19a: ("And out of the ground the Lord God formed every beast of the field, and every fowl of the air"), omitting, for the sake of consistency, the phrase "every fowl of the air" (for they have already been created from the sea on day five):

> [1:24] God said,
> Let th' Earth bring forth Soul living in her kind,
> Cattle and Creeping things, and Beast of the Earth,
> Each in their kind. The Earth obey'd, and straight
> Op'ning her fertile Womb teem'd at a Birth
> Innumerous living Creatures, perfet forms,
> Limb'd and full grown: [2:19a] out of the ground up rose
> As from his Lair the wild Beast where he wons
> In Forest wild, in Thicket, Brake, or Den.
>
> (7.450b–58)

By thus pulling verse 2:19a into the orbit of 1:24 (and deleting the problematical reference to birds), Milton disposes of the half-verse's chronological disproportions; having done so, he may now conclude his redaction of the first half of day six by attending to Genesis 1:25a.

---

omits the crucial word *for:* the misleading effect of his omission is to disguise Milton's taking issue with the logic of his source.

Actually the poet has already begun to do so, for lines 456b–58 echo the first part of 1:25a ("And God made the beast of the earth after his kind") as much as they do 2:19a. At lines 459–92, therefore, Milton incorporates the rest of verse 25a, completing, for chronological consistency's sake, another set of adjustments to the biblical text.[14] He is not yet quite done with verses 24–25, however, for three additional (and only partly chronological) difficulties remain in the Authorized Version's redaction of the creation of the land animals. As we shall see in the next section, reckoning with them required the poet to exercise his utmost art.

III. GENESIS 1:24–25 AND 3:1A

Anyone who has read Genesis 1–3 en bloc is struck with the arresting notice, at the outset of the third chapter, that "the serpent was more subtil than any beast of the field which the Lord God had made" (3:1a). But what sort of animal is this special creature? The Authorized Version implies that he is not a beast of the field (for were he, the translators would have written "the serpent was more subtil than any *other* beast of the field," a distinction not lost on the lynx-eyed editors of the Revised Standard Version).[15] Nor, obviously, is the animal fish or fowl or cattle or—as the curse on him at 3:14 so clearly implies—creeping thing. Not knowing the serpent's *differentia specifica* creates moreover a second difficulty: on which day was he created? Genesis 1 nowhere mentions the beast—not surprisingly, for its authors, as the documentary hypothesis amply demonstrates, themselves knew nothing of the animal's complicity in the tragic fall of man and so have no reason to take special note of him. Milton, however, could not construe the matter by referring to independent authorship of chapters 2 and 3; nor, given his homocentric bias, could he afford to ignore what the Bible ignores in his expansion of chapter 1. Instead he found it convenient to graft the serpent-lore of 3:1a onto his elaboration of 1:25a, a transplantation easier for Milton to accomplish than for me to analyze.

The following schematization of Milton's treatment of Genesis 1:24–25 and 3:1a will help make the details of my analysis clearer:

Genesis 1:24	=	*PL* 7.450b–56a ("Cattle," "Creeping things," and "Beast of the Earth")
1:25a	=	456b–59 (beasts of the earth)
	=	460 (cattle)

14. I have reserved lines 449–50a for discussion below in section VIII.
15. Thus they translate, "Now the serpent was more subtile than any other wild animal that the Lord God had made."

	=	461a (beast of the earth)
	=	461b–63a (cattle)
	=	463b–74 (beast of the earth)
	=	475–76a (creeping things—"Insect of Worm")
	=	476b–79 (insects)
	=	480–81a (worms)
	=	481b–84a (serpentine worms)
	=	484b–89a (ants)
	=	489b–92a (bees)
	=	492b–94a (insects and worms)
3:1a	=	494b–97a (the serpent)
1:25b	=	497b–98 (periphrastically)

To justify affiliating the two verses Milton must, to be consistent with the zoological categories of 1:25a, declare the serpent to be either beast, cattle, or creeping thing. He naturally chooses the first, by having Raphael "correct" (albeit all unwittingly) the stylistic "infelicity" of the Authorized Version: when the angel speaks of "The Serpent subtl'st Beast of all the field" (7.495), his substitution of the superlative ("subtl'st") for the Bible's comparative ("more subtle than") effectively includes the animal among the nonbovine noncreeping field dwellers.[16] Happily, moreover, the language of 3:1a ("beast of the field") closely resembles that of 1:25a ("beast of the earth"); this fortuitous circumstance makes it seem more natural for the poet to intertwine biblical verses that derive from otherwise quite alien contexts.

Nevertheless, a third problem remains: although it is appropriate, for the reasons just given, for Raphael to cite the serpent in his discussion of day six, the question remains, at what point ought he to do so? Genesis itself offers a likely solution, one implied in a stylistic eccentricity of 1:24–25a:

> And God said, Let the earth bring forth the living creature after his kind, *cattle*, and *creeping thing*, and *beast of the earth* after his kind: and it was so. And God made the *beast of the earth* after his kind, and *cattle* after their kind, and *every thing that creepeth upon the earth* after his kind.
> (Emphasis mine)

What strikes me about this passage is the way that verse 25a reverses 24b: thus the last sort of land animal whose existence God commands is the first to be made (though last in expression, the beast of the earth is first in execution). This fact is not lost on Milton: following the biblical paradigm with a care that borders on scrupulosity, he first

16. Raphael's correction is "unwitting" because the Bible does not exist from his point of view. The same is true at 9.560, where Eve knows the "Serpent" to be the "subtlest beast of all the field."

repeats the order of 1:24 ("Cattle and Creeping things, and Beast of the Earth" [7.452]) to articulate God's command that the earth bring forth such animals; then, in a more leisurely narrative of the parturitional process itself, Milton emulates the chiasmus of 1:25a, describing seriatim the birth of "the wild Beast" (457), "The Cattle" (460), and lastly "whatever creeps the ground" (475). One would therefore expect Raphael to mention the serpent early in his narrative of the land animals, by inserting Genesis 3:1a at lines 457ff., where other beasts of the field are dutifully itemized.

Nevertheless, the angel says nothing about the serpent at this juncture. Given that animal's contribution to the fall of man, the fact that Raphael's narrative exists for Adam's sake, and the further facts that in Genesis 1 last is best[17] and in Genesis 3 the serpent is the best (because the subtlest) nonhuman sentient creature—for all these reasons, it would be decidedly anticlimactic for the angel to discuss the beast in an antepenultimate position, but decidedly appropriate for Raphael to engage in comment on serpents at the very end of his lengthy expansion of 1:24–25a (7.450–92) as a last climactic concern. This, of course, is precisely what happens in *Paradise Lost*, and without any violation of the sequential imperatives of Genesis 1:25.[18] Consistent with that verse, at lines 456b–92 Raphael moves from wild beasts through cattle to creeping things, which he subdivides into "Insect or Worm" (476). To the two members of this third category he pays the closest attention: after briefly characterizing first the one (476–79), then the other (480–81), the angel distinguishes creeping worms according to size (481–84). He next gives equal time to insects, both those that creep—citing the provident ant (484–89)—and those that can also fly—citing the exemplary bee (489–92). Finally, Raphael summarily concludes his elaborate redaction of 1:24–25a by observing that "the rest [of whatever creeps the ground] are numberless" (492).

Now the significance of Raphael's taxonomic efforts resides in what he says of the larger creeping worms, for his language there is the middle term that enables him and Milton to achieve an effortless transition from creatures that creep to the most important noncreeping beast of the field—"the Serpent sly / Insinuating [that] wove with Gordian twine / His braided train" (4.347–49): "not all" worms, says Raphael, are

---

17. Milton recognizes this when he writes of the second half of day six, "There wanted yet the Master work, the end / Of all yet done" (7.505–6), where "the end" means "the last" but also "the purpose or object" of all previously created things.

18. In 7.387–448, describing the creation of sea beasts and fowl on the fifth day, Milton is similarly scrupulous in following the sequence given in Genesis 1:20–23.

> Minims of Nature; some of Serpent kind
> Wondrous in length and corpulence involv'd
> Thir Snaky folds, and added wings.
>
> (7.481–84)

The topic at hand is, I repeat, things that creep—just as Genesis 1:25a says it ought to be; but as is obvious, the angel's diction also reverberates with echoes of 3:1a and therefore suggests not only serpentine creeping worms but also beasts of the field in general and the serpent in particular. These echoes jog Raphael's memory—not that they remind him of Genesis 3:1a, which he has not read, but that they cause him to think of the serpent, whom he mentions ten lines later as a relevant afterthought arrived at by free association:

> nor unknown
> The Serpent subtl'st Beast of all the field,
> Of huge extent sometimes, with brazen Eyes
> And hairy Mane terrific.
>
> (494b–97a)

The context of Raphael's remarks—at the conclusion of his extended paraphrase of Genesis 1:25a—enables the angel simultaneously to imply (1) the snake's identity as a beast of the field, (2) his creation on the sixth day, and (3) his special stature as the last-created nonhuman animal. Thus, in a single stroke of considerable poetic compression, Milton disposes of the three difficulties of the Authorized Version's account of the land animals.

One additional problem remains, however—or rather, in the process of resolving the three difficulties in his received text, Milton introduces into *Paradise Lost* a fourth crux evidently absent from Holy Writ: he has Raphael append to his description of the serpent a disclaimer that the beast is terrifying and indeed the counterassertion that serpents are "to thee [that is, Adam] / Not noxious, but obedient at thy call" (497b–98). Now on the one hand the angel's point is well taken: for although both Milton's and the Bible's Adam know that man has "Dominion . . . / Over . . . / . . . every living thing that moves on the Earth" (532–34, echoing Genesis 1:26b and 28b); and although Milton's God assures Adam that *all* the animals will "pay thee fealty / With low subjection" (8.344–45); and although *no* "Beast . . . durst enter" (4.704) the "blissful Bower" (690) of our grandparents—"Such was thir awe of Man" (705)—still, Raphael's adverting in admiration to the serpent's "brazen Eyes / And hairy Mane terrific" might make the animal *appear* something less than man's best friend. Ever the "affable Arch-angel" (7.41), Raphael therefore assures Adam of the serpent's docility even before our father can have begun to infer the (erroneous) opposite impression from the angel's words. But on the other hand, given our knowledge of the subtle beast's ultimate instrumentality in the deception of Eve, it is difficult for us not to construe Raphael's disarming of Adam and Eve ("whatever you do, DON'T beware of serpents," he seems to be saying) as at best a sardonic dramatic irony that implicates him—and God and Milton too—in the fall of man (though of course, since Raphael does not know that Satan will use the serpent as the instrument of fraud, the irony is lost on him).

Time serves not now to show that on the contrary Raphael's words actually support Milton's intention to justify God's ways vis-à-vis the transgression of Eve—for my present theme is creation in Genesis and in *Paradise Lost*, not creation and fall.[19] Suffice it to say that the poet has arranged for Raphael to speak as he does in deference to the ethics (albeit not to the idiom) of Genesis 1:25b, which in context reads: [25a] "And God made the beast of the earth after his kind, and cattle after their kind, and every thing that creepeth upon the earth after his kind: [25b] *and God saw that it was good*" (emphasis mine). Milton deals with the first half of verse 25 by subjoining to it Genesis 3:1a; but then, as if to compensate for this interpolation, he deletes verse 1:25b ("and God saw that *it was* good") from Raphael's narrative—or rather he substitutes a kindred expression that would appear to render the same ethical verdict periphrastically by denying its opposite (the serpent is "Not noxious, but obedient at [Adam's] call," where the phrase "is *Not* noxious" may be construed as equivalent to "*is* good").

Very well, but why should Milton make Raphael resort to a non-scriptural periphrasis at precisely this juncture? The poet of *Paradise Lost* is not one to modify his inspired source on a whim, even when—as in the arbitrary chiasmus of Genesis 1:24–25a—the Authorized Version permits itself a modicum of seemingly whimsical vicissitude. What characterizes 1:25b, moreover, is not its stylistic whimsicality but rather its studied predictability as the penultimate instance of a semantic unit first introduced at the end of day one ("And God saw the light, that *it was* good" [1:4a]), repeated verbatim fully five more times as the creation proceeds apace, and reiterated a final time, in a climactic variation of the original phraseology ("And God saw everything that he had made, and behold, *it was very* good" [1:31a; emphasis mine]), at the conclusion of the six days' work. Milton faithfully reproduces six of the Bible's seven exemplars;[20] why, at 1:25b, should he opt for the anomalous circumlocution "it was *Not* noxious" over the familiar apothegm "it *was* good"?

19. For a defense of Raphael and God in the present context, see my "More Theirs by Being His: Teaching Milton to Undergraduates" and Chapter Two, passim.

20. At *PL* 7.249, 309, 337, 352–53, 395, and 549 and 556–57 (both of which repeat 1:31).

That Milton does so can be traced to the enormously problematical consequences of his having previously adopted the position that not the serpent but rather Satan in the serpent tempts Eve at Genesis 3:1–6a. Again it is beyond the scope of the present chapter to rehearse all the difficulties vis-à-vis the problem of theodicy that Milton encounters (and adjudicates) by affiliating himself with the traditional but exegetically unparsimonious opinion that "Th' infernal Serpent" (1.34a) and not "The Serpent subtl'st Beast of all the field" (7.495) first seduced Eve. I must, however, essay to engage a number of these matters in order fully to account for Milton's periphrastically rendering the biblical notice "God saw that *it was* good," for his reasons derive exclusively from the Satan-serpent displacement.

Baldly stated, the poet's problem was to find a way to mediate the contradiction created by his confirming on the one hand the scriptural assertion that every thing that God had made was very good (Gen. 1:31a = *PL* 7.548–49), and by his deducing on the other hand (from the biblical curse on the serpent at 3:14–15) that the poor beast becomes entirely bad—"vitiated in Nature" (10.169a)—notwithstanding his unwitting (and therefore also his unwilled) complicity in the fall of Eve.[21] Certain Renaissance biblical commentators had sought to reckon with this dilemma by noticing that whereas God blesses the fish and fowl created on the fifth day, and whereas he similarly blesses man and woman after their creation at the conclusion of day six, enjoining irrational and rational animal alike to "Be fruitful, and multiply" (1:22a, 28a), no such blessing climaxes the formation of the land animals. This omission was ingeniously explained by some exegetes in terms of Genesis 3:1a. Deducing therefrom (as does Milton) that the serpent was among the beasts of the field created on the sixth day, they concluded that God could not properly bless the animal because he was ultimately to be cursed as the sad instrument of all our woe.[22] Milton's way of handling the enigmatic status of the serpent pivots not, however, on some such "simple" omission as this (although he too omits to have God bless the land animals) but rather on his transforming the Bible's notice *the land animals were good* into Raphael's observation *the serpent is not bad*. To understand how this can be the case, we must look ahead to the poet's account of the curse on the subtle animal.

In *Paradise Lost* Milton "justifies" God's punishing the serpent for a crime he never committed ("Conviction to the Serpent none belongs,"

21. Satan finds the animal fast asleep and possesses him without disturbing his repose (9.182–91). Being unaware of what is happening to him, the serpent can hardly assent to it.

22. This interpretation is recorded by Williams, *Common Expositor,* 60–61. The problem with it is that while he does not bless the earth animals, the God of Genesis recognizes that they are good (1:25b).

Messiah himself declares [10.84]) by deliberately and flamboyantly begging the entire question.[23] After Eve (repeating Gen. 3:13b) alleges that "The Serpent me beguil'd and I did eat" (10.162), we are told that

> without delay
> To Judgment [God] proceeded on th' accused
> Serpent though brute, unable to transfer
> The Guilt on him who made him instrument
> Of mischief, and polluted from the end
> Of his Creation; justly then accurst,
> As vitiated in Nature.
>
> (163b–69a)[24]

That Milton believed the curse on the serpent to be just I do not for a moment doubt; but that he thought his explanation of God's justice in thus anathematizing the animal to be other than finespun sophistry—false rules prankt in reason's garb—would be a death to think: a mere brute is somehow justly accursed though falsely accused, and cursed moreover without delay, because the Lord God Almighty is unable to transfer the guilt onto Satan, the truly guilty malefactor. This casual casuistry does not compute, nor does Milton mean it to, as he proceeds at once to make clear: "more to know / Concern'd not Man (since he no further knew) / Nor alter'd his offense" (169–71). Here the question-begging parenthesis (an evident circularity) subverts the pseudological progress of the larger unit in which it occurs, challenging the reader to accept the curse on the serpent for what it must seem to be to anyone who believes, as Milton does, that Satan tempted Eve: an inexplicable (but divine and therefore just) fiat.

What is the relevance of this discussion to Milton's requiring Raphael to substitute the periphrastic "to thee / Not noxious" for the biblical "God saw that *it was* good"? As we have just seen, the poet cannot logically mediate the contradiction *all creatures are entirely good, the* (sinless) *serpent is entirely bad.* He can, however, render this puzzling state of affairs poetically palatable by asserting the serpent's God-given goodness on the one hand, while simultaneously discrediting the beast on the other (through oxymoronic innuendo) *even before* Satan pollutes him. Thus, from the very beginning we encounter a Janus-like serpent in *Paradise Lost:* in Book 4 Milton writes of him,

23. In a note at 10.83–84, Hughes glosses *Conviction* as "formal proof of guilt." If he means that the serpent's guilt is so obvious that formal declaration of it would be supererogatory, Hughes has in my opinion missed Milton's point.

24. It is possible to construe *unable* (165) as modifying *Serpent* rather than *God;* since, however, God is the adjudicator throughout the passage, any transferring of guilt would appear to be exclusively his prerogative.

> close the Serpent *sly*
> *Insinuating,* wove with Gordian twine
> His braided train, and of his *fatal guile*
> Gave *proof* unheeded.
>   (347b–50a; emphasis mine)

What makes these lines ominous for Adam and Eve and prejudicial to the serpent is not so much the reader's prescience, conferred on him by the Book of Genesis, that the animal will soon occasion the fall of man, as it is the pejorative connotations of the words I have italicized. Where the Authorized Version uses the encomiastic adjective *subtil* to characterize the serpent's intelligence, Milton calls the beast *sly,* which also implies his evasiveness, furtiveness, and duplicity; moreover *Insinuating,* while etymologically meaning "to move by windings and turnings"—and so used by Milton to describe the serpent's harmless meanderings—also connotes "slyly hinting or suggesting, usually in order to ingratiate oneself or to defame another." As for *fatal,* it derives from the Latin *fatum,* "to have spoken." In the context of *Paradise Lost,* therefore, it implies creation by the Word of God and has the force of "God-willed" or "God-destined" (thus the Deity can aver that "what I will is Fate" [7.173b]). On one level, then, Milton is merely observing that the *guile* (that is, the craftiness) of the serpent is God-willed and so entirely good; but *fatal* also means "disastrous" or "lethal" (as in *a fatal blow*), and *guile* often implies deceptive cunning in dealing with others.[25] The net effect of Milton's diction—in Book 4 and elsewhere—is thus to describe a creature that is at once the quite innocent (for such God made him, from sin and blame entire) "Serpent subtl'st Beast of all the field" (7.495) that Raphael so admiringly calls to Adam's attention, but that is also the quite nocent "wily Snake" (9.91) that he will assuredly become after Satan discerns, in the unpolluted animal's "wit and native subtlety" (93), reasons to adjudge him the "Fit Vessel, fittest Imp of Fraud" (89).

The moment therefore that Satan—that "Inmate bad" (495)—decides to enter the creature, Milton drastically accelerates the rhetorical discrediting that he has begun as early as Book 4, swiftly transforming the good/bad serpent of a week ago into a thoroughly perverse "spirited [that is, possessed by the Devil] sly Snake" (613), a "wily Adder, blithe and glad" (625), even a "dire Snake" that "into fraud / Led Eve our credulous Mother" (643–44). Finally, Satan's deceptive scheme having been consummated, Milton abandons any pretense of retaining even vestiges of the equivocal language of Book 4. The richly ambiguous "Serpent sly / Insinuating" of unfallen Paradise

25. For the range of relevant connotations, see *OED*, s.v. *sly*, A.1.a and 3.b; *insinuate*, 1.c; *fatal*, 1 and 6.a; *fate*, 3.a and 4.b; and *guile*, 1.

becomes now, thanks to Satan, the unequivocally "guilty Serpent" of the postlapsarian world, which "Back to the Thicket slunk" (784–85).

We have at last sketched out the necessary context in which to comprehend why, at the conclusion of his discussion of the land animals, Raphael calls the serpent "not / Noxious" instead of echoing the explicit biblical language "*it was* good": unbeknownst to the angel, his diction is the precise middle term whereby Milton negotiates the oxymoronic terrain staked simultaneously by the conflicting claims of the explicit "all creatures are good" in Genesis 1 and the implicit "the serpent is bad" in Genesis 3. When Milton remarks, a split second before Satan expropriates the beast, that the serpent is "Not yet in horrid Shade or dismal Den, / Nor nocent yet" (185–86), readers familiar with the poet's ambiguous manipulation of negative particles throughout *Paradise Lost* will beware of prematurely assuming that they have encountered a straightforward litotes, which they may proceed blithely to paraphrase by affirming the contrary of what Milton has denied, namely, that the Edenic serpent resides innocently in open fields, far from deceit and guile; for while I concede that such a reading would be true as far as it goes, it would altogether eviscerate the semantic force of Milton's strategy of negation. The poet wants his utterance to participate, as much as it possibly can, in the very reality it supposedly serves to deny: the serpent is "Not *yet* in horrid Shade . . . / Nor nocent *yet*," but the pathetically weak disclaimer effected in the repeated doublet "Not yet . . . / Nor . . . yet" is itself a virtual litotes signifying the quite opposite notion: "Not yet in horrid Shade— but almost," Milton implies, "Nor nocent yet—but almost nocent." How nigh the serpent's change approaches!—and how fittingly Milton's language mimics the animal's altogether equivocal status. The beast occupies the center of a circle of ethical indifference; he moves about in worlds not realized, in a twilight zone midway between good and evil; neither good nor bad, the animal is strangely both at once. Milton's language therefore oscillates between two universes, one (the unfallen) about to give way to the other (the fallen), which is, however, *not yet* quite ready to be born.

Now just this state of affairs pertains in Book 7, wherein Raphael tells Adam that the serpent is "Not noxious": for while this phrase assures Adam (and us) of what the beast is *not*, it does not provide any unequivocal assurance of what the animal *is* (in this light, it is stunningly appropriate that Raphael should begin his disquisition on serpents by telling Adam "*nor unknown* / The Serpent subtl'st Beast of all the field" [7.494–95; emphasis mine]). Moreover, while it is possible that "Not noxious" is the semantic equivalent of "entirely good," so that the phrase may be construed as doing in *Paradise Lost* what verse

25b does in Genesis 1, the phrase also has precisely the force of "Not noxious . . . *yet*," even though Raphael, unaware that the serpent will be corrupted, can nowise be permitted to think this adverb, much less to utter it. In short, the angel's periphrasis is seen to be an artful adjustment of the biblical text that, taken in conjunction with its stylistic equivalent at *Paradise Lost* 9.185–86, serves the significant purpose of mediating the contradiction between Genesis 1:24–25 and 3:1a. It is, if I may venture to repeat myself, another stroke of considerable—infinite—poetic compression.

IV. A First Conclusion

Having, therefore, in the space of some three hundred lines adjusted or expanded whatever portions of Genesis 1:1–5 and 14–19 require clarification in relation to themselves and to one another; and having, moreover, eliminated the chronological inconsistencies between Genesis 1:11–13 and 2:5–6, on the one hand, and between 1:20–25 and 2:19a, on the other; and having, finally, adjudicated the chronological, taxonomic, and ethical ambiguities of 1:24–25 in relation to 3:1a, our poet has earned the right to conclude his recension of these verses by proffering a six-line recapitulation of the six days' work:

> Now Heav'n in all her Glory shone, and roll'd
> Her motions, as the great first-Mover's hand
> First wheel'd thir course; Earth in her rich attire
> Consummate lovely smil'd; Air, Water, Earth,
> By Fowl, Fish, Beast, was flown, was swum, was walkt
> Frequent.
>
> (7.499–504)

It is an artful summation; nevertheless, Milton's work is not yet done, any more than his God's is: "and of the Sixt day yet remain'd" (504), the poet writes, alluding of course (1) to the creation of man at Genesis 1:26–29; (2) to the quite different account of this event at 2:7 and 2:15–25; and (3) to the problematic institution of the Sabbath at 3:1–3. Milton, as I shall now demonstrate, attends to these matters with unparalleled success.

V. Genesis 1:26–29 and 2:7–9a; Genesis 2:16–17

In a recent stylistic analysis of Milton's paraphrase of Genesis, Ernst Häublein has suggested that the "technique of blending [by which Milton describes the making of man] entails a radical transformation and condensation of the Bible unique within the paraphrase. It seems that the last act of creation was viewed by [the poet] as a challenge for his utmost craftsmanship."[26] I am not sure that Milton's rewriting of Genesis 1:26–29 is *unique* relative to his treatment of verses 1–25, but I quite agree that *Paradise Lost* 7.505–47 proceeds from the hand of a master craftsman, as the following summary of Milton's treatment of Genesis 1:26–29, 2:7–9a, and 2:16–17 suggests: Prolegomenon = *PL* 7.505–16a; Genesis 1:26a = 516b–18; 1:26 = 519–23; 1:27a = 524; 2:7a = 524–26a; 1:27a = 526b–28a; 2:7b = 528b; 1:27b = 529–30a; 1:28 = 530b–34; 2:8 = 535–38a; 2:9a = 538b–39; 1:29 = 538b–39 and 540–42a; 2:16 = 540–42a; 2:17 = 542b–47.

In the Authorized Version, Genesis takes up the creation of man with the words, "And God said, Let us make man in our image, after our likeness: and let them have dominion over the fish of the sea, and over the fowl of the air, and over the cattle, and over all the earth, and over every creeping thing that creepeth upon the earth" (1:26). Milton, however, begins his account with a twelve-line prolegomenon (505–16) that renders explicit what is only implied in Genesis— namely, that man is "the Master work, the end / Of all yet done" (505–6). He then attends to a notorious crux created by his source's enigmatic use of the plural ("Let us") to describe the contemplative activity that immediately precedes the making of man. God's hortatory gesture has been said to smack of everything from polytheism to proto-Trinitarianism;[27] Milton (as might be expected, given the Johannine logos-Christology that informs his account of the six days' work) opts for a reading that allows his non-Trinitarian God to be nevertheless the one and the many. Man being "chief / Of all his works," the Father himself descends to oversee his creation; thus, where Genesis has it simply that "God said," Milton writes:

> [1:26a] th'Omnipotent
> Eternal Father (For where is not hee
> Present) thus to his Son audibly spake.
> (516b–18)

This passage neatly resolves the biblical crux by eliminating the ambiguity of "us." It also emphasizes the actual (as opposed to the merely virtual) participation of the Father in man's making ("to his Son" he "audibly spake"), which in turn implies the special dignity of man (his

26. "Milton's Paraphrase of Genesis: A Stylistic Reading of *Paradise Lost*, Book VII," 119.

27. Speiser disposes of these implications by boldly translating the relevant verse, "I will make man in my image, after my likeness," a decision he justifies as follows: "Heb. employs here plural possessives. . . . Yet no other divine being has been mentioned; and the very next verse uses the singular throughout; cf. also ii 7. The point at issue, therefore, is one of grammar alone, without a direct bearing on the meaning. It so happens that the common Heb. term for 'God,' namely Elohim . . . is plural in form and is so construed at times" (*Genesis*, 7, n. 26).

creation is not delegated), the ubiquity of God ("he also went / Invisible, yet stay'd [such privilege / Hath Omnipresence]" [588–90]), and the subordination of the Son (unlike his ubiquitous Father, he must return to Heaven, from whence he had come into Chaos in order to create).

Having made these four points in fewer than three lines, Milton now repeats the rest of Genesis 1:26 almost verbatim (519–23); but whereas the Bible exhibits a possible redundancy in the phrase "in our image, after our likeness," Milton's God says, "Let us make now Man in our Image, Man / In our similitude" (519–20). If the scriptural *likeness* is not a mere tautological reflex of *image*, it may imply a distinction between the soul and the body and so emphasize that in both respects man is Godlike. Milton perhaps detected such a nuance, which he may have heightened (by substituting "In our similitude" for "after our likeness") in order to distinguish the human "mind / And inward Facultie" on the one hand from man's "outward" and bodily features on the other (8.541–43).[28]

But this is to conjecture; what happens next in Genesis, however, is not a conjecture: moving uninterruptedly from deliberation to execution, "God created man in his own image, in the image of God created he him" (1:27a). Milton's God does the same thing, when Raphael declares that he "form'd thee, *Adam*, thee O Man" (7.524). The angel's words bear some resemblance to 1:27a, but their primary referent is Genesis 2:7, "And the Lord God formed man *of* the dust of the ground, and breathed into his nostrils the breath of life; and man became a living soul." In order to make Genesis 2 appear to conform once again to the normative chronology of its predecessor, Milton now weaves all of 2:7 into his redaction; and in order to make his stitching and unstitching seem a moment's thought, he systematically staggers his references, quoting now from the one chapter, now from the other, in the event effecting a pleasing synthesis of the two:

> [1:27a and 2:7a] This said, he form'd thee, *Adam*, thee O Man
> [2:7a] Dust of the ground, and in thy nostrils breath'd
> The breath of Life; [1:27a] in his own Image hee
> Created thee, in the Image of God
> Express, [2:7b] and thou becam'st a living Soul.
>
> (524–28)

By adding the word *Express* to the Bible's "in the image of God," Milton suggests that Adam and Eve resemble God corporeally as well as intellectually—thus confirming what we have learned in Book 4,

---

28. In the *Christian Doctrine* Milton writes, "*God is said to have created man in his own image, after his own likeness*, Gen. i.26, and not only his mind but also his external appearance" (*YP* 6:135).

wherein even Satan can discern that "in thir looks Divine / The image of thir glorious Maker shone" (291–92), and still earlier, when a blind Milton nostalgically laments his inability to visualize man's "human face divine" (3.44). Otherwise the lines serve the self-evident but not inconsiderable purpose of fusing two quite different creation stories "Easier than Air with Air" into a seamless "Union of Pure with Pure" (8.626–27).

Paradise Lost next essays a less than self-explanatory return to the second half of Genesis 1:27 ("male and female created he them") and to all of 1:28, wherein God begins to apportion man prerogatives over the rest of the terrestrial world: "And God blessed them, and God said unto them, Be fruitful, and multiply, and replenish the earth." These verses Milton repeats—not, however, without making a subtle adjustment in the biblical wording:

> [1:27b–28a] Male he created thee, *but thy consort*
> *Female for Race;* then bless'd Mankind, and said,
> Be fruitful, multiply, and fill the Earth.
> (7.529–31; emphasis mine)

Whereas, in typical paratactic fashion, Genesis merely *implies* a relationship between gender and procreation, the reader being required to infer it from the collocation of 1:27b and the command to "be fruitful and multiply," Milton renders explicit the procreative rationale of sexual differentiation (woman is "Female *for Race*"). At the same time, he disabuses his audience of the misogynistic opinion that Eve was made primarily for reproductive purposes: God did not make Adam's "consort / . . . for Race," but rather his "consort / *Female* for Race." Evidently she exists primarily for nobler reasons, a point to which I shall return.

At this juncture *Paradise Lost* turns once again to Genesis 2, continuing the pattern of oscillating interfusion that characterizes the entire narrative of man's creation. According to 2:8–9a, "the Lord God planted a garden eastward in Eden" consequent upon Adam's creation. He then "put the man whom he had formed" into the garden, and only then "made the Lord God to grow every tree that is pleasant to the sight, and good for food." Milton, to be sure, agrees that the Deity did all these things, but the context in which he reports them implies a different chronology from the Bible's:

> [2:8] Wherever thus created, for no place
> Is yet distinct by name, thence, as thou know'st
> He brought thee into this delicious Grove,
> This Garden, [2:9a = 1:29] planted with the Trees of God,
> Delectable both to behold and taste.
> (535–39)

In this passage, Milton fuses the notice "God planted a garden" with its analogue "made the Lord God to grow every tree," thereby metamorphosing the Bible's simple preterites ("planted," "made to grow") into the past participial phrase "This Garden, *planted* with the Trees of God": consistent with the poet's view that the vegetable world antedates the creation of man by three days, his grammatical transformations suggest (contrary to Genesis 2:8–9a) that Adam is brought into an already created garden replete with already planted trees. To reinforce the point Milton now returns to Genesis 1 again (and so to its chronology), a transition rendered smoother by the fact that the just-cited notice at 2:9a about the delectable loveliness of the plant world closely resembles the passage at 1:29 where God decrees man's vegetarianism. After paraphrasing this latter verse (540–42), Milton turns yet once more to Genesis 2, so that Raphael can repeat God's sole command regarding the tree of prohibition (2:16b–17). Since verse 16b ("Of every tree of the garden thou mayest freely eat") echoes the generous sentiments of 1:29 ("I have given you . . . every tree, in which *is* the fruit of a tree yielding seed"), the transition again seems utterly effortless; happily so, for by skillfully interjecting the forbidden fruit near the conclusion of his narrative of the six days' work, Milton enables Raphael to reserve for the climactic position certain redundant facts (the phrase "as thou know'st" at line 536 has already declared what follows to be ancient history for Adam) that nevertheless serve those vital admonitory purposes for which the angel has descended in the first place:

> [1:29 = 2:16b] freely all thir pleasant fruit for food
> [God] Gave thee, all sorts are here that all th' Earth yields,
> Variety without end; [2:17] but of the Tree
> Which tasted works knowledge of Good and Evil,
> Thou may'st not; in the day thou eat'st, thou di'st;
> Death is the penalty impos'd, beware,
> And govern well thy appetite, lest sin
> Surprise thee, and her black attendant Death.
>
> (540–47)

On this cautionary note Raphael concludes his redaction of Genesis 1:26–29.

In his version of man's creation Milton thus settles a number of perplexing biblical questions, ranging from the apparent plurality of gods in the Bible through the wherefores of human sexuality. The most striking characteristic of *Paradise Lost* 7.505–47, however, is the subtle art that insinuates Genesis 2:7–9a and 16–17 into the temporal context of 1:26–29 without a trace of Procrusteanism. Milton's technique of interfusion is not unlike what we have seen him do elsewhere, but the

degree of blending effected in the passage just discussed has no parallel in Book 7: within the brief space of forty-three lines the poet shifts
back and forth between his source's divergent creation accounts an
astonishing seven times, splicing eight and one-half biblical verses
into an esemplastic unity whose grateful vicissitude evidences in no
small measure Milton's integrative artistry.

There remains, nevertheless, a cluster of verses from Genesis 2 so
manifestly at odds with chapter 1 as steadfastly to resist the sort of
reconciliation we have thus far encountered; I refer of course to the
creation of Eve at 2:18–25. With its idiosyncratic chronology, its emphasis on etiology, its anthropomorphic Deity, and the atmosphere of
morally problematic interiority with which it suffuses both God and
man, chapter 2 stands in diametric opposition to its more succinct
analogue at 1:26–29, an opposition heightened by the intimate jux-
taposition of the one with the other. Fully sensitive to the radical
incompatibility of the two versions, Milton wisely declines essaying to
conflate them into a single, internally consistent linear formulation.
Instead he tears the two narratives quite asunder, relegating the details
of Eve's birth to Adam's recollections in the second half of *Paradise Lost*
8. The interposition of some 425 lines between Raphael's terse paraphrase of 1:26–29 and Adam's more leisurely exfoliation of 2:18–25
mitigates the intrinsic incoherence of the two versions viewed—as
they must be in the Bible—as adjacent episodes in a narrative continuum. Milton's buffering also enables him to confer upon the latter
story a certain degree of chronological autonomy. Freed thereby for
once from the troublesome bondage of temporal coincidence, the poet
can, at the minimal expense of a modest anachronism, attend to more
substantive cruxes in the creation of Eve, and most notably to eliminating the programmatic misogyny wherewith the patriarchal authors
of Genesis 2 sought to institutionalize their conviction that a woman's
proper place is as a fruitful vine in some obscure corner of her spouse's
home.

Because the problems I am about to address are of such magni-
tude, and because they require correspondingly complex Miltonic solutions, I will divide the following discussion into two parts: section
VI will repeat certain relevant portions of Raphael's version of the
creation of man in order to consider them further in the light of Genesis 2:15–17 and *Paradise Lost* 8; and section VII will then focus on the
problem of Eve.

VI. GENESIS 1:26–29 AND 2:7–9; GENESIS 2:15–17

Even though, as we have seen, Raphael modifies Genesis 1:26–28
by filling its interstices with the autochthonous details of 2:7 (7.516–

34), he does not alter the overriding impression—sustained throughout his narrative of the six days' work—that we are still very much in the stylized, scrupulously symmetrical cosmos of the first chapter. Milton's second treatment of Genesis 1:26–29, 2:7–9, and 2:15–17 may be schematized as follows: Genesis 1:26–27 = *PL* 8.253–91; 2:7 = 253–91; 2:15a = 292–318; 2:8 = 292–318; 2:15b–16 = 319–22; 2:17a = 323–26; 2:9b = 323–26; 2:17 = 327–37; 1:28–29 = 338–41. Consistent with this primary source, Raphael asserts that God made man—both "Male" and "Female"—simultaneously, as separate but equal reflections of the same divine image, and only *"then* bless'd Mankind" (529–30; emphasis mine) by decreeing Adam's and Eve's hegemony over the whole earth. The angel then rehearses certain supposedly subsequent details from chapter 2: God next brought man and woman into the garden of Eden and gave them leave to touch and to taste all the fruit thereof, interdicting only the Tree of Knowledge (535–44). Now the sexual egalitarianism and the chronological sequencing with which Raphael affiliates himself faithfully mirror Genesis 1,[29] but they are contradicted by the implications of 2:15–25, the view that Milton himself partially adopts, in startling departure from his habitual tendency to prefer the protocols of chapter 1. The poet mediates the contradiction by separating Raphael's account from the later Adamic variant (so that the angel's may sound authoritative at the moment of its utterance) and by denying Raphael an omniscient point of view vis-à-vis the work of the sixth day (so that Adam's narrative may sound authoritative at the moment of *its* utterance).

According to Raphael he was not an eyewitness to the creation of man (8.229–46). Without a doubt his absence that day reflects Milton's concern to observe the grand masterpiece, decorum: Adam is eager to tell his story (198–216)—not that he feels competent to do so adequately, but that he seeks a pretext to delay his angel visitor's departure (250–53)—and Raphael, providentially ignorant of the details, is equally eager to hear them: "Say therefore on" (228), he decorously urges, "for I attend, / Pleas'd with thy words no less than thou with mine" (247–48). But beyond averting the narrative inconvenience that would attend Adam's reciting and Raphael's hearing a twice-told tale, the angel's ignorance also enables us to adjust his brief report at 7.505–47 in the retrospective light of Adam's more accurate version—without, however, accusing the "affable Arch-angel" (7.41) of either inadvertency or disingenuousness, for he speaks the truth as far as he knows it. Moreover, the transition from his version to Adam's is further mediated by the close family resemblance between the two.

29. Elsewhere, however, Raphael echoes Milton's view (4.295–311) that Eve is ontologically subordinate to Adam: see, for example, 6.909 and 8.560–94.

Thus Adam explains that he was created outside the garden of Eden (8.253–91) and thence by God led into it (292–311). After identifying himself (312–18), God proceeded, just as Raphael has said, to transfer the garden and its fruits to Adam "To till and keep" (320), excepting only "the Tree whose operation brings / Knowledge of good and ill" (323–24). This sounds isomorphic with Raphael's version, but it differs in two crucial respects, as comparison with its source at Genesis 2:15–17 will make evident:

> And the Lord God took *the man*, and put him into the garden of Eden to dress it and to keep it.
> And the Lord God commanded the man, saying, Of every tree of the garden thou mayest freely eat:
> But of the tree of the knowledge of good and evil, thou shalt not eat of it: for in the day that thou eatest thereof thou shalt surely die.
> (Emphasis mine)

The point, of course, is that the God of Genesis 2 puts *man only* in the garden, for from its authors' point of view woman has yet to be made. Milton agrees with their formulation, a decision whose ramifications are legion; the first of them requires the poet quite simply to disagree with the view of Genesis 1:28–29—a view erroneously seconded by Raphael (7.530–34)—that outside the garden, directly after their creation, God blessed man and woman alike. On the contrary, as 2:15–17 imply, the benediction that the Bible records was uttered inside Paradise, after man alone was created, and therefore in Adam's presence only—not indeed to exclude Eve from the aboriginal land grant, but rather to balance Adam's recapitulation of God's "Sternly . . . pronounc'd" and "dreadful" "rigid interdiction" (8.333–35) with a signal instance of the Deity's more characteristically "gracious purpose" (337):

> [Genesis 1:28] Not only these fair bounds, but all the Earth
> To thee and to thy Race I give; as Lords
> Possess it, and all things that therein live,
> Or live in Sea, or Air, Beast, Fish, and Fowl.
>
> (338–41)

At this point Milton concludes his second redaction of Genesis 1:26–29, this time in the authoritative light of 2:15–17.

VII. GENESIS 2:18–25

Having thus for once—and only once—adjusted Genesis 1 to bring it within the chronological penumbra of chapter 2, Milton proceeds to confront the far more formidable burden of transubstantiating the admittedly subtle but morally dubious chauvinist etiologies of 2:18–25 into a thoroughly rational justification of God's ways to man—and to woman too. To grasp the nature of the task before him, we must see the passage in its entirety:

[18] And the Lord God said, *It is* not good that the man should be alone; I will make him an help meet for him.
[19] And out of the ground the Lord God formed every beast of the field, and every fowl of the air; and brought *them* unto Adam to see what he would call them: and whatsoever Adam called every living creature, that *was* the name thereof.
[20] And Adam gave names to all cattle, and to the fowl of the air, and to every beast of the field; but for Adam there was not found an help meet for him.
[21] And the Lord God caused a deep sleep to fall upon Adam, and he slept: and he took one of his ribs, and closed up the flesh instead thereof;
[22] And the rib, which the Lord God had taken from man, made he a woman, and brought her unto the man.
[23] And Adam said, This *is* now bone of my bones, and flesh of my flesh: she shall be called Woman, because she was taken out of Man.
[24] Therefore shall a man leave his father and his mother, and shall cleave unto his wife: and they shall be one flesh.
[25] And they were both naked, the man and his wife, and were not ashamed.

I will not pause to engage in protracted scrutiny of this extraordinary passage; it has, of course, been the object of infinite commentary, and I happily refer my reader to the recently published (and in my view unsurpassed) analyses of Robert Alter.[30] At the risk of oversimplifying, I wish merely to itemize what I believe Milton perceived as the nine problems of Genesis 2:18–25. The following schematization of Milton's treatment of Genesis 2:18–25 will help in sorting out these problems: Genesis 19b = *PL* 8.338–56; 2:20 = 352–444; 2:18 = 444–51; 2:21 = 452–68; 2:22a = 469–77; 2:22b = 478–90; 2:23 = 491–97a; 2:24 = 497b–99; 2:25b = 500–522; 2:25 = 523–611; 2:24 = 612–29.

To begin with a chronological matter, (1) the passage describes creation according to the sequence *man, land animals, fowl,* and finally *woman,* whereas Genesis 1, adopting a roughly evolutionary developmental progression, moves along what would later be denominated the great chain of being, from *fowl* through *land animals* to *man* and *woman;* (2) the biblical God seems not to foreknow the proper names of the animals, which he brings (in ignorance?) to Adam "*to see* what he would call them"; (3) the names the animals acquire seem to be purely arbitrary signifiers contingent only upon the first man's whimsy (for "*whatsoever* Adam called every living creature, that *was* the name thereof"); (4) the passage suggests divine inadvertency, God first pro-

30. See his *The Art of Biblical Narrative,* 27–32 (on the creation of Eve) and 141–47 (on inconsistencies between the account of her creation and the details of chapter 1).

viding the animals to satisfy Adam's need for a "help meet," then learning (ex post facto) that they will not suffice, and only *then* hastening to remedy the situation by creating Eve; (5) therefore, as Alter has appropriately observed, the narrative misogynistically "imagines woman as a kind of divine afterthought, made to fill a need of man, . . . made, besides, out of one of man's spare parts" (p. 141), and made, to that extent, radically imperfectly; (6) in Genesis 1 *nothing*, adventitious or otherwise, is permitted to intervene between God's deliberative and executive acts ("God said, . . . and it was so"), but here the creation of inferior creatures interposes between the Deity's stated intention to ameliorate man's single imperfection and his fulfilling that promise; (7) once created, Eve is brought to Adam to be named, just as the animals have been: she seems therefore scarcely better than they and no less subject to the man's dominance, not to say his despotic power; (8) verse 24 indulges in a gross hyperbole when it suggests that marriage can make a man and woman "one flesh"—an exaggeration immediately (and inconsistently) undercut by the grammatical plurality of verse 25 ("*they* were *both* naked, the man *and* his wife"); and finally, (9) it can be inferred from the naked unashamedness of Adam and Eve that they are childlike and indeed innocent—or rather ignorant—of human sexuality, a peculiar circumstance for presumably rational creatures enjoined in Genesis 1 to "be fruitful and multiply."

Now *Paradise Lost* reckons with these nine problems brilliantly, and for the most part within the brief confines of Adam's autobiography. I will discuss Milton's solutions in a series of triads.

As to the first three cruxes in Genesis 2:18–25, (1) we know that in Book 7 Milton follows the chronological order of chapter 1; he therefore omits Genesis 2:19a from Adam's story, describing instead how God brings the *long-since* created "Bird[s] and Beasts" (8.342), of whose prior existence Adam has likewise known long since (263–65), to his onomastic attention (342–48); (2) although Milton's Adam does indeed name the animals at God's behest (342–45; cf. 6.73–76), he does not do so independently of God's providential prescience: "I named them," he tells Raphael, "with such Knowledge *God* endu'd / My sudden apprehension" (352–54; emphasis mine); (3) nor, therefore, are the names conferred upon the animals merely conventional epithets. "I named them," says Adam, "and understood / Thir Nature" (352–53), an echo of Raphael's instancing that "thou thir Natures know'st, and gav'st them Names" (7.493): in the prelapsarian cosmos of *Paradise Lost* we discern a causal nexus between *signum* and *res* rather than a merely casual contiguity.[31]

31. In *The Common Expositor*, Williams argues that in the Renaissance, commentators believed that biblical Hebrew signifies naturally by, among other things, ety-

Turning now to the second triad, (4) as to the more damaging charge of divine inadvertency vis-à-vis God's proffering the animals as companions for Adam, and as to its implications, namely, that (5) Eve is an expendable commodity built with "second thoughts"—just as Satan would believe the entire visible universe to have been built (9.99–102)—and that (6) God's inadvertency necessitates an embarrassing delay in the swift, sure realization of the divine will, Milton eliminates these difficulties in a single poetic stroke. In *Paradise Lost* God arranges for "each Bird and Beast" to be christened in pairs— "Approaching two and two" is how Adam puts it (8.349–50). By means of this quite unbiblical detail, Milton's Deity intends to apprise Adam of his anomalous solitude. Indeed his stratagem works: "in these / I found not what methought I wanted still" (354–55), Adam tells Raphael, both his desire for companionship and the inadequacy of the animals being inferred after the fact, to be sure, but by Adam, not by God. What follows next is an elaborate debate between God and man, with the Creator playfully urging his latest image to find solace among the beasts (369–75; 399–411), and with Adam retorting (deferentially, of course) that only rational fellowship will suffice (379–97, 412–33). The debate concludes when God, in what amounts to a reconstructive commentary on Genesis 2:18–22, explains that he has orchestrated the whole scenario as a test of Adam's self-knowledge:

> Thus far to try thee, *Adam,* I was pleas'd,
> And find thee knowing not of Beasts alone,
> Which thou hast rightly nam'd, but of thyself,
> Expressing well the spirit within thee free,
> My Image, not imparted to the Brute,
> Whose fellowship therefore unmeet for thee
> Good reason was thou freely shouldst dislike,
> And be so minded still; *I, ere thou spak'st,*
> *Knew it not good for Man to be alone,*
> *And no such company as then thou saw'st*

---

mological transparency: the commentators "proved" this "by the names in Genesis. Thus, *Adam,* the name of the first man, means 'man.' *Eve* means 'life.' *Cain* means 'from' or 'by the Lord,' so that only in Hebrew does Eve's statement at the birth of Cain, 'I have gotten a man from the Lord,' make any sense." These features in Hebrew enabled the commentators to conclude that "in the beginning man was given a perfect language to go with the perfect nature in which he was created" (228). They were at least partly right, as modern exegesis has demonstrated. Thus, for example, at Gen. 2:7, where "Yahweh God formed man from clods in the soil," there is a play on the words *adam* ("man") and *dama* ("soil" or "ground"). As Speiser has argued, "This should not . . . be mistaken for mere punning. Names were regarded in ancient [Semitic] cultures not only as labels but also as symbols, magical keys as it were to the nature and essence of the given being or thing. . . . The writer or speaker who resorted to 'popular etymologies' was not interested in derivation as such" (*Genesis*, 16, n. 5). Milton would agree.

> *Intended thee,* for trial only brought,
> To see how thou couldst judge of fit and meet:
> What next I bring shall please thee, be assur'd,
> Thy likeness, thy fit help, thy other self,
> Thy wish, exactly to thy heart's desire.
>
> (437–51; emphasis mine)

It is characteristic of Milton's genius that here, as elsewhere, he makes a virtue of the necessity (forced upon him by the inconveniences of Genesis) to depart radically from the received text. He assures us that, far from being inept, the biblical God presciently "Knew it not good for man to be alone" and that, appearances to the contrary notwithstanding, he never "Intended" that Adam seek "fellowship" among the beasts. Eve, therefore, far from being an afterthought, was foreordained for Adam *ab ovo:* as Genesis 1 implies, man (both male and female) was always first in intention though last in execution—even if unfallen Adam erroneously concludes that God's omega cannot also be his alpha (he believes that Eve was not "intended first, [but] after made / Occasionally" [555–56]); nor does her having been derived from man's "spare" rib derogate from her perfection—even if fallen, self-extenuating Adam misogynistically calls her a "fair defect / Of Nature" (10.891–92) made from a "Rib / Crooked," "sinister," and "supernumerary" (884–87) to boot. Milton's Eve, on the contrary, is perfect, both without (in a logical solecism the poet calls her "the fairest of her Daughters" [4.324]) and within (unfallen Adam insists that she was "Created pure" [5.100] and that she remains free "from sin and blame entire" [9.292]). Moreover, she, unlike Adam, was created in Paradise. Nor, finally, does Milton retain the disparity in Genesis between God's *verbum*—"I *will* make him an help meet for him" (where the modal auxiliary implies determination as well as simple futurity)—and *factum*—"*but* for Adam there *was not* found an help meet for him" (where the adversative conjunction is as much a reluctant and discouraged concessive as it is a factual adversative). Whereas, in Genesis, two verses describing the creation and naming of the animals (2:19–20a) intervene between the Bible's mournful litany "an help meet" (18b) / "not . . . an help meet" (20b), in *Paradise Lost* Milton relegates verse 19a to Book 7.456–58, begins his account of the making of Eve by expanding 2:19b–20a (8.338–436), and only then attends to the *inclusios* "help meet" / "not . . . meet"—reversing, however, the biblical order of insertion: after declaring (not finding) that the "fellowship" of the animals was always "unmeet" (442) for Adam, God explains that the lengthy colloquy attendant upon the just-completed naming ritual was educative and exemplary, God's intention having been to determine whether *Adam* (not God) "couldst judge of fit and meet" (448). Having successfully educed "the spirit within [Adam] free" (440) in ample manifestation of the first man's "complete / Perfections" (5.352–53), God now—and only now—repeats the promise of Genesis 2:18b (8.449–51), a promise he proceeds at once—for "Immediate are the acts of God" (7.176)—to fulfill (8.452–77). The effect of Milton's artful reconstruction is to eliminate the quantum gap in Holy Writ between divine intention and execution, an effect I will highlight by summarizing Milton's rearrangement of the relevant verses of Genesis 2:

> [19b = *PL* 8.338–56] and [God] brought [the animals] unto Adam to see what he would call them; and whatsoever Adam called every living creature, that *was* the name thereof.
> [20 = 8.352–444] And Adam gave names to all cattle, and to the fowl of the air, and to every beast of the field;[32] but for Adam there was not found an help meet for him.
> [18 = 8.444–51] And the Lord God said, *It is* not good that the man should be alone; I will make him an help meet for him.

At this point Milton's God does just that (2:21–22 = 8.452–90), there being no untidy biblical gap between *his* word and deed.

We come now to the third and final triad of cruxes in the biblical creation of Eve, those deriving from Genesis 2:21–25, wherein God finally gets round to forming her. To do so, as Robert Alter felicitously observes, he works in "the anthropomorphic métier of a sculptor in the medium of flesh and bone":[33]

> [21] And the Lord God caused a deep sleep to fall upon Adam, and he slept: and he took one of his ribs, and closed up the flesh instead thereof.
> [22] And the rib, which the Lord God had taken from man, made he a woman, and brought her unto the man.
> [23] And Adam said, This is now bone of my bones, and flesh of my flesh: she shall be called Woman, because she was taken out of man.

Since (like the animals) Adam's spouse is brought to him by God, whereupon Adam names her (just as he has the animals), does it not logically follow (7) that Eve stands in relation to her husband precisely as the animals do—namely, as his decided inferior ripe for subjugation? This inference gains plausibility from the fact that Genesis 2:22 resembles the well-known passage in the Babylonian creation epic, the *Enuma elish,* wherein the god Marduk forms man out of the remains (and so in the image) of a just-slain god, but only to be a slave

---

32. Notice that Genesis says nothing about Adam naming the fish—as if, in a departure from 1:26–29, man does not have dominion over these creatures of the sea. Milton eliminates this silent inconsistency by having God assure Adam that he has hegemony over the "Fish within thir wat'ry residence, / Not hither summon'd, since they cannot change / Thir Element to draw the thinner Air" (8.346–48).

33. *Art of Biblical Narrative,* 29.

"charged with the service of the gods / That they might be at ease."[34] Since Eve, too, will be cursed to subjugation once fallen ("thy desire *shall be* to thy husband, and he shall rule over thee" [3:16b]), does not the Bible's allusion to its Near Eastern analogue proleptically indict Adam's future "help meet" as the guilty occasion of his mortal transgression?

Perhaps so, but even if this reading seems congenial, it would never have occurred to Milton, who of course knew nothing of Genesis's Mesopotamian literary antecedents. Unlike the ignoble and ignominious ritual servitude that the *Enuma elish* enjoins on both man and woman, the God of *Paradise Lost* forms Eve, no less than Adam, "upright with Front serene" freely to "Govern," not slavishly to serve (7.509–10), in fulfillment of his promise to bring the first man "Thy likeness, thy fit help, thy other self" (8.450). While, therefore, it is true that Adam and Eve are "not equal, as thir sex not equal seem'd" (4.296), it does not follow—as self-depreciating Eve humbly alleges— that her husband "Like consort to thyself canst nowhere find" (448): for Eve is Adam's "likeness" (8.450), and both of them reflect "The image of thir glorious Maker" (4.292).

Consequently Milton graciously endues Eve—on the analogy with Genesis 2:19b–20a—with an exquisite onomastic facility not unlike her mate's: witness fallen Eve's nostalgically apostrophizing the "flow'rs" that she "bred up with tender hand / From the first op'ning bud, *and gave ye Names*" (11.273–77; emphasis mine). By thus conferring upon woman the status of *anthropos onomastikos,* Milton delicately mitigates whatever innuendo of tyrannical male domination may be thought to surface in Genesis 2:21–23; he also takes advantage, for the sake of further liberating Eve, of a scriptural nuance I have thus far slighted. Whereas the God of Israel displays the animals before Adam *in order* that he might name them (and so, by implication, might rule over them), the Bible observes of Eve (rather more noncommittally) only *the fact* that Adam christens her. This subtle distinction, wire-drawn in Genesis to aery thinness, becomes explicitly dichotomized in *Paradise Lost.*

On the one hand, Milton's God summons the creatures "to receive / From [Adam] thir Names" "In sign" of their "fealty" and "low subjection" (8.342–45) to him; but on the other hand, the naming of Eve has a quite different symbolic purport: for whereas the beasts approach Adam "cow'ring low / With blandishment," while "each Bird" likewise "stoop'd on his wing" (350–51) in awestruck deference to him, Eve's advent is replete with the lofty dignity of a Catullan epithalamion:

34. Cited in J. B. Pritchard, ed., *Ancient Near Eastern Texts Relating to the Old Testament,* 68.

> On she came,
> Led by her Heav'nly Maker, though unseen,
> And guided by his voice, nor uninform'd
> Of nuptial Sanctity and marriage Rites:
> Grace was in all her steps, Heav'n in her Eye,
> In every gesture dignity and love.
>
> (484b–89)[35]

This is a far cry indeed from its source's laconic notice "[God] brought her unto the man"; it is also the harbinger of a radically modified onomastic ritual: left breathless by Eve, this "fairest . . . / Of all [God's] gifts" (493–94), Adam declares,

> *I now see*
> Bone of my Bone, Flesh of my Flesh, *my Self*
> Before me; *Woman is her Name,* of Man
> Extracted.
>
> (494b–97a; emphasis mine)

Here, where Genesis has "This *is now* bone of my bones," as if Eve's Adamic origin somehow depended upon her husband's perception thereof, Milton writes, "*I* now *see* / Bone of my Bone," subtly transforming the biblical Adam's perlocutionary power into the more modest recognition of Eve's autonomy. The point is reinforced in what follows: in Genesis, Adam legislates his wife's dictatorial "Woman is her Name," which amounts, again, to a simple acknowledgment that Eve's nature is such-and-such. Finally, Adam's merely recognizing what his prototype virtually creates (in imitation of the biblical God's creating a world out of words) is mediated by his addition of the phrase "my Self" to Genesis 2:2a: "my equivalent," he means, if not indeed "my equal." Milton's Adam—as we learn in Book 9—will never demand submission from such an unfallen "help meet," much less seek to subjugate her after the fashion of a mere brute.

This point is reinforced if we remember that at 4.295–311 Milton says that Eve's hair "impli'd / *Subjection, but* requir'd with sway" (307–8; emphasis mine). The adversative conjunction *but* negates the pejorative implication of *Subjection*—as does the oxymoron at 9.376–77, wherein unfallen Eve has the last fatal word prior to separating from her husband against his wishes, if not his will: "So spake the Patriarch

35. Cf. 5.358–60: "Nearer [Raphael's] presence *Adam* though not aw'd. / Yet with submiss approach and reverence meek, / As to a superior Nature, bow[ed] low." Unlike the animals vis-à-vis himself, Adam is not awestruck at Raphael's appearance, for both he and the angel are rational creatures; but like the animals, the first man bows in submission to his decided superior. That Eve does not analogously curtsy to Adam suggests that she is not *qualitatively* inferior to her husband: they share the same (human) nature. But see also note 29.

of Mankind [Eve's father, no less!], *but* Eve / Persisted, *yet* submiss, *though* last, repli'd" (emphasis mine). The oxymoronic nature of Eve's unsubmissive submission is experienced more elegantly in the contradictory description that she (4.449–91) and Adam (8.484–520) give of their nuptials: both accounts are true, though Eve attributes to native narcissism what Adam perceives as sweet reluctant amorous delay. He *will* not interfere with her freedom of choice.

Two cruxes remain in the account of Eve's creation. The first concerns whether we are to take the phrase "they shall be one flesh" (Genesis 2:24) literally—especially in the contradictory light of the subsequent verse's grammatical plurality ("*they* were *both* naked, the man *and* his wife" [2:25]): (8) does the Bible *really* intend that sexual intercourse in marriage could bridge the chasm that—from Adam on down—has divided *I* from *Thou*? Saint Paul seems to ridicule this interpretation by remarking that even whoremongers could quite readily conform to the Mosaic letter construed as such (I Corinthians 6:16). Since the letter killeth, Paul elsewhere prefers to read Genesis 2:24 as an analogue of Christ's intimate oneness with the Church (Ephesians 5:31–32). But Milton deploys a more complex figurative strategy than Paul's for accommodating the passage to rational exegesis: for him, to read it literally would postulate a metaphysical impossibility, as Raphael's comments on the love of angels imply: "Whatever pure thou in the body enjoy'st," he tells Adam,

> we enjoy
> In eminence, and obstacle find none
> Of membrane, joint, or limb, exclusive bars:
> Easier than Air with Air, if Spirits embrace,
> Total they mix, Union of Pure with Pure
> Desiring; nor restrain'd conveyance need
> As Flesh to mix with Flesh, or Soul with Soul.
> (8.622–29)

The contrast between angelic and human sexuality could not be more pointed: neither flesh nor human soul can love as angels do; Genesis 2:24 cannot mean what it says.

Milton therefore makes Adam adjust the language of Scripture to suggest a figurative reading of "they shall be one flesh":

> for this cause [man] shall forgo
> Father and Mother, and to his Wife adhere;
> And they shall be one Flesh, *one Heart, one Soul.*
> (8.497–99; emphasis mine)

Adam's appositional glosses imply precisely that human dimension to Eve's personality in the absence of which the animals could not be what she decidedly is for him—a companion "fit to participate / All rational delight" (390–91). The first of them also mediates the contradiction between the Bible's "one Flesh" and Milton's "one Soul," for the "Heart" is the fleshly tabernacle of the human spirit: "Marke in my heart, O Soule, where thou dost dwell, / The picture of Christ crucified," cries Donne in a relevant sonnet.[36] Adam and Eve cannot be "one Flesh" per se, but neither are they consigned to the apparent doom of their biblical counterparts, namely, to be "the bifurcated halves of a primal self . . . trying to recapture [its] impossible primal unity."[37] Through the holiness of their hearts' affections—by loving one another as God loves them—Milton's unfallen man and woman can become, as Adam says, "one Heart, one Soul." But in what sense?

Various passages in *Paradise Lost* 4 make it clear that by "one Soul" Adam means simply that he and Eve—whether "Imparadis'd in one another's arms" (4.506) or not—can aspire without impediment to a marriage of true minds. Admittedly, given Milton's traducianism, Adam might appear to intend "one Soul" literally;[38] but the most likely evidence, his plaintive lament "Part of my Soul I seek thee, and thee claim / My other half" (487–88), sounds suspiciously like a Petrarchan lover's sigh-blown quotation of some learned precedent from an *ars amatoria;* moreover, Milton elsewhere assures us that Adam and Eve are merely of one mind—"unanimous" (736), a word that literally translates the phrase "one Soul." Buoyed by their unanimity, Adam wittily and punningly mimics it when he blends the cognates *part* and *partner* with the homonyms *sole* and *soul* into the solution sweet of denominating Eve the "Sole partner and sole part of all [the] joys" of Eden (4.411). Finally, in the first human instance of love at first sight, Adam desiderates his newborn wife "by my side / Henceforth an individual solace dear" (485–86). Editors often gloss the word *individual* as meaning "inseparable," but of course it also equivocally suggests precisely the opposite—"existing as a single, separate, thing or being." Adam naturally does not intend this meaning, but he experiences the full force of his double entendre in Book 9 when he accedes, correctly if ambivalently, to Eve's desire to tend the garden alone; for she cannot be an individual *solace* without first becoming a separate individual. In such wise does Milton construe the Bible's dictum "they shall be one flesh."

Let us turn now to the last crux in Genesis 2:18–25, (9) the sexual

---

36. "What if this present were the worlds last night?" in *The Complete Poetry of John Donne,* ed. John T. Shawcross.

37. Alter, *Art of Biblical Narrative,* 31.

38. Williams has suggested a possible traducian implication of this passage; see *The Common Expositor,* 87.

naïveté implicit in the notice that Adam and Eve were naked but knew not shame (2:25). This brief verse is more an appendage to than the climax of the creation of Eve, part of a separate etiology deployed to foreshadow the fall and to account for fallen man's newly acquired knowledge of good and evil in terms of his concomitant sexual awareness (3:7, 10–11). Milton, on the contrary, believes that man acquired only "guilty shame: dishonest shame / Of Nature's works, honor dishonorable" (4.313–14) by eating the fruit: his Adam and Eve are sophisticated prelapsarian adults whose informed sexuality the poet memorializes in the celebrated epithalamion "Hail wedded Love" (750–70). They love unashamedly not because they think not of sex but because, being "Virtue-proof" (5.384), "they thought no ill" of it (4.320). Why, then, should the Bible suggest that they think of it not at all?

For Milton the answer may derive from the vagaries of oral formulaic poetry as he probably understood them. Raphael apprises Adam of what "was done / From the beginning, that posterity / Inform'd by thee might know" (8.637–39), but we may presume that Adam, once fallen, would have been inadequate to the task. Is it not likely that behind Genesis 2:25 lay a tale of prelapsarian human sexuality that, eroded by time and the human proclivity for fictionalizing history, was recorded finally as "they were both naked, the man and his wife, and were not ashamed"? Given the evidence I have discussed thus far, Milton appears to have regarded all of Genesis as at best a highly elliptical and at worst a badly botched vestige of some such *Ur*-text as Raphael's narrative. Our poet, gifted protégé of the all-knowing "Spirit" who "Wast present" at the creation (1.17–22), presumes to reconstruct that *Ur*-text, recording, among other things, the exemplary matrix whence issued Genesis 2:25.

Milton does so, moreover, precisely where a reader of Genesis would expect him to—when Adam appends to his redaction of 2:18–24 the quite innocent (but ominously foreboding) confession that his passion for Eve inclines him to uxoriousness (8.523–59). Since precisely this tendency will occasion his fall (9.997–99), Raphael takes the opportunity, if not to rebuke Adam, at least to remonstrate "with contracted brow" (8.560) against his inappropriate submissiveness to an inferior (761–78). Then, to drive the point home, the angel arbitrarily (and incorrectly) hypothesizes that the issue at hand is sexual passion, an assumption he seizes upon to castigate Adam for supposedly regarding intercourse as the ne plus ultra of earthly bliss:

> But if the sense of touch whereby mankind
> Is propagated seem such dear delight
> Beyond all other, think the same voutsaf't

> To Cattle and each Beast; which would not be
> To them made common and divulg'd, if aught
> Therein enjoy'd were worthy to subdue
> The Soul of Man, or passion in him move.
>
> (579–85)

Since Genesis 1 enjoins both man and beast to be fruitful and multiply, and since both kinds of creatures reproduce sexually, the naked unashamedness of 2:25 might be taken to imply less a childlike innocence than a virtual parallelism between human and brute sexuality. Indeed Raphael concludes with a kindred observation: "carnal pleasure" is essentially bestial, he tells Adam, "for which cause / Among the Beasts no Mate for thee was found" (593–94). Apart from its impact on Adam (to which I shall attend in a moment), the angel's rebuke is a corrective commentary on Genesis that cautions *us* not to construe 2:24 as meaning that human love and bestial lust are equivalent.

Adam is said to be "half-abash't" (595) at Raphael's well-intentioned but misplaced reprimand. The word *abash* derives from a Middle English verb (*abaisen*) that means "to gape in surprise" or "to be dumbfounded," and Adam is indeed astonished at the affable archangel's unwontedly austere and not at all sweetly "contracted brow"; but *abash* also means "to inflict with a sudden loss of self-confidence and a growing feeling of shame," emotions inappropriate to unfallen man. That is why Milton writes "*half*-abash't": he means "abash't etymologically speaking," for Adam is surprised, yes, but disconcerted, no, at Raphael's censure, since he has nothing to be ashamed about, as his spirited self-defense (596–611) amply demonstrates. Milton thus completes his apologetic expansion of Genesis 2:18–25 by speculating that verse 25 derives from the transformation of "half-abash't" into the litotes "not ashamed." It is a fit conclusion to his account of Eve's creation, and the glory of it all is that the poet shapes his defense of Scripture without a trace of defensiveness: Genesis is never mentioned in the course of Adam's and Raphael's colloquy, for it is hardly *their* concern to practice hermeneutic apologetics; meanwhile the biblical reverberations of the episode will be experienced by the learned reader of *Paradise Lost* as waves of implication that continue the task of making Genesis safe for Miltonic orthodoxy.

VIII. A Second Conclusion: Genesis 1:31—2:3

Let us return now briefly to the first creation account and to its concluding verses:

> [1:31] And God saw every thing that he had made, and, behold, *it was* very good. And the evening and the morning were the sixth day.

[2:1] Thus the heavens and the earth were finished, and all the host of them.
[2:2] And on the seventh day God ended his work which he had made; and he rested on the seventh day from all his work which he had made.
[2:3] And God blessed the seventh day, and sanctified it: because that in it he had rested from all his work which God created and made.

This passage accounts etiologically for the cult practice of celebrating the Sabbath, whose observance it "invests with all the reality of creation itself" and "represents . . . as a fundamental law of the world order."[39] But the four verses also contain at least two cruxes: (1) they imply that God finished creating on day six but assert that he ended "on the seventh day"; and (2) they say that God rested on the Sabbath, implying that an omnipotent Deity can somehow experience fatigue.[40] Again, to appreciate Milton's handling of these cruxes, the following schematization of his treatment of Genesis 1:31–2:3 may be useful: Genesis 1:31b = *PL* 7.449–50, 504; 2:1 = 548; 1:31a = 548–49; 1:31b = 550; 2:2a = 551–53; 1:31a = 554–57; 2:2a = 558–81; 1:31b = 568; 2:2 = 581–92; 2:3 = 592–634; 1:31b = 601.

Raphael eliminates the first difficulty by fiat, declaring that "The Sixt [day], . . . of Creation *last* arose" (7.449; emphasis mine; cf. 568, 601). He later makes the same point less obtrusively by reversing the sequence of Genesis 1:31–2:1:

> [2:1] Here finish'd [God], [1:31a] and all that he had made
> View'd, and behold all was entirely good;
> [1:31b] So Ev'n and Morn accomplish'd the Sixt day.
> (548–50)

Raphael now takes up the matter of God resting; first, preveniently: day six was "accomplish'd," true,

> [2:2a] Yet not till the Creator from his work,
> Desisting, though unwearied, up return'd
> Up to the Heav'n of Heav'ns his high abode.
> (551–53)

The phrase "though unwearied" (an echo of Isaiah 40:28) says it all, of course, although its connection to Genesis 2:2b–3 becomes apparent only some 40 lines later: "on Earth the Seventh / Ev'ning arose" (581–82), when the Son, resituated now at the right hand of the Father, "sat him down" (584–88),

39. See *The Interpreter's Bible*, ed. George Arthur Buttrick et al., 1:489.
40. Doubtless the notion of God resting at all found its way into Genesis on account of its central importance in the *Enuma elish*. There, too, though for reasons of their own, the gods rest before, during, and after the creation of heaven, earth, and man. See Pritchard, ed., *Ancient Near Eastern Texts*, 60–72.

[2:2b] and from work
Now resting, [2:3a] bless'd and hallow'd the Sev'nth day,
[2:3b] As resting on that day from all his work.

(591b–93)

This passage subtly concludes Milton's reworking of Genesis 1–2 by adjusting the Authorized Version one last time: where the biblical God hallows the Sabbath *"because* that in it he had rested from all his work,"* Milton writes *"As* resting on that day." Does God repose on the Sabbath? In the *Christian Doctrine* Milton affirms it: "If it is said that God rested, let us not deny it";[41] and *Paradise Lost* 7.591–92 ("and from work / Now resting") certainly agrees; but if we construe "As" in the next line as introducing a simile, it is only *as if* Messiah seeks refreshment from labor. It is a strange way to conclude an account that has otherwise, and with a zeal approaching fanaticism, made intricate seem straight.

IX. CONCLUSION

Source analysis of the sort I have essayed in this opening chapter is risky in at least two respects. First, one must attempt to specify the author's source for a given literary motif. Does Milton's conception of Sin in *Paradise Lost* 2 derive from Spenser, from Ovid, from Hesiod, or from a handbook of mythology?[42] Second, the comparativist may draw unwarranted inferences about compositional processes and authorial intentions from his inventory of source modifications. The work of Allen H. Gilbert is paradigmatic of the pitfalls confronting one who would speculate, in the absence of draft manuscripts, about the stages by which a poem got put together, and the leap from what an allusive author modifies to why he adjusts his sources will smack to many of the intentional fallacy.[43]

The very existence of these dilemmas nevertheless adds credibility (and, I hope, a certain urgency) to the task of studying Genesis and *Paradise Lost* comparatively. On the one hand, verbal parallels demonstrate to a moral certainty that Milton's source for the creation is the Bible in the Authorized Version.[44] Moreover, I would assert (with the previous pages to back me) that it is in source analysis (if anywhere) that critics relying primarily on textual evidence can hope to speculate least speculatively on matters of composition and intentionality. James Sims has accounted for the divagations between Milton's and the Authorized Version's accounts of the creation as resulting from "the work

41. *YP* 6:135.
42. See my " 'Real or Allegoric': The Ontology of Sin and Death in *Paradise Lost*."
43. Gilbert, *On the Composition of "Paradise Lost": A Study of the Ordering and Insertion of Material*.
44. See the sources cited in note 1.

of composing poetry from the prose of Genesis."[45] I would argue, on the contrary, that they proceed from the more profound, programmatic, and problematic determination to order the compressed cacophonies of Scripture in the service of a theology that is rational root and branch. In that determination, and in some of the methods by which he proceeds, Milton reveals himself to be astonishingly like the modern practitioners of higher biblical criticism.

By affiliating themselves with a modification of the Graf-Wellhausen hypothesis, the editors of *The Interpreter's Bible* have managed to rationalize essentially all the cruxes in Genesis 1–2. The inconsistencies between the two creation narratives, chronological and otherwise, become trivial upon the assumption of composite authorship. As for the troublesome irrationalities of Genesis 2:4b–25, modern exegesis has elegantly disposed of them by rewriting the received text in a manner not unlike Milton's reliance upon interpolation, paraphrase, and linear rearrangement. On the assumption that the primordial narrative from which Genesis 2 is presumably redacted must have made logical sense, the editors in question have sought to construct a hypothesized *Ur*-text by deleting eleven verses as impertinent late additions. I cannot pause to rehearse the rationales offered for their various emendations,[46] but it will be instructive to repeat the editors' reconstructed version of the creation of woman, for it strikingly resembles the Miltonic recension that I analyzed above:

> [2:18] And the Lord God said, *It is* not good that the man should be alone; I will make him a help meet for him.
> [2:21] And the Lord God caused deep sleep to fall upon Adam, and he slept; and he took one of his ribs, and closed up the flesh instead thereof.
> [2:22] And the rib, which the Lord God had taken from man, made he a woman, and brought her unto the man.

The mere deletion of verses 19–20, which *The Interpreter's Bible* justifies on seven separate grounds,[47] has the parsimonious consequence of eliminating the hints of divine inadvertency and implicit misogyny that characterize the received text. Milton, more cautious than the modern exegetes whose methods he anticipates, would not boldly excise verses from sacred Scripture; but as we have seen, he produces the same rationalizing effect by relegating 2:19a to Book 7 and by positioning 2:18 between verses 20 and 21. If I may hazard a generalization from this typical coincidence, Milton is a higher biblical critic without a well-formed documentary hypothesis on which to ground his reconstructive efforts.

---

45. *The Bible in Milton's Epics*, 33.
46. For the full account see *The Interpreter's Bible*, 1:491–501.
47. Ibid., 1:497–99.

What, finally, are we to make of Milton's redaction of Genesis? I am awed by the poet's zeal for logic and stupefied by his skillfully accomplishing such an apparently effortless interfusion of contradictory sources. But in the end, his rage for order may have been gratified at too great a price, for the harmonies Milton desiderates seem to distort the biblical world view beyond recognition. Robert Alter has provocatively suggested that the authors of Genesis deliberately and artfully juxtaposed the two creation accounts, not because they piously and inartistically regarded their inherited materials as canonical and so unalterable, but because they

> had certain notions of unity rather different from our own, and because the fullness of statement they aspired to achieve as writers in fact led them at times to violate what a later age and culture would be disposed to think of as canons of unity and logical coherence. The biblical text may not be the whole cloth imagined by pre-modern Judeo-Christian tradition, but the confused textual patchwork that [proponents of the Graf-Wellhausen hypothesis have] often found to displace such earlier views may prove upon further scrutiny to be purposeful pattern.[48]

It is just possible that the radical discontinuities of Scripture represent the conscious intention of a final redactor rather than a slipshod concomitant of composite authorship. If Alter is right, Milton may have been more consumed with the lust of logic than smit with the love of sacred song, and his version of Genesis might be less an uncommon work of art than the common gloss of a theologian. Indeed the rationalizing zeal with which the poet continues his deconstruction of Genesis as regards the fall of man—the subject of my next chapter—may confirm (for some) just such a judgment against the poet of *Paradise Lost*.

---

48. *Art of Biblical Narrative*, 133.

2

Fall
The Trope of Deception
in *Paradise Lost*

You are the devil's gateway . . . . *you* are the first deserter of the divine law;
you are she who persuaded him whom the devil was not valiant enough to
attack. *You* destroyed so easily God's image, man. On account of *your*
desert—that is, death—even the Son of God had to die.
                                        —**Tertullian,** *On the Apparel of Women*

Thomas Browne fittingly begins his encyclopedic *Pseudodoxia Epide-mica* with perplexed ruminations on the original vulgar error in human history, the deception of Eve in Genesis 3. The event is not well motivated by the laconic brevity of the inspired text: an ontologically inferior serpent, merely bestial if most subtle, facilely persuades the first woman to swallow lies against her maker and a fruit whose very touch is the kiss of death (3:1–6). Although the Christian tradition sought to ameliorate the Bible's hypotrophic rendering of this archaic cataclysm by inspiriting the sly serpent with the vastly superior prevaricating propensities of the Father of Lies, Browne is not convinced that the substitution adequately enfleshes the motivational interstices of Genesis: Eve was

> deceived by Satan; and that not in an invisible insinuation, but *an open and discoverable apparition,* that is, in the form of a Serpent; whereby although *there were many occasions of suspition, and such as could not easily escape a weaker circumspection, yet did the unwary apprehension of Eve take no advantage thereof.* It hath therefore seemed strange unto some, she should be deluded by a Serpent, or subject her reason to a beast, which God had subjected unto hers. It hath empuzzled the enquiries of others to apprehend, and enforced them unto strange conceptions to make out, how without fear of doubt she could discourse with such a creature, or hear a Serpent speak, without suspition of Imposture. *The wits of others have been so bold, as to accuse her simplicity . . . .*[1]

1. *Pseudodoxia Epidemica,* in *The Works of Sir Thomas Browne,* ed. Geoffrey Keynes, 2:17–18 (emphasis mine). All citations of Browne are to this volume. All citations of

This passage is hardly complimentary to gullible Eve, and if Browne does not accuse her of imbecility (which he does not), neither does he eradicate the impression (reinforced in those portions of his narrative that I have italicized) that her inexplicable deception is suffused with inexcusable culpability. Elsewhere Browne concedes, "There was no inconvenience in the [serpentine] shape [Satan] assumed, or any *inconsiderable* impediment," nor any "*material* impediment" in a mindless brute's essaying "vocal conference with Eve" (pp. 344–45; emphasis mine); but *some* impediment there was, he implies, registering an irreducible "empuzzle[ment]" of his own that Adam's wife unwarily and blasphemously accepted lies put forth by a mere serpent. Browne provisionally attributes this paradox to "the condition of Sex, and the posteriority of Cremation [*sic*]" (p. 18)—a grudging misogynistic concession that also predestines Eve to (sinful) deceit *ab ovo*.

I have perhaps overstated Browne's implicit misogyny (his major concern is to rescue Genesis as a well-wrought Aristotelian plot)—but only to foreground the literary and theological cruxes related to Eve's deception that Milton so masterfully manages in *Paradise Lost*. Why does the woman not discern fraud in the serpent? Why does neither she nor Adam discern the Satan-serpent identity until Book 10—if at all? Why does only the man discern Satan's complicity in her fall at the outset?[2] When does original sin occur? Who sinned more, Adam or Eve? Antecedent to these difficult questions, and governing our adjudication of them, is the issue of deceit in Milton's epic, its provenance in prelapsarian life, its complicity in the fall of man, and its concomitant applications in the juridical spheres of crime and punishment, guilt and retribution, and damnation and regeneration. Meditation on deceit, as axiomatic to the fall of Eve but as antithetical to the transgressions of angels and of Adam, will lead us into the midmost heart of Milton's intention in *Paradise Lost;* will rescue Eve (at Adam's ethical expense) from an ensemble of odious entitlements ranging from sheer stupidity to a perverse "will to deceit";[3] and will extricate Milton from the oft-repeated but baseless charge that he himself is a misogynist.[4]

In order to indicate my line of argument, I want to consider briefly the first two of the rhetorical questions posed above before proceeding with other discussions. The issue posed in these questions may seem trivial to some, but Adam's inability to arrive at apodictic knowledge of

Paradise Lost in this chapter are to *John Milton: "Paradise Lost,"* ed. Alastair Fowler, whose interpretations I address in this chapter.

2. At 9.904–5 he knows that "Some cursed fraud / Of enemy hath beguiled thee, yet unknown."

3. William Kerrigan, *The Sacred Complex: On the Psychogenesis of "Paradise Lost,"* 16.

4. I discuss (and refute) the charge at various junctures throughout this chapter, as I do in Chapter One. See also the Conclusion.

the details of Satan's deceit (even when confronted with Michael's unequivocal testimony) is critical to Milton's exoneration of Eve from blamable deception. Intimations of this become clearer when we remember that at 9.904–5 and 947–51 unfallen Adam knows only that Satan has somehow overcome Eve; at 1067–70 fallen Adam is no longer sure that the Devil has expropriated the beast in any sense, for he is "in subjection now / To sensual appetite" (1128–29); and at 1172–73 he again connects Satan with Eve's trespass. At 10.175–81 Adam hears the protevangelium, which initially implies that the serpent acted independently, and at 10.867–71 and 877–80 he reaches the limits of postlapsarian contraction with respect to the Satan-serpent connection, actually *denying* any affiliation between them. Eve inadvertently stimulates her husband to rethink the issue at 10.924–27, which he does at 1029–36, inferring only that "Satan . . . *in* the serpent hath contrived / Against us this deceit": *in* the serpent need not, however, mean *assuming the form* of the animal. At this point Adam has made only a slight perceptual advance beyond what he knows at 9.947–51.

At 11.425–28 Michael actually implies that Eve and Adam "with the snake [not with Satan] conspired." The angel's subsequent comments on the protoevangelium emphasize the identity of the woman's seed, not the Satan-serpent collaboration (for example, see 12.148–51, 232–35, 310–14, 325–27, 368–69, 541–44). At 12.312 Michael refers to "the adversary serpent," thus implying the devil's and the snake's identity *to the reader,* but not to Adam. The fallen man is at this point preoccupied only with "the woman's seed" (376–85), and he infers only that "must *the serpent* [not Satan] now his capital bruise expect." Michael's response (386–95) identifies Satan as him on whom the bruise will fall (compare 429–33), and the angel is even more explicit at 454, calling Satan "The serpent, prince of air"; but Adam never responds to these overtures. It is not clear in *Paradise Lost* that he *ever* understands that Satan actually possessed the serpent. Why not? Because "in the wily snake, / Whatever sleights *none* would suspicious mark" (9.91–92; emphasis mine), and because "more to know [than that the devil somehow defrauded Eve] / Concerned not man" (10.169–70). It is precisely this careful treatment of detail that allows Milton to exonerate Eve, as I shall argue in what follows.

I. The Woman Was Deceived

> Wommennes conseils been ful ofte colde;
> Wommannes conseil broghte us first to wo,
> And made Adam fro Paradys to go,
> Ther as he was ful myrie and wel at ese.
> —**Chaucer, "The Nun's Priest's Tale"**

We are taught in Holy Scripture, that the devil "rangeth abroad like a roaring lion, still seeking whom he may devour" [I Peter 5:8]: and as in several shapes, so by several engines and devices he goeth about to seduce us; sometimes he transforms himself into an angel of light [II Corinthians 11:14], and is so cunning that he is able, if it were possible, to deceive the very elect.

—**Burton,** *The Anatomy of Melancholy*

I will begin (and end) with I Timothy 2:11–15, a seminal deutero-Pauline passage concerned with the observance of decorum at worship services:

Let a woman learn in silence with all submissiveness. I permit no woman to teach or to have authority over men; she is to keep silent. For Adam was formed first, then Eve; and Adam was not deceived, but the woman was deceived and became a transgressor. Yet woman will be saved through bearing children, if she continues in faith and love and holiness, with modesty. (RSV)

A. B. Chambers believes that "Milton merely accepts and employs" this commentary on Genesis 3:1–6 to motivate the falls of Adam and Eve;[5] but in fact the poet steadfastly repudiates its misogyny: where the New Testament alludes censoriously to Eve's deception, which it minimally counterbalances with an astonishing parturitional soteriology, Milton remarks matter-of-factly, in an elliptical revisionary critique of I Timothy, that "The infernal serpent['s] . . . guile / . . . deceived / The mother of mankind" (1.34–36). This passage tends to deflect blame from the deceived to the deceiver, and it dignifies Eve as the progenitrix of the human race instead of demeaning her as a secondary and derivative creation. Moreover, by predicating motherhood of the woman before her fall (compare 5.388–91), Milton proleptically neutralizes the punitive consequences of her future transgression: whereas in the Bible childbearing *causes* a grudging postlapsarian commutation of capital punishment ("woman will be saved *through* bearing children"), in *Paradise Lost* the fact that woman's primordial vocation precedes her original sin (for Satan deceived not Eve but "The mother of mankind") implies her redemption before her fall (deceived or not, she is saved *for* motherhood as much as *by* it; compare 10.1013–40).[6]

As is thus already evident, and as Chapter One has already confirmed, Milton characteristically expropriates whatever he borrows from ancient sources, biblical or otherwise, transforming his predecessors almost beyond recognition—and this less out of the anxiety of influence than in the interest of making them safe for his zealously

5. "The Falls of Adam and Eve in *Paradise Lost*," 118.
6. The preceding paragraph is repeated from my review of Timothy J. O'Keeffe's *Milton and the Pauline Tradition*, in *Milton Quarterly* 16 (1982): 99–101.

rational theodicy. He transforms the Bible almost beyond recognition, but not quite: the core of I Timothy's chauvinist exegesis (and only the core)—that "the woman was deceived" "but Adam was not deceived"—survives Milton's radical surgery to become the *tropus ex machina* whence the poet engineers the fall. It also challenges his utmost art: Milton must metamorphose deutero-Pauline misogyny into something other than a pretext for feminine subjugation (his egalitarian theology demands *this*), and he must simultaneously render the true fact that "The serpent [Eve] beguiled and [she] did eat" (10.162) as a plausible state of affairs consistent with the decorum of verisimilitude (his Aristotelian poetic demands *that*). The difficulty is suggested by commentators' repeated allusions to the intractability of the Genesis material (not to mention deutero-Paul);[7] the success of *Paradise Lost* resides in the care with which a great and good poet lovingly negotiates this virtually inaccessible terrain.

To proceed in reverse order, I turn first to the problem of verisimilitude. Eve must fall deceived, but how? Milton immeasurably complicates the task by equipping her with prelapsarian bliss, an extraordinary intellect, mountains of supererogatory information about her enemy (transmitted by Raphael), repeated warnings not to eat the bad fruit, and circumstantial apprisals, both theoretical (for example, 7.537–47) and instinctual (5.8–11), of the baneful consequences of transgression. Thus forewarned, how can Eve possibly be deceived?

The answer pivots on the role of Uriel in *Paradise Lost*.[8] In the Bible this angel, whom John the Divine "saw also in the sun" (3.623; Revelation 19:17), warns fallen men of the coming apocalypse (12:7–12); Milton wishes that he had likewise cautioned unfallen Adam and Eve about the imminent intrusion of Satan into Eden and its Garden (4.1–8). In the event the poet assigns this admonitory function to Raphael (5.219–47)[9] and redeploys Uriel as a cosmic Baedeker (3.722–35). But this is merely a deceptive ruse: Milton hardly required the angel to facilitate the Devil's journey to Paradise (its ostensible motive). A demon who could traverse the dark unbottomed infinite abyss of Chaos with the dubious help of its anarchic superintendents could surely map his way to Eden through the concentric Ptolemaic spheres of the visible cosmos without the assistance of the regent of the sun. Far from being a redundant road map, Uriel is actually the

7. See, for example, Basil Willey, *The Seventeenth Century Background*, 237–58; and the dubious cogitations of Michael Lieb, "*Paradise Lost* and the Myth of Prohibition." I have yet to discover candid discussion of the intractability of I Timothy.

8. To my knowledge never discussed in detail heretofore. Dennis Burden has some useful observations on this angel in *The Logical Epic*, 100, 109–10.

9. For which see Chapter Three, passim.

paradigm of how unfallen rational creatures can fall into (sinless) deception unaware:

> He drew not nigh unheard, the angel bright,
> Ere he drew nigh, his radiant visage turned,
> Admonished by his ear, and straight was known
> The archangel Uriel.

$$(3.645-48)$$

This astonishing passage prefigures the deception of Uriel through syntactic sleight-of-hand. "He drew *not*": the negative adverb momentarily denies that Satan moves at all, an impression at once corrected by the adverb *nigh,* which makes Milton appear to be saying that while the Devil advances, he does not get that close to Uriel. The appearance of *unheard* (another slippery negative) requires, however, a second adjustment: Satan does draw nigh to the archangel, but not without being heard by him. (Similarly, at 9.516–28, the demon attracts Eve's [subconscious] aural attention before effecting a visual epiphany.) "He drew not nigh unheard, the angel bright": is *angel bright* in apposition with *He* (that is, the Devil), as it appears to be (for *He* is after all disguised as a luminescent "stripling cherub" [636])? The answer is no, though the apparently appositional phrase hovers briefly between uncertain alternatives. "Ere *he* [that is, *Satan,* clearly] drew nigh, *his* radiant visage turned [whose visage? the Devil's? or Uriel's?], / Admonished by his ear." At this uncertain juncture we arrive at a temporary stasis, clarifying antecedent ambiguities, confident at last that excellently bright Uriel, alerted by his ear, hears *someone* approach and about-faces to identify the intruder. "[A]nd straight was known . . . ." Who was known? All signs point to *Satan,* for *Uriel* has become the active aggressor in the identity crisis underway. The end-of-line position of *straight was known,* abetted by its grammatical passivity, reinforces this expectation. It is, however, forthwith disappointed by the rude shock of the next half-verse: "and straight was known / *The archangel Uriel.*" Since his "goodness thinks no ill / Where no ill seems" (688–89), the angel bright cannot even suspect Satan, much less penetrate his disguise: *Uriel,* not the Devil, is "straight . . . known," because the deceitful demon, cherubically accoutered, "makes intricate seem straight, / To mischief swift" (9.632–33).

I am no innocent partisan of affective stylistics, but my description of the reader's exfoliating response to *Paradise Lost* 3.645–48 shows these lines to be indeed a syntactic mimesis of the forthcoming deception of Uriel.[10] Though "one" of God's "eyes" (648–50), the archangel

10. As are 3.588–624, which show also that Uriel, unlike Satan, is always an open and discoverable apparition. Compare the angel's undisguised arrival at Paradise (4.555–88). My reading of 3.645–48 is based on the theoretics of Stanley E. Fish, *Sur-*

is light years distant from being the "all-seeing" "eye / Of God," whose "heart / Omniscient" is therefore impossible to "deceive" (10.5–7). In fact Uriel is, if anything, more vulnerable to deceit by the "Artificer of fraud" (4.121) than Eve herself, for *she* has been repeatedly forewarned by Raphael to beware of the enemy, whereas *he*, "Admonished" only by his fallible "ear," is never cautioned to beware at all. Hearing and seeing are believing in his case, as indeed they must be:

> For neither man nor angel can discern
> Hypocrisy, the only evil that walks
> Invisible, except to God alone,
> By his permissive will, through heaven and earth:
> And oft though wisdom wake, suspicion sleeps
> At wisdom's gate, and to simplicity
> Resigns her charge, while goodness thinks no ill
> Where no ill seems.
>
> (682–89)

Just as Abdiel's defiance (5.809–48) and Eve's dream (4.799–809) are paradigms of sinless temptation in *Paradise Lost,* the beguiling of Uriel is *the* paradigm of sinless deception. Milton's prevenient substitution of this archangel (for prelapsarian Eve) in the passive dimension of the-one-beguiled corresponds to the Christian tradition's substitution of the archdemon Satan (for the scriptural serpent) in the active dimension of the-one-beguiling. Thomas Browne need not have sought a priori misogynist rationalizations for Eve's failure to discern satanic fraud in the wily machinations of the subtle serpent; Milton accounts for her "ineptitude" with an a priori of his own: he conjures up Uriel, who is no less impotent than she for being "The sharpest sighted spirit of all in heaven" (691).

The deception of this angel allows us to see—long before her temptation and fall—that Eve's intelligence is equivalent to that of Adam. But apart from certifying her mental acuity, the passage more importantly renders plausible—*though it does not cause*—Eve's transgression. She must be deceived (Genesis and Timothy tell us so), but Aristotelian norms of tragic verisimilitude (*Poetics* 15) require her sinless deception (and sinful fall) to be endogenous correlatives of plot structure rather than exogenous visitations *ex machina*. In this respect Milton actually benefited from Thomas Browne's less sympathetic treatment in *Pseudodoxia Epidemica*. By way of exorcising a related vulgar error (one barely exceeding Eve's deceit in enormity), Browne criticizes those, such as Peter Comestor,[11] who say "that Sathan

---

prised by Sin: The Reader in "Paradise Lost." My profound disagreements with Fish consist not in his methodology, but in its abuse.

11. Comestor's *Historia Scholastica,* Lib. Gen. XXI in *Patrologiae cursus completus*

appeared not unto Eve in the naked form of a Serpent, but with a Virgin's head, that thereby he might become more acceptable, and his temptation find the easier entertainment" (p. 344).[12] Since the Bible maintains an inscrutable silence on the question of serpentine physiognomy, its determination is a matter of plot plausibility alone, and Browne rejects a hominoid serpent on the literary ground of verisimilitude: "the assumption of humane shape," he argues, "had proved a disadvantage unto Sathan; affording . . . a suspicious amazement in Eve, before the fact, in beholding a third humanity beside her self and Adam" (p. 344). Eve cannot be allowed to be *suspicious* and *amazed* at the same time, Browne contends, for the fateful conjunction of these adjectives would enable her to penetrate Satan's disguise, which would in turn require her to fall undeceived, a denouement at once implausible and uncanonical.

Similar problems complicate the biblical phenomenon of a speaking serpent. If a zoomorphic beast will obviate wary astonishment in Satan's intended victim, will not a vocal reptile produce this very affect? William Perkins thinks not: anticipating Thomas Browne, this Renaissance exegete clears Eve of prelapsarian imbecility by locating her proneness to deception in invincible ignorance of the serpent: "the naming of the creatures, which argues knowledge of them, was not giuen to Eue, but to Adam."[13] Browne indeed feels the same way: surely the woman "would be *amazed* to hear a Serpent *speak*" (p. 345; emphasis mine), and the doctor wonders how this could occur without arousing some concomitant "*suspition* of Imposture" (p. 18; emphasis mine). To avoid reintroducing simultaneous suspicion and amazement into the equation of Eve's temptation, Browne, like Perkins, rationalizes her susceptibility to a vocal animal by referring to her "inexperience[d] . . . ignorance of [the animals'] natures" (p. 345).

This maneuver solves the problem of verisimilitude, but it also damns Eve with faint praise: Perkins and Browne purchase her susceptibility to deceit at the (misogynistic) cost of denying her intellectual sufficiency. In *Paradise Lost*, however, Milton addresses the issues of serpentine physiognomy and language on the one hand, and the related human affects of suspicion and amazement on the other, with much more tact, subtlety, and sympathy for Eve than do his predecessors. Roland Frye believes that the poet could not "put a 'lady visage' on his Tempter without seeming to some readers to invite [a misog-

---

. . . *Series Latina*, ed. J.-P. Migne, 198, is the oldest extant literary reference to this motif.

12. The pictorial tradition is discussed by Roland M. Frye, *Milton's Imagery and the Visual Arts*, 101–5.

13. *The Whole Treatise on the Cases of Conscience*, in *Workes*, trans. Thomas Pickering, 2:57.

ynistic] identification of the devil with women."[14] Frye is probably right, but in this instance concerns of verisimilitude surely outweigh proto-feminist anxiety. Milton therefore insists—and it is as if he had Browne in front of him—that the Devil comes forth to seduce Eve *"Mere* serpent in appearance" (9.413; emphasis mine), thus succinctly announcing his departure from a vulgar error spawned in the Middle Ages. As to the issue of "Language of man pronounced / By tongue of brute" (9.553–54), the poet resolves this problem without denying Eve the status of *anthropos onomastikos:* as I mentioned in Chapter One, she names the flowers (11.273–79), and she is a first-rate herpetologist. She knows perfectly well that serpents cannot speak (9.553–57), but that a snake could *acquire* linguistic facility is by no means implausible. If, as Adam notes, human reason is "To brute denied" (9.240), God has also declared that the animals "know, / . . . reason not contemptibly" and have their own "language" (8.373–74)—information that disarms Eve's suspicions at encountering a reasoning, speaking reptile (10.588–61).

Moreover, Milton is careful, just as Browne says he should be, to segregate *amazement* from *suspicion* in the temptation scene. Satan has largely neutralized any astonishment in advance (1) by first attracting Eve's visual and auditory attention to his inarticulate but audible insinuations (9.516–28), and (2) by beginning his "fraudulent temptation" (531) with the brilliantly disarming imperative "Wonder not" (532). "Though at the [serpent's] voice much marvelling" (551), Eve, Milton craftily remarks, is merely "Not *un*amazed" (552; emphasis mine) at this vocal apparition: the poet's double negative occupies a linguistic twilight zone between the denial and the assertion of an affective state that might indeed, were Eve unequivocally amazed, arouse her suspicions.[15]

By this time Milton has already solved a number of problems that Thomas Browne identifies in the biblical account of the fall of Eve. In that text, temptation begins with a transparent prevarication: "Did God say, You shall not eat of any tree in the garden?" (Genesis 3:1), the serpent asks, rushing headlong into vocal utterance and suspiciously exaggerating the prohibition against a single tree to God's pusillanimous banning of them all (compare 2:16–17). Browne is rightly astonished that Eve could receive such a "Temptation so coldly; and when such specious effects of the Fruit were promised, as to make them like God [3:4–5], not to desire, at least not to wonder [that the serpent]

---

14. *Milton's Imagery,* 104.
15. "Not *un*amazed" no more means *amazed* than "not *un*happy" means *happy.* Compare "half his strength he put not forth" (6.853), which tells us only what Messiah did *not* do (an all-powerful Deity cannot exercise *half* his strength: omnipotence halved is still *omni*potence). See my *"Paradise Lost* and the Greek Theogony," 141–42.

persued not that benefit himself, [or to ask]: If the tast of this Fruit
maketh the eaters like Gods, why remainest thou a beast?" (p. 18). I
am anticipating here, for Milton does not permit Satan to utter the
scriptural temptation (3:4–5) until line 655, fully 124 verses after he
first accosts Eve (532). But that is just the point: the Bible's haste (a
mere five verses from temptation to sin) is incommensurate with a
plausible fall into deception and transgression, as both Browne and
Milton understand. Milton obviates this plot inconvenience by the
tactic of delay. And he handles Browne's objection that the serpent has
not himself eaten so desirable a fruit by focusing Eve's "Not unamazed" attention on a related question, the failure to ask which
Browne misogynistically refers to her ignorance: the great "wonder"
of how the animal became "speakable of mute" (563) now "claims [her]
attention due" (566).

Diane McColley, the best analyst of Eve's prelapsarian sufficiency,
speculates that "if she had [inquired] vigilantly" as to "how the Serpent acquired the consummate gift of speech," "she might have penetrated [Satan's] disguise."[16] But first, the disguise is *impenetrable*; second, unfallen Eve has *no reason* at this juncture to exercise vigilance
with respect to serpents; and third, she *does* inquire about how the
beast became articulate. Milton handles both McColley's and Browne's
objections in a single stroke. Eve asks the very question the former
desiderates—emphatically and repeatedly (553–66)—and receives an
answer that makes irrelevant the suspicious interrogation the latter
requires: in *Paradise Lost* the serpent allegedly acquires speech and
reason by eating an unspecified fruit (568–612), and Satan will eventually persuade the woman to repeat his overreaching by asserting the
specious but plausible analogical argument that upon eating it, she
"should be as gods, since I as man, / Internal man, . . . proportion
meet" (710–11). By neglecting at first to identify the magical plant as
the forbidden tree of knowledge, Satan moreover slyly avoids prematurely arousing Eve's suspicions, for to introduce the issue of disobedience at this point would make her wary and abort his fraudulent
temptation.

Eve is said to be "Yet *more* amazed *unwary*" (614; emphasis mine) at
this juncture: she has leapt the Miltonic quantum gap between *not
unamazed* and *more amazed* without traversing the intermediate space of
amazement, but the leap does not violate Brownean verisimilitude by
landing her in an oxymoronic field of *suspicious* amazement. She is
now unwary, potential suspicions about a vocal animal having been
plausibly displaced by innocent (and quite apposite) curiosity about

16. *Milton's Eve*, 196.

the unnamed fruit (615–24) itself. *Unwary amazement,* as Thomas Browne well knew, is psychologically compatible with a fall into deception and is therefore precisely the affect Satan requires in his first human victim. Milton relies on the same affect; he does so not to victimize Eve, however, but merely to render her plausibly susceptible to deception.

Some readers will nevertheless object that by now Eve *ought* to be suspicious—of the many satanic flatteries insinuated throughout lines 532–48 and 568–612. Satan calls her the "sole wonder" (533) of the universe; he identifies her with Messiah (she is the "Fair*est* resemblance of [her] maker fair" [538; emphasis mine]); he euhemerizes her as a "goddess" (547); she deserves angelic servitude (548). The fiend is appealing to her supposed narcissism,[17] successfully it would appear, for the only rejoinder that Eve can muster in response to his hyperboles is the ambiguous disclaimer, "Serpent, thy overpraising leaves in doubt / The virtue of that fruit" (615–16). If she is indeed not *un*amazed at a vocal serpent and *yet more* amazed to discover whence he has acquired speech, should she not beware of such untoward flatteries as he has heaped upon her?

The answer is no, because while Eve hears the Devil overpraise the fruit, she does not hear him flatter *her*.[18] Although Satan's "glozing" (3.93 = 9.549) appeals to her assumed vanity work their "way" "Into the heart of Eve" (550), she remains sinlessly unaware that this has happened; not that she is stupid or vain, but that she listens selectively, for reasons that a parallel example from Sophocles will illustrate. When Teiresias confronts the Theban king in *Oedipus Tyrannos,* he fairly delivers the tyrant over to self-incrimination, accusing him— in plain Attic Greek—of both parricide and incest. But Oedipus does not internalize the more damaging claim of incest until much later; instead he rages at the prophet for adducing the blamable but lesser charge of murder. Why is Oedipus not incensed at the more grievous allegation? Because he has not heard it. Preoccupied with the accusation that he is a murderer and with the anterior question of his parents' identity, about which he has had doubts since childhood, Oedipus seeks, with the rigor characteristic of his superior and uncompromising intellect, to track *that* conundrum to its inmost cell: "Who are my parents?," he asks, unwittingly closing his ears and

17. *Supposed* only, because if Eve loves her own image at 4.460–91, she does not know that it is an image and is soon taught to distinguish appearance from reality.

18. 9.615–16 may refer, however, to the serpent's "overpraising" of Eve. But even if they do, the substance of the following paragraph is not vitiated. The woman is far too absorbed in the mysteries of a vocal serpent and a magic plant to attend *warily* to potentially suspicious ontological hyperboles: "suspicion sleeps / At wisdom's gate," for Eve's "goodness [*not* her imbecility] thinks no ill / Where no ill seems" (3.686–89).

mind to the Teiresian decree that calls him "brother and father to the children that he loves." Oedipus is indifferent to the issue of incest, but *only because he does not know that the issue has been raised*.[19] It is the same with Milton's Eve. Smarter by far than her postlapsarian Theban grandson, she focuses her amazed attention on the arresting (if not urgent) riddles of how the serpent acquired speech and whether a mere plant can be of "virtue" (616) to make a beast wise. Eve is indeed unwary of satanic flattery, but only because she is unaware of it at all.

Given the evidence assembled thus far, it is no wonder that the unfallen woman fails to detect satanic fraud in a speaking serpent, no wonder that, later on, even after she has discovered that the fruit in question is forbidden, she can say—and believe—that the beast is an "author [i.e., informant] unsuspect, / Friendly to man, far from deceit and guile" (771–72). Like the encyclopedia salesman who makes you *want* his books before he puts a (prohibitive) price tag on them, Satan first inclines Eve's desire toward an apparently innocuous fruit, and only *then* reveals its immeasurably inflated cost. Moreover, disguised as a serpent he is not, contra Browne, "an open and discoverable apparition" (p. 3). Milton works hard to prove that not even Uriel could have discerned fraud in Satan. Satan shrewdly mobilizes the subtle animal as the sad instrument of all Eve's woe because, as Saint Augustine had noted, "being slippery, and moving in tortuous windings, it was suitable for his purposes."[20] Naturally endowed "with subtle wiles" (9.184), the animal will not arouse any untoward suspicions in her; it is therefore the perfect vehicle for hypocritical deception. Neither Adam nor Eve has any reason to notice, much less to suspect, the serpent's wiles:

> close the serpent sly
> Insinuating, wove with Gordian twine
> His braided train, and of his fatal guile
> Gave proof unheeded.
>
> (4.347–50)

This passage is full of ethical double entendres, but its postlapsarian linguistic ambiguities are unavailable (and irrelevant) to unfallen man.[21] Moreover, any (paranoid) anxieties the serpent might otherwise engender are dispelled by Raphael long before Satan decides to inspirit him:

19. Sophocles, *Oedipus Tyrannos*, trans. and ed. Luci Berkowitz and Theodore F. Brunner, 11–12.
20. *The City of God*, 14.11, trans. Marcus Dods, in *Great Books of the Western World*, 18:386. All citations of Augustine are to this volume.
21. Burden, *Logical Epic*, 153, wrongly claims that "through Man's fault" the beast's "slyness" "went unheeded." Why should he notice it, since the animal is harmless?

> nor unknown
> The serpent subtlest beast of all the field,
> Of huge extent sometimes, with brazen eyes
> And hairy mane terrific, though to thee
> Not noxious, but obedient at thy call.
>   (7.494–98)

Appearances notwithstanding, these lines do not implicate Raphael in the fall of man.[22] *They do, however, motivate the sinless deception of Eve.* On the one hand, Milton himself confirms Raphael's diagnosis of the animal's innocence: it lives "Not yet in horrid shade or dismal den, / Nor nocent yet" (9.185–86). Even if the litotes-like phrase *nor nocent yet* loudly anticipates the fall by ominously implying the opposite of its propositional content ("nor nocent *yet* . . . but *almost* nocent"), the serpent is *as yet* utterly harmless, the "Fearless unfeared" benign denizen of "the grassy herb" (186–87).[23] But on the other hand, both Raphael and Milton certify Satan's judgment, distilled from "meditated fraud" and sevenfold circumnavigation of the globe, that the animal is "Most opportune [to] serve his wiles" (9.55, 63–66, 76–85):

> Him after long debate, irresolute
> Of thoughts revolved, his final sentence chose
> Fit vessel, fittest imp of fraud, in whom
> To enter, and his dark suggestions hide
> *From sharpest sight:* for in the wily snake,
> Whatever sleights none would suspicious mark,
> As from his wit and native subtlety
> Proceeding, which in other beasts observed
> Doubt might beget of diabolic power
> Active within beyond the sense of brute.
>   (87–96; emphasis mine)

Whereas for Thomas Browne the serpent afforded "many occasions of suspition, and such as could not easily escape a weaker circumspection [than Eve's]" (p. 3), Milton attributes to his reptilian subtlety "sleights [that] *none* would suspicious mark."

Not even Uriel. The beast is indeed a "Fit vessel" in whom to conceal "dark suggestions" "From sharpest sight"—even from the eyes and mind of "the sharpest sighted spirit of all in heaven" (3.691 = 9.91). Satan knows infallibly that he can "Le[a]d Eve" "into fraud" (9.643–44), for this demonic confidence man has long since "beguiled / Uriel, though regent of the sun" (3.689–90). Just as *sharpest sight* at 9.91 hearkens back to the deception of Uriel, *beguiled* at 3.689 looks ahead to

22. See my "More Theirs by Being His: Teaching Milton to Undergraduates," 7.
23. See Chapter One for further discussion of Milton's use of litotes in descriptions of the serpent.

the deception of Eve, whom "The Serpent . . . beguiled and [she] did eat" (10.162). Milton's cross-referencing identifies the two events *as isomorphic with respect to the issue of sinless deception*.

Stella Revard, justly seeking to refute the groundless charge that unfallen Eve is insufficient to withstand satanic temptation, argues persuasively that she is indeed up to that task and so must bear independent responsibility for her sinful transgression. But like Diane McColley, Revard wonders wistfully whether Eve might "have unravelled the coils of Satanic rhetoric, have separated the plausible from the true, and unmasked Satan in the Serpent."[24] Decidedly not! Even unfallen Adam, who is not deceived, and who recognizes at once that "Some cursed fraud / Of enemy hath beguiled [Eve], yet unknown" (904–5)—even he does not recognize Satan *in* the serpent. It has recently been suggested, as I have pointed out in my Introduction, that *yet unknown* modifies *enemy*, so that Adam does not even know that the Devil is the foe in question. I do not endorse this ingenious reading,[25] but it adds a certain weight to Milton's plain and perspicuous intention: *some* satanic fraud has deceived Eve, but the nature of the deception (namely, that Satan has possessed the serpent) is as yet unclear to Adam. Given the experience of Uriel, how could it be otherwise? Fallen Eve is therefore entirely correct to tell Adam that he could "not have discerned / Fraud in the serpent" (9.1149–50): for "Neither man nor angel can discern / Hypocrisy" (3.682–83) before the fact, as Uriel sinlessly discovers only after the fact (4.114–30).

Complementing the impenetrability of Satan's disguise as a factor in Eve's deception, Milton provides a number of psychological concomitants that further bespeak the event's plausibility—indeed, its inevitability. Although both Raphael and Adam have cautioned Eve "to beware / [She] swerve not too secure" (5.237–38), the much-maligned separation scene (9.201–384),[26] in which Adam struggles manfully to admonish his wife about the duplicity of Satan, issues in, innocently but pathetically, precisely the opposite effect: Eve is more than adequately "forewarned" (378) of imminent danger, but she departs from her husband "Secure [neither] to single or combined" (339) deception, but rather "too secure [that is, careless]" to beware at

24. Revard, "Eve and the Doctrine of Responsibility in *Paradise Lost*," 76.

25. Jean Gagen, "Adam, the Serpent, and Satan: Recognition and Restoration." The article's thesis is defended by repeated beggings of the question. Gagen does so to rescue Eve from imbecility by minimizing Adam's perceptual acuity. The author does not perceive the Satan-serpent identity in Book 9, but he certainly knows that the Devil has defrauded Eve: see 9.253–56, 274–75, 306–8, 351–56, 360–64, and (especially) 947–51 and 1171–73. The contrary evidence of 1067–69 and 10.867–80 is irrelevant, since Adam is now fallen and *therefore* reasoning badly (compare 9.1120–31).

26. Diane McColley lists numerous misreadings of this scene in *Milton's Eve*, 182–83, nn. 3–5. But McColley herself misreads it, as I shall argue.

all. Unable (witness Uriel) to unmask the artificer of fraud, she does not "much expect / A foe so proud will first the weaker seek" (382–83). She therefore attacks her garden work "mindless the while" (9.431), attentive to her horticulture but not to the enemy, and is indeed—psychologically speaking—"opportune to all [Satan's duplicitous] attempts" (481). Her own (sinless) state of mind and the serpent's native subtlety join to cause the sinless peripeteia Adam has already fervently predicted:

> reason not impossibly may meet
> Some specious object [i.e., the serpent] by the foe suborned,
> And fall into deception [not into sin] unaware,
> Not keeping strictest watch, as she was warned.
>
> (360–63)

Ignorant of the experience of Uriel, Adam erroneously thinks that deceit can be mastered by intellectual discernment; he is dead wrong (*no* wariness can prevent a "fall into deception"), but Eve's inattentive daydreaming certainly facilitates the beguiling that occasions her fall: it must, because the Bible says the woman was deceived.

Excursus on the Separation Scene

Such theoretical acuity as Adam manifests in the just-cited passage has deceived certain readers into inferring that *he* is proof against deception. Georgia Christopher, repeating the errors of Perkins, Browne, McColley, Revard, and others, suppresses the deception of Uriel and Eve's onomastic skills to assert that "the interpretive acuity that Adam showed in labeling the beasts according to their natures would have enabled him to see the verbal serpent as a fraud."[27] This mistaken opinion—a misogynistic one, for it implies that unfallen Eve is an innately inept exegete of the word—has persisted so tenaciously in the literature as to merit further rebuttal; so I will conclude this section with a relevant and decisive example of Adam's prelapsarian susceptibility to beguiling—his crucial misperception of his wife's intentions in the separation scene. Eve, in a repetition of her inquisitive husband's "sudden mind" (5.452), spontaneously suggests that they divide their garden labors for efficiency's sake (9.201–25). Christopher calls her labor ethic "a left-handed [i.e., sinister]" violation of "God's word," a specifically interpretive "offense."[28] But on the contrary: Eve's proposal, articulated with reasoned candor, is entirely innocent and charmingly aggressive—a rare instance in *Paradise Lost* of female seizure of initiative.[29] It is also

27. Christopher, *Milton and the Science of the Saints*, 159.
28. Ibid., 154.
29. The first such sinless seizure occurs at 5.321–30. See my "*Summa contra Pastorem et Lectorem.*"

erroneous, but to err in Paradise is not offensive—witness Uriel.

From Milton's point of view, Eve's gesture proceeds from an exigency of plot: having decided, with the mainstream exegetical tradition, to orchestrate the temptations of woman and man sequentially and independently,[30] the poet must somehow effect the separation of this perpetually "Handed" (4.739) couple. He must do so plausibly and—as Diane McColley has proven—in a way that manifests "Eve's [prelapsarian] sufficiency" to withstand temptation alone.[31] Certain critics have recently taken exception either to the woman's desire to separate or to Adam's insistence that it is imprudent for her to do so. Georgia Christopher calls "departure from her spouse's side against advice" "Eve's proto-sin"—casuistical imprecision that is ethically meaningless and antitheodicial.[32] Joan S. Bennett blames both man and woman: she faults Adam for apodictically dismissing Eve by "substitut[ing] his own authority for a truly free decision from her"; and she criticizes Eve for breaking "a particular law" (Adam's desire that she remain by his side) "in deference" not "to a rationally understood higher purpose of the whole law" but to some doubtfully voluntarist antinomian impulse (the wish to garden alone) reflecting what Eve "sincerely feels at the moment to be right."[33] Diana Benet, on the other hand, anxious to secure Eve's continuing rectitude at the moment of separation, says that Adam lets her depart because "he does not know" "whether to go or stay" "is the better course" of action. But Eve is said to know: adopting (it is alleged) an Abdelian temptation paradigm, the woman argues (correctly, Benet believes) that just as this faithful angel stands alone, "Unshaken, unseduced, unterrified" (5.899) by Luciferean fraud, she too must face the tempter "Alone, without exterior help sustained" (9.336); she too must demonstrate independently that her "firm faith and love / Can [not] by his fraud be shaken or seduced" (286–87).[34]

The Abdiel parallel is, however, not precise: first, he is an angel; and second, *he is not deceived*, for Lucifer's temptation is an open and discoverable apparition: he presents the angels with a naked proposal to rebel. In point of fact, the appropriate paradigm for both Adam and Eve is not Abdiel's single sufficiency—which demonstrates merely that it *is possible* to circumvent temptation on one's own—but his cautionary

30. McColley, *Milton's Eve*, 181–82, n. 1, cites representative Renaissance commentators who thought they were seduced together.

31. Ibid., 141.

32. *Milton and the Science*, 151.

33. "'Go': Milton's Antinomianism and the Separation Scene in *Paradise Lost*, Book 9," 398–99.

34. "Abdiel and the Son in the Separation Scene," 130, 132–33.

adjuration to his colleagues not to succumb to Luciferean fraud. Abdiel is to Lucifer's legions what Adam and Eve might have been to one another had they confronted Satan as a family unit. To be tempted alone is not sinful, but a one-on-one encounter with evil renders *either* man or woman less likely to resist temptation, as "the event perverse" (9.405) of the fall amply testifies.

My thesis is that in separating from Adam, Eve makes an innocent strategic error occasioned by sinless self-deception. Why else would Milton call this solitary woman a "fairest unsupported flower, / *From her best prop* [i.e., Adam] *so far,* and storm [that is, Satan] so nigh" (432–33; emphasis mine)? Why else would he describe her, in perhaps the finest epic simile in Western literature (633–45), as about to be "swallowed [!] up and lost, *from succor* [i.e., Adam again] far" (642; emphasis mine)? Milton's plot requires him to arrange human temptation as a sequence of independent events, but nothing obliges him to endorse the ominous scenario as an ethical desideratum ("I now *must* change / Those notes to tragic" [5–6; emphasis mine]). Although God gave Adam a "native innocence" that might have kept him from being our "true *Epimetheus,*" it does not follow that Eve, his "consummat and most adorned [unfallen (4.708–19)] *Pandora,*" might not have been, if not "the nurse and guide of," at least an admonitory adjunct (9.308–14, 357–58) to, "his arbitrary happinesse and perseverance."[35] Nor does it follow, as Eve mistakenly thinks, that she and her husband are "endued / Single with *like* defense" (9.324–25; emphasis mine), or that they are *equally* "secure to single or combined" (339) assault. Far from it. As Joseph Summers has argued apropos of a related passage (4.288–318), "the democratic assumption that ideally every individual *should* be self-sufficient and our tendency to define 'perfection' as eternal self-sufficiency complicate our difficulties"[36] in understanding what I call Milton's theory of ethical synergism. Adam and Eve are created in "single imperfection" (8.423); God knows "it not good for man to be alone" (445). They do not *require* each other to resist satanic temptation ("Perfect within, no outward aid require" [8. 642]), but mutual support would not be supererogatory: "Subtle he needs must

35. *The Doctrine and Discipline of Divorce,* YP 2:293. The passage is nicely analyzed by Burden, *Logical Epic,* 68–70. I have deliberately misread it to emphasize my point. Milton is not identifying *Pandora* (Greek *all-gifted*) with Eve in this passage, because only in the fall does she become in any sense Adam's "nurse and guide," and even then the "[*un*]happiness" to which she seduces him is still his own arbitrary choice. Unfallen Eve is not a Pandora; she is "more lovely than" the Hesiodic temptress and "O too like [her only] / In sad event" when, after her fall, "she ensnared / Mankind" (4.714–18). Before the fall she might, however, have supported Adam in temptation, just as he might have supported her.

36. *The Muse's Method: An Introduction to "Paradise Lost,"* 95.

be, who could seduce / Angels, *nor think superfluous others' aid"* (307–8; emphasis mine). Adam, not Eve, is thinking of Abdiel,[37] who comes to the timely rescue of Lucifer's troops—futilely, as it happens (so much the worse for them), but not superfluously.

The issue of prelapsarian ethical synergism being so critical to Milton's theodicy, and bearing so directly, as I shall argue, on the theme of deception in *Paradise Lost*, I will take up one additional preliminary argument before essaying an analysis of the separation scene itself. There is a supposed parapraxis in *Areopagitica*: "our sage and serious poet *Spencer*, . . . describing true temperance under the person of Guion, brings him in with his palmer through the cave of Mammon, and the bowr of earthly blisse that he might see and know, and yet abstain."[38] Since in *The Faerie Queene* Guyon is not accompanied by the Palmer into the Cave of Mammon (2.7), Milton is thought to have forgotten a plot detail in his original's epic. On this supposition, certain bizarre theories about the anxiety of influence have been concocted to account for the bard's supposed amnesia.[39] Milton, however, rarely forgets, and he is certainly not anxious lest Spenser's authority entrammel him in slavish discipleship. In addition to adding the Palmer to the Mammon episode, he confers the adjective *earthly* on Spenser's "bowr of . . . blisse," anticipating a further metamorphosis of his source's diction that, some fifteen years later, will enable him to characterize the terrestrial "blissful Bower" (4.690) of unfallen Adam and Eve. In *Areopagitica* Milton is anxious not about influence (he certainly does not have "the guilty conscience of the student who has diverged from his teacher")[40] but about the temptation protocols appropriate to orchestrating the "event perverse" whence "the knowledge of good and evil as two twins cleaving together leapt forth into the World" (p. 514).

37. Benet's argument ("Abdiel and the Son," 132–33) turns on the linguistic similarity between 5.899 ("Unshaken, unseduced") and 9.287 ("shaken or seduced"). But if Eve actually intends to argue along Abdelian lines, why does she do so only surreptitiously? Why not allude to this servant of God more explicitly, as Adam does? Since Eve does not think that she can be seduced *at all* (9.285–89), the farthest thing from her mind is the salient fact that Lucifer's troops are led astray *in spite* of Abdiel's admonitions. Benet's supposed parallel is the ingenious concomitant of her desire to defend Eve by rejecting Milton's (and Adam's) sensible commitment to ethical synergism.

38. *YP* 2:516.

39. See Harold Bloom, *A Map of Misreading*, 128. Maureen Quilligan, *Milton's Spenser: The Politics of Reading*, 65, argues ingeniously that "Guyon's phantom companion becomes the prototype of Milton's reader." John Guillory, *Poetic Authority: Spenser, Milton, and Literary History*, 133, more sensibly locates Milton's "parapraxis" in retrospective anxiety about "the Lady of *Comus*, who cannot stand alone except in passive resistance." I agree, except that *Areopagitica* makes it clear that Milton's fundamental proof text is Genesis 3.

40. Guillory, *Poetic Authority*, 134.

If, "As . . . the state of [fallen] man *now is*," Milton "cannot praise a fugitive and cloister'd virtue, unexercis'd & unbreath'd, that never sallies out and sees her adversary,"[41] as the state of prelapsarian man *then was*, he cannot endorse (though he does not *censure*) a "Virtue" (9.335) that "rash[ly]" (9.780)[42] exposes itself to satanic guile: "Seek not temptation, then, which to avoid / Were better [true]." "Trial will come unsought [absolutely true: compare 412–21]" (364–66). Moreover, although Guyon survives the descent to Mammon's cave (though not unscathed [2.7.65–66]), Milton, anticipating the fall of Eve, cannot believe it plausible that he does so unsustained by the help of the Palmer. Like Dante, the poet himself dare not enter "the wide womb of uncreated night" (1.150) unassisted: rather he is taught "by the heavenly Muse to venture down / The dark descent, and up to reascend, / Though hard and rare" (3.19–21). If he requires the aid of a "celestial patroness" (9.21) to fathom Hell, and if Guyon requires the assistance of the Palmer to resist the mere *earthly* enchantments of Acrasia, ought not the knight logically to rely on the squire to facilitate his more dangerous descent into eschatology? Spenser naively believes that Guyon survives the temptation to avarice and ambition by autonomously recollecting his uprightness and past successes: "And evermore himselfe with comfort feedes, / Of his own vertues, and prayseworthy deeds."[43] But Milton, who, like the knight of temperance, perseveres "In darkness, and with dangers compassed round, / And *solitude*" (7.27–28 = 2.801 = *FQ* 2.7.20.9; emphasis mine), survives "*not alone*," nor by his own virtue, but only while Urania "Visit'st [his] slumbers nightly" (7.28–29; emphasis mine). *That* is why he calls upon the Palmer, who guides Guyon through the Bower of Bliss, to support the knight's dangerous journey into Hell as well. Virtue may indeed be sufficient unto itself, but it will be more sufficient if an Abdiel or a Palmer or an Adam or an Eve offers aid and comfort in virtue's hour of critical need.

Without an exterior prop, the fall of either Adam or Eve is more likely to occur. Far from endorsing the prudence of separation, Milton therefore merely permits it, not only because his plot requires this concession, but also because independent temptation makes Eve's fall more plausible. For these reasons the poet chooses to follow majority

41. *YP* 2:514–15; emphasis mine. Ernest Sirluck has a sensible discussion of Milton's divagation from Spenser in "Milton Revises the *Faerie Queene*."

42. Just as, after long deliberation, "her rash hand in evil hour / Forth reaching to the fruit, [Eve] plucked, she ate" (9.780–81), Eve's separation from Adam is ill-considered. Imprudence is not, however, a sin (or an imperfection) in *Paradise Lost:* it is a blameless concomitant of prelapsarian susceptibility to deception.

43. *The Faerie Queene*, 2.7.2.4–5, in *Spenser: Poetical Works*, ed. J. C. Smith and E. De Sélincourt.

opinion on the question of whether the woman succumbed to the serpent in her husband's absence. The inspired biblical text says that "she took some of [the] fruit and ate it; and she also gave some to her husband, *who was with her*, and he ate it" (3:6; emphasis mine). It requires considerable ingenuity to infer separate and independent temptation from this text;[44] Milton does so, not because he feels pressured to conform to tradition, but because the artist in him would have been hard pressed to orchestrate Eve's deceived transgression and Adam's undeceived repetition of it as virtually simultaneous events transacted in a single space of shared temptation. When Adam counsels his wife against the prudence of departing, he unwittingly anticipates just this potential plot difficulty, projecting Milton's artistic dilemma onto Satan himself: the fiend has "hope to find / His wish and best advantage, us asunder, / Hopeless to circumvent us joined" (257–59). Adam does not mean that he and Eve *cannot* be seduced together, but he intuitively understands what Satan soon confirms (421–26, 479–88): that the Devil is as little hopeful of defrauding the couple simultaneously as he is of encountering "what so seldom chanced, . . . / . . . Eve separate" (423–24). If he finds her alone, "to his wish, / Beyond his hope" (423–24), this peripeteia does not correspond to Milton's theological preferences. *He* wishes, "Beyond *his* hope," that "innocent frail man" "had . . . / . . . scaped / . . . [Satan's] mortal snare" (4.6–8), a nostalgic fantasy that shared temptation might well have justified. Accepting, however, ancient history's inexorable necessity, the poet seeks to render plausible a tragic outcome he cannot undo. That is why he fashions the separation scene. The dialectic that comprises this portentous event enables him, moreover, to eradicate misogyny from the deutero-Pauline deception ethic. Without compromising his sinless couple's intelligence or integrity, Milton shows, in the separation colloquy, how frail indeed they are, for Eve's departure turns not on the question of who is to blame for it, but on shared prelapsarian susceptibility to innocent self-deception.

Adam responds to Eve's desire to absent herself from felicity awhile by (correctly) endorsing it in principle (9.227–36) and by (correctly) positing certain distinctions designed to confirm that Edenic "labor" (236) is not meant to be "toilsome" (4.439) or "irksome" (9.235–47). Adam is forever teaching Eve, as he shall try—futilely—to teach her in the colloquy that follows. First, however, he falls into deception unaware: "but if much converse perhaps / Thee satiate, to short absence I could yield" (247–48). In prelapsarian Paradise, how-

---

44. To do so the RSV deletes the clause "who was with her" from the text of Genesis. I therefore cite this passage from the New American Bible. AV has "and gave also unto her husband with her," which leaves the issue clouded in some ambiguity.

ever, surfeit is a purely hypothetical construct (5.451–52, 636–39); the first human encounter with gluttony occurs at the fall, when Eve "Greedily . . . engorged without restraint" and becomes "satiate at length" (791–92; compare 1004–11). Her husband is self-deceptively searching for a rationale to occasion the libertarian opinion that his "individual solace" (4.486) is entitled to the psychological "space" needed to make her also a separate individual. Moreover, Milton requires Adam's concessive *but* for his own reasons, for without it the colloquy would cease, and husband and wife would turn to their garden labors "joint hand[ed]" (244).[45] But beyond acquiescing to the inexorability of plot, Adam's tentative imposition of hidden motives on Eve contributes to the theme of deception in *Paradise Lost*. The woman who can say "with thee conversing I forget all time" (4.639) is not likely to become satiated with "talk between, / Food of the Mind" (9.237–38; compare 8.39–58). Beguiled by his affection for a woman he is loath to offend, Adam projects a subconscious, or at any rate a language-mind dichotomy, onto his unfallen spouse. He has misread her concern that "discourse . . . intermits / Our day's work" (223–24)—which it surely does—as unspoken ennui at conversation itself. The point is that Adam's attribution of sinless deceit (disguised motives) to Eve is itself an instance of blameless error—he is plainly wrong, the victim of innocent self-deception.[46] If Eve is first to suggest separation, it is her husband, not she, who keeps the issue an issue.

Having gotten himself into this difficulty, Adam correctly urges the imprudence of separation under the present circumstances: the "doubt" that "possesses" him (251) corresponds (though he does not know it) to the danger of the serpentine "imp of fraud" (89), whose "brutal sense / . . . possessing [Satan has already] inspired / With act intelligential" (188–90). Adam's point is that since a "malicious foe" (253) "seeks to work us woe and shame / By sly assault" (255–56), he and his wife ought (prudentially speaking) to remain "joined, *where each / To other* speedy aid might lend at need" (259–60; emphasis mine). But Eve sinlessly misinterprets this incisive assessment of human ethical synergism as an "unkindness" (271): her selective

45. Without the *but* Adam would get the last (definitive) word, as he does at 4.660–88 (clarifying Eve's astronomical speculations) and 5.95–128 (interpreting her satanic dream). This pattern changes (sinlessly) at 5.308–30, where Eve corrects Adam's inadvertent opinion that she has a pantry. If he is expert in gardening protocols (and he is), she is the unsurpassable mistress of cuisine. Eve's taking of initiative at 9.204–25 is likewise sinless, a natural development from her earlier experience. The basis upon which she argues for separation is faulty, but no more blamable than Adam's naive apperception that one requires a storehouse for victuals in the garden of Eden.

46. Benet, "Abdiel and the Son," 131, claims that he "is alert even to [Eve's] unexpressed feelings when he refers to the emotional boredom that he fears might underlie her proposal." But prelapsarian Eve is an open book: she has nothing to hide.

attention transforms Adam's "doubt . . . lest harm / Befall thee sev-
ered from me" (251-52)—which is exactly what happens—into
"doubt" of her "firmness . . . / To God or thee" (279-80). The woman is
propelled thereby to the further inference that her husband fears that
her "firm faith and love / Can by [Satan's] fraud be shaken and
seduced" (286-87)—which of course is *exactly* what happens; but she
objects to this conclusion as "misthought of her to thee so dear" (289).
At this point Eve, defensively rebutting charges of insufficiency that
have never been filed against her, has concluded not only that she is
capable of withstanding independent temptation, but also that she is
invincible to satanic deceit. Milton is preparing her (psychologically) for
a fall into deception by having her rebut Adam's prudential admonitions with exaggerated assertions of prelapsarian infallibility.

Adam now attempts to correct Eve's misinterpretation with "heal-
ing words" (290). He is not "diffident" (293) of his wife; reiterating the
theme of ethical synergism, he labors only "to avert / From [Eve] *alone*"
(302-3; emphasis mine) what they can better face together. He benefits
from the woman's "influence," deriving therefrom "Access in every
virtue" (309-10); should she not likewise "trial choose" "when [he is]
present" (315-16)? Indeed she should, for, as Adam understands, Eve
is dangerously (though not sinfully) close to underestimating the
"false guile" of the enemy (306-8). Diagnosing her unwarranted sense
of security, Adam therefore presses the urgency of remaining "joint
hand[ed]" (244).

Milton absolutely endorses these sentiments (318-19); "but Eve
. . . thought / Less attributed to her faith sincere" (319-20). *She,* not her
husband, has "misthought," in a sinless repetition of the mistaken
Adamic perceptions that have occasioned the colloquy in the first
place and that punctuate its every exchange. She now thinks that a
fragile prelapsarianism, "straitened by a foe" (323), is inconsistent
with human tranquility: "Frail is our happiness, if this be so, / And
Eden were no Eden thus exposed" (340-41). But paradisaical bliss *is*
"frail" (4.11, 9.340); man and woman *are* "exposed"—or shortly will
be—to a dangerous "foe" (327). *In order to sustain her conviction in faith
that she is indeed happy in the garden of God, Eve insists that she is "secure
to" (339)—by which she means "incorruptible by"—independent temptation.*
Her innocent mind, deceived because she is not God, has reverted to
Adam's naive pre-Raphaelian notion that he cannot "want obedience
. . . / To [God], or possibly his love desert" (5.514-15). Eve thinks,
moreover, that "faith, love, [and] virtue" are blank and excremental
unless tested "Alone, without exterior help sustained" (335-36),
whereas in fact the sun-clad power of temperance, as Guyon demonstrates, requires only that it be uncloistered and exercised, not that it

be assayed "Alone." Diane McColley believes that Eve's argument "recaptures moral clarity and turns the tide in her favor with a succinct compendium of *Areopagitica*," "on the principle of [which] . . . [she] is right."[47] *But nothing in Milton's excoriation of prepublication censorship justifies Eve's preference for a solitary, unaided psychomachia,* and the evidence of Guyon suggests that the woman is rashly defending a prudentially untenable temptation ethic. Why does Eve persist in this attitude? She is "loth to be thought not circumspect or firm enough, [and] urges her going apart, the rather desirous to make trial of her strength" (*The Argument*). As John S. Diekhoff has argued, "Eve's use of the arguments from [postlapsarian] *Areopagitica* in a [prelapsarian] context where they do not apply is but the rationalization of her desire—the desire for temptation."[48]

Eve's desire is innocent (343–47, 373–75), the blameless concomitant of human (not specifically female) proclivity to deception; but it is also dangerous, for she is rapidly acquiring the attitudinal overconfidence that will make her fall into satanic deception a fait accompli. This point may be clarified by a final detail from Spenser. The most striking feature about the Mammon episode is that this "God of the world and worldlings" (*FQ* 2.7.8.1) is an open and discoverable apparition: he calls himself "Great Mammon" (2), and his otherworldly kingdom is peopled by the mournful shades of those who have succumbed to avarice. The climactic temptation that Guyon repudiates comprises "golden apples" (54.1) depending from a forbidden tree in "the Garden of Proserpina" (53.1). The knight, however, easily repudiates Mammon's solicitation that he pluck the "fruit of gold" (63.7), for he is not deceived into misconstruing its fallacious force:

> he was warie wise in all his way,
> *And well perceived his deceiptfull sleight,*
> Ne suffred lust his safetie to betray;
> So goodly did beguile the Guyler of the pray.
> (64.6–9; emphasis mine)

Eve, however, *cannot* expose satanic fraud: "Whatever sleights [= *FQ* 2.7.64.7] *none* would suspicious mark." The Milton who deploys the Palmer to ameliorate Guyon's resistibility to undeceived temptation would surely endorse Adam's desire to assist Eve in withstanding diabolical guile.

Adam therefore replies "fervently" (342) to the woman's apparent indictment of divine providence (343–48). "Impelled by her obvious errors," he "responds with true reason."[49] He now occupies the slot

47. *Milton's Eve*, 172, 177.
48. "Eve, the Devil, and *Areopagitica*," 434.
49. Summers, *The Muse's Method*, 174.

that earlier required Raphael to respond "with contracted brow" (8.860) to the man's apparent uxoriousness (528–659). If Adam must "Accuse not nature" (561), Eve must accuse not "God" (9.344)—which in fact she has not *quite* done. Emphasizing "the danger" (349) of false security, Adam twice speculates—clairvoyantly—that unwary carelessness might occasion a fall into deception (351–56, 360–63). For these reasons he rehearses—for the last time—the Miltonic theme that shared temptation is preferable to single combat with the Father of Lies: "Not then mistrust, but tender love enjoins, / That I should mind thee oft, *and thou mind* [i.e., admonish and *re*mind] me" (357–58; emphasis mine). Since the falls of both our grandparents will comprise not sinful deception but culpable amnesia (10.12–16), the Augustinian art of memory is precisely the anodyne that Adam and Eve require as they approach their fateful moment of prelapsarian choice. What better mnemonics can they devise than to be "Imparadised in one another's" (4.506) solemn admonitions?

Adam now "close[s]," not "the encounter,"[50] but his account of ethical synergism, urging, in terms just this side of a direct command, that his wife "sever not" (366) from him. Prelapsarian decorum and the requirements of Milton's plot, translated psychologically into respect for Eve's independence, prevent Adam from "more" than "admonish[ing]" Eve,

> foret[elling]
> The danger, and the lurking enemy
> That lay in wait; beyond this [would be] force,
> And force upon free will hath here no place.
> (1171–74)

Fallen Adam is often guilty of specious self-extenuation, but his retrospective summation of this aspect of the separation scene is entirely apposite. Raphael has cautioned him to cling to "wisdom, she deserts thee not, if thou / Dismiss not her" (8.564–65), but he has never adjured Adam to require *Eve's* uninterrupted presence at his side (witness Eve's sinless separation at 8.39–63). Man's "woe" begins with "effeminate slackness" (11.632–34), but *not yet*: the first resignation of manhood in *Paradise Lost* occurs when Adam, presented with the sinful apparition of his fallen daughter, "dropped" "From his *slack* hand" a "garland wreathed for Eve" (892–93; emphasis mine). At this juncture in the separation scene, however, he is far from "slack"; nor does he "fair dismiss" (1159) his wife, as she will retrospectively allege in a "vain" (1189) extenuation of her own. Having more than adequately

50. Bennett, "'Go': Milton's Antinomianism," 400.

followed Raphael's advice to "warn / Thy weaker" (6.908–9), Adam can do no "more" (9.1170) to protect her.

He therefore allows the separation colloquy to issue in Eve's conditional dismissal. After mobilizing all the right arguments, he repeats the concessive gesture by which he kept separation an issue at the outset, concluding with a valedictory *But* that gives Eve (and Milton) the entree requisite to effect her departure. Having sought, over the space of some two hundred lines, to persuade her of the hazard of "leav[ing] the faithful side / That gave [her] being" (265–66), Adam ambivalently concedes Eve's right independently to enact certain specious premises that his exhortations have failed to exorcise from her innocent but fallible consciousness:

> But *if thou think*, trial unsought may find
> Us both securer than thus warned thou seem'st,
> *Go;* for thy stay, not free, absents thee more.
>
> (370–72; emphasis mine)

Joseph Summers believes that in this passage Adam "suddenly dismisses reason, ignores his 'better knowledge,' abdicates his responsibility," and "tells [his wife] to go."[51] But in fact he is formulating a last-ditch effort to secure Eve's "stay"; she has leave to "Go" through her husband's goodness—but if, and only if, *she* believes ("if *thou* think") that the couple ("Us both") will be even more careless ("securer") by passively awaiting temptation than she now appears to be ("than . . . thou seem'st"), notwithstanding Adam's repeated admonitions ("thus warned"). The conditional modality of his *if* implies (a) Adam's intention to make separation a matter for which Eve, not he, must bear final responsibility;[52] and (b) his forlorn hope that the rational power of his protasis will—even at this late juncture—persuade her to disregard the far-from-unconditional force of his apodosis. Other readings of these difficult lines are of course possible,[53] so it is no wonder that Eve, like many of Milton's critics, erroneously transforms them into an apodictic dismissal:

51. *The Muse's Method*, 174.
52. Excellent commentary on this point by Burden, *Logical Epic*, 89ff. Also Fowler, *John Milton: "Paradise Lost,"* 458–59, who errs, however, by implying that the separation issues from man's defective intellect.
53. The lines may mean that "trial unsought may find / Us both securer than thus warned thou seem'st [to think]," but Eve clearly does not think Adam and she are secure [i.e., careless] in one another's company. Her point is that joint temptation is too easily rebuffed to be meritorious (335–36). They are *too* secure (that is, safe) from attack while together; she thinks them *very* (if not equally) "secure to single or combined" assault (339). Adam knows that she is wrong and therefore specifies her already dangerous security, which he is trying "fervently" (342) to eradicate.

> With thy permission then, and thus forwarned
> Chiefly by what thy own last reasoning words
> Touched only, that our trial, when least sought,
> May find us both perhaps far less prepared,
> The willinger I go.
>
> (378–82)

Adam has said, in effect, "*I* think you should stay because joint trial will find us less secure [careless]; but if *you* persist in thinking the reverse is true, you may go." Eve, however, by now anxious to depart, confers imperative force on the reluctantly concessive (and almost subjunctive) predicate *Go*,[54] a metamorphosis she mediates by regarding as *his* opinion ("*thy own* last reasoning words") what Adam has merely hypothesized as *hers* ("if *thou* think"), and what he firmly hopes is *not* her opinion: "that our trial, when least sought, / May find us both perhaps far less prepared." She repeats this error (sinfully) after her fall, speciously extenuating her own trespass by alleging that Adam did "not much gainsay [false], / Nay didst permit [true], approve [false], and fair dismiss [false]" her (1158–59). Contrary to Diane McColley, "her going forth alone is a considered, deliberated, [but *not* an] informed choice."[55] Eve is deceived, both as to Adam's intentions and as to the meaning of his words—just as, at the outset of the colloquy, he erroneously read satiety into her work ethic. Both are deceived, neither blameworthily; the separation scene thus begins and ends in innocent human error, for deception (witness Uriel) is a (sinless) fact of prelapsarian life.

I Timothy 2:11–15 is therefore right: the woman *was* deceived—but so was the man.

II. The Woman Was Deceived and Became a Transgressor

As long as the state of innocence continued, it was impossible for the human intellect to assent to falsehood as if it were truth. . . . Though the woman was deceived before she sinned in deed, still it was not till she had already sinned by interior pride.

—Aquinas, *Summa Theologica*

[Temptation] and [transgression] we know in the field of this World grow up together almost inseparably; and the knowledge of [temptation] is so involv'd and interwoven with the knowledge of [sin], and in so many cunning resemblances hardly to be discern'd, that those confused seeds

54. Bennett, a true daughter of unfallen Eve, likewise regards *Go* as an apodictic imperative ("'Go': Milton's Antinomianism," 400). This reading is, however, impossible to validate. Bennett asserts it to force Adam into the Procrustean bed of voluntarist antinomianism.
55. *Milton's Eve*, 154.

which were impos'd on *Psyche* as an incessant labour to cull out, and sort asunder, were not more intermixt.

—*Areopagitica*

Man falls because he is deceived by Satan.
—**B. Rajan**, *Paradise Lost and the Seventeenth Century Reader*

In Timothy, however, Eve is not sinlessly deceived. The pseudo-paratactic collocation of "the woman was deceived *and* became a transgressor" suggests more than mere temporal succession or casual contiguity between deception and sin: to deutero-Paul the two phenomena are ethically implicated as the yolk and white of one cataclysmic theological shell. The force of their interconnectedness is obscured in the Revised Standard Version, as it is in most English translations. A better rendering of the Greek text might be "Adam was not deceived at all, but the woman got into deception and so was in transgression and remains in it."[56] (This reading is intimated, interestingly enough, in the King James Bible, which reads, "the woman being deceived was in the transgression.") Eve was beguiled *and therefore* sinned—which is why subjection to their husbands is enjoined upon her many daughters.

Such an exegesis of I Timothy found wide support in the Middle Ages and beyond. Saint Augustine believes that "our first parents fell into open disobedience because they were already secretly corrupted; if [Eve's] will had remained stedfast . . . , the woman would not have believed the serpent spoke the truth."[57] His opinion survived intact into the seventeenth century. John Donne must serve as spokesperson for innumerable others: for him, the mere fact of Eve's deception "implies a weakness [if not indeed a sin] in the woman, that she is *the weaker vessell*, and that Adam [because less weak] *was not deceived*."[58] Eve was fooled and *therefore* fell: for an unfallen "human intellect," according to Thomas Aquinas, cannot "assent to falsehood as if it were truth."[59]

For Milton, however, the unfallen mind of "weaker" (6.909) Eve can and does assent to numerous sinless prevarications—but not because it is weak or culpable. In a revisionary critique of his biblical source and the tradition it spawned, he insists that the beguiling of Eve merely occasions her disobedience. How indeed could it be otherwise, since prelapsarian deception, as Uriel discovers, is inevitable? When

56. For a justification of such a reading based on the Greek New Testament, see below.
57. *City of God*, 387.
58. *The Sermons of John Donne*, ed. George R. Potter and Evelyn M. Simpson, 2:344–45.
59. *Summa Theologica* 1.94.4, trans. the Fathers of the English Dominican Province, 100–101.

Eve departs from Adam, Milton addresses her in apostrophic valediction: "O much deceived, much failing, hapless Eve, / Of thy presumed return! Event perverse!" (404–5). This couplet syntactically mimics the very deception it bespeaks: *deceived, failing,* and *hapless* are parallel attributive adjectives and appear to imply that deceit ipso facto entails hopeless sinful transgression. But the next line corrects this impression: Eve is innocently deceived with respect to the present circumstance only—her "presumed return"—for she has just promised Adam "To be returned by noon amid the bower" (401) to serve him dinner, when in fact at that very moment she will be about to serve herself the forbidden fruit (739–43). Deception makes her "hapless" indeed but not at all morally culpable. And it never will.

The same point is suggested after the fall when Milton observes that Satan "in the serpent, had perverted Eve, / Her husband she, to taste the fatal fruit" (10.3–4). The lines seem to say that the Devil makes the woman a pervert, a transgression she apparently repeats by perverting Adam. But the poet's syntax momentarily disguises his actual semantic intent: Satan merely occasions Eve's fall by turning her mind toward sin (*per*vert being the antonym of *animad*vert), just as she merely seduces (i.e., leads) Adam into temptation without causing him "to taste the fatal fruit." Contrary to Augustine and Aquinas, Eve is without fault even after she has been deceived, flattered, and led by Satan, in a willed but innocent surrender of initiative, "to the tree / Of prohibition" (644–45).

In *Surprised by Sin,* the hard gemlike flame of Stanley Fish's intellect nevertheless misapprehends the process by which Uriel exonerates Eve even at this late stage. Does Milton expect the woman to be more discriminating than the regent of the sun? Fish thinks he does, and he relegates the opposite opinion to impercipient readers:

> The reader who has answered the question [should Eve be sharper-sighted than Uriel?] (in the negative) before he asks it *will have forged another link in the chain which leads Eve to the tree* [exactly!]. Yet only an instant's reflection serves *to discredit the parallel* [between Uriel and the woman] and to illuminate the conditions of Eve's temptation by emphasizing *the differences* between the two situations. *Hypocrisy is not a problem for Eve* [!] since she need only recall what God has said in response to any tempter no matter what his appearance [true enough]. Uriel's failure is excusable [true]. . . . *But* Eve's failure is a failure of the will [false!] . . . .[60]

This analysis is a paradigmatic example of failure to maintain the requisite casuistical distinctions: (1) Milton, not the reader, proves (by the example of Uriel) that Eve cannot be more discriminating than the

60. *Surprised by Sin,* 233; emphasis mine.

angel bright; (2) Milton, *not the reader*, thus deploys the angel to forge "another link in the chain" that inexorably draws "Eve to the tree" (Fish, who elsewhere correctly distinguishes the insufficiency of her intellect to discern fraud from the sufficiency of her will to withstand temptation, here collapses the crucial distinction, chastising readers who think Uriel dooms Eve to be deceived, and anteriorizing her fall by implying that she is culpable for consenting to deception—but she is *doomed* to this fate by a well-wrought chain of antecedent causality; to be deceptively seduced ["Lead then, said Eve" (631)] to a forbidden fruit is not, as Fish implies, to be led into sin); (3) contrary to Fish, the parallel between Uriel and Eve on the issue of deception is isomorphic: both are absolutely beguiled, for the created intellect cannot discern satanic fraud before the fact; (4) the *point of difference* between the angel and the woman consists only in the fact that Satan does not seduce Uriel *into temptation* (he never invites him to disobey God), whereas he is about (*about*, notice), in what appears (*appears*, notice) to be a Miltonic divagation from the Lord's Prayer,[61] to suggest that Eve transgress; (5) hypocrisy is therefore a real and insurmountable problem for Eve's intellect (not her will), for the potency of satanic deceit prevents her from exposing fraud at this or at any later prelapsarian juncture; and (6) when Eve sins it will indeed, as Fish argues, be traceable to "failure of the will," but in this passage the critic either asserts on his own behalf, or at any rate attributes to the supposed defects of fallen readers, the notion that a willed lapse accounts for Eve's continuing entanglement in Satan's net of deception.

Nevertheless, the fact remains that invincible ignorance alone, caused by satanic "deceit and lies" (5.243) and innate creaturely propensity to deception, seduces Eve—yet sinless—to "the root of all our woe" (9.645). And she remains faultless even beyond her arrival at the tree. Having brought her to this ominous pass, Milton at last grafts the scriptural temptation scenario (Genesis 3:1–6) onto his own narrative. Whereas in the Bible temptation begins with certain words of the serpent (1b), *Paradise Lost* reverses the potentially damaging implications of this fact: Eve sees the prohibited tree and *she* speaks first, confirming her inner rectitude and momentarily recapturing lost initiative by informing the snake that she cannot eat the bad fruit (9.647–54). Milton now repeats the biblical serpent's opening gambit (655–58 = Genesis 3:1b), after which he introduces Eve's biblical response, adding however the pregnant prolegomenon, "To whom thus Eve yet sinless" (659). Since she has long since been beguiled by

61. The prayer asks only that *God* "lead us not into temptation." But he never does in *Paradise Lost*. Lucifer tempts Abdiel, Abdiel tempts Lucifer (as I shall show), Satan tempts Eve, and Eve tempts Adam.

Satan, the poet has already departed from Augustine and Aquinas on the issue of culpable deceit: *his* Eve is *yet sinless*. Like Uriel's, her unfallen "human intellect" can "assent to falsehood as if it were truth."

But why does Milton call the woman blameless *at precisely this juncture,* preveniently exonerating her from sin with respect to Genesis 3:2–3, which she is about to repeat? The answer turns once again on the misogyny of Thomas Browne and others. The biblical verses read, "We may eat of the fruit of the trees of the garden; but God said, You shall not eat of the fruit of the tree which is in the midst of the garden, neither shall you touch it, lest you die." Browne chauvinistically finds mortal sin in these words: the woman

> either mistook, or traduced the commandment of God [citing 2:16–17]. Now Eve upon the question of the Serpent [3:1b] returned the Precept in different terms: *You shall not eat of it, neither shall you touch it, lest perhaps you die.* In which delivery, there were no less than *two mistakes, or rather additional mendacities;* for the commandment forbad not the touch of the Fruit; and positively said Ye shall surely die: . . . And therefore although it be said, and that very truely, that the Devil was a liar from the beginning, yet was the Woman herein the first express beginner: and falsified twice, before the reply of Satan. *And therefore also, to speak strictly, the sin of the Fruit was not the first Offence: They first transgressed the Rule of their own Reason; and after the commandment of God.* (pp. 18–19; emphasis mine)

But "to speak strictly" (the issue is far from a quibble), Milton believes that "the sin of the Fruit" was the *only* "offence." He calls Eve "yet sinless," a fact he elsewhere confirms by insisting, in propria persona, that Adam and Eve are indeed "Charged not to touch the interdicted tree" (7.46; compare 9.651, 925). Moreover if, as Browne says, Eve "extenuat[es]" by transforming the apodictic "you shall die" (Genesis 2:17) into a hypothetical "lest ye die" (9.663 = Genesis 3:3b), *for Milton prelapsarian extenuation is blameless:* "To whom thus Eve *yet sinless.*" She *wants* to eat (the biblical "tree which is in the midst of the garden" has become "this *fair* tree" [661; emphasis mine]), but desire is not sin: touching the fruit is. Finally, whereas the woman in the Bible matter-of-factly refutes the serpent's allegation that all trees are forbidden by remarking, "We may eat of the fruit of the trees of the garden" (3:2), Milton's Eve says (pointedly): "Of *each* tree in the garden we may eat" (660; emphasis mine), thus emphasizing God's generosity. These are not the words of one who has already "traduced the commandment of God."[62]

When does Eve sin? Thomas Aquinas is kinder to her than Thomas Browne with respect to this theodicial crux. Although he agrees that it

62. Cheryl Fresch does a good job of refuting Browne in "Milton's Eve and the Problem of the Additions to the Command."

was not the Father of Lies but "sinful pride"—an inordinate coveting of her own excellence—"that corrupted Eve into deception," Aquinas locates the moment of sin later than Browne, just after Genesis 3:4–5: "This," he says, "does not mean that pride preceded the promptings of the serpent, but that *as soon as the serpent had spoken his words of persuasion*, her mind was puffed up, the result being that she believed the demon to have spoken truly."[63] If we follow Aquinas, Milton's Eve sins at the moment Satan completes his lengthy expansion of the blasphemous untruths uttered by the biblical serpent (679–732 = 3:4–5). She certainly believes "the demon to have spoken truly": the tempter is "replete with guile" (733); his "words [are] impregned / With reason, to her seeming, and with truth" (737–38); and indeed they *are* "persuasive." In Eve's unfallen dream (4.799–809), to cite a relevant analogue, Satan does not corrupt her—cannot corrupt her[64]— but he does deceive her. Although the tree of knowledge is merely a conventional "sign of . . . obedience" (4.428),[65] Satan, overhearing the prohibition, transforms a forbidden *plant* into "*knowledge* forbidden" (515; emphasis mine), as if the tree had the indigenous power to enhance intelligence. In the dream he repeats this adjectival shift (moving *forbidden* from a vegetative sign [*tree*] to the epistemological reality it mysteriously signifies [*knowledge*]), as is proven when his victim, recounting her nightmare to Adam, now speaks of "the tree / Of *interdicted knowledge*" (5.51–52; emphasis mine). This is Eve's second extramural beguiling in *Paradise Lost*,[66] one that prepares her to believe in Book 9 that the tree of prohibition "gives . . . life / To knowledge" (9.686–87). She is thus hopelessly deceived long before she encounters Satan in the serpent; as Thomas Browne claims, she has "transgressed the Rule of her own Reason"; her "mistake is" indeed "that she believes the words of a creature against those of the Creator"[67]—is she beyond hope? "Puffed up" (Aquinas) with *superbia*? Decidedly *not*. Browne wonders why, at this critical juncture, Eve does not peremptorily terminate her temptation with the following rejoinder: "If the

63. *Summa Theologica* 2.2.163.1; in *The "Summa Theologica" of St. Thomas Aquinas, Second Part of the Second Part, QQ. CXLI-CLXX*, 254; emphasis mine. Had Aquinas read *Paradise Lost*, he would have located Eve's sin as early as 9.550–66, for her unfallen intellect has already assented to a falsehood (that is, that a serpent can speak).

64. One cannot sin in a dream, for reason and free will are dormant in dormition. See my "Beyond the Oedipus Complex."

65. Kerrigan, *The Sacred Complex*, 249–55, shows, however, that the tree has special force, though not the power to confer knowledge of good and evil—except in the negative sense suggested at 4.220–22 and 9.1069–73. God (8.323–24) and Raphael (7.542–44) actually obfuscate the tree's onomastic significance, rendering Eve more susceptible to deceit in dream.

66. The first, of course, is her confusion of appearance and reality at birth (4.449–91): *to be sinlessly beguiled is the birthright of all prelapsarian creatures.*

67. Christopher, *Milton and the Science*, 160.

tast of this Fruit maketh the eaters like Gods, . . . we are so already. If thereby our eyes shall be opened hereafter, they are at present quick enough, *to discover thy deceit*" (p. 18; emphasis mine). Maureen Quilligan, inadvertently aligning herself with the misogynistic tradition, believes that Eve's "interpretive experiences [at 4.489–91] ought to have made her proof against the tempter's ploy [citing 9.686–90]," as if the lessons she acquires at birth about appearance and reality ought to make her impervious to subsequent deceit.[68] But this is exactly the point at which Milton departs from the tradition: witness Uriel! "*Whatever* sleights"—even satanic blasphemy itself—"*none* would suspicious mark." This is why Milton's God says that "man falls deceived / By [Satan] *first*" (3.130–31; emphasis mine), which I take to mean "Eve is *first* deceived by the artificer of fraud; *then* she falls, sinful not *thereupon* but *thereafter*." Prelapsarian deception is undiscoverable in *Paradise Lost*, and it is not sinful.

Nearly every critic I have consulted on this issue locates Eve's sinful lapse at some point before she physically disregards the commandment "not to touch the interdicted tree" (7.46). Cheryl Fresch insists that by "the time the Tempter concludes [lines 679–733], the 'evil desire' which Milton argued was what the 'first parents were originally guilty of' has established itself."[69] But what is the context of the passage to which Fresch alludes? In the *Christian Doctrine* Milton distinguishes sin (as opposed to temptation), both original and actual, into

> two subdivisions, whether we call them degrees or parts or modes of sin, or whether they are related to each other as cause and effect. These subdivisions are evil desire, or the will to do evil, and the evil deed itself. James i.14, 15: *every man is tempted when he is drawn in and enticed by his own lust* [Eve up through line 733 and *well beyond*, as I shall argue]: *then, when lust has conceived* [the will to do evil], *it brings forth sin*.[70]

Milton indeed insists, as Fresch indicates, that "it was evil desire that our first parents were originally guilty of," but he never says that their "will to do evil" *preceded* their actual sin. In fact he goes on to argue that "this evil desire, this law of sin, was not only inbred in us [as *our* original sin], but also took possession of Adam *after his fall*, and *from his point of view could not be called original*" (*YP* 6:388–89; emphasis mine). What can this mean but that, for Milton, prelapsarian creatures can create the evil desire (what we call original sin) that they bequeath to posterity only by engaging the "second subdivision of sin, after evil desire, . . . the evil action or crime itself, which is commonly called 'actual' sin" (p. 391)? In the fallen world desire may be per se sinful, but in Paradise man cannot experience *culpable* desire except by executing an *antecedent originating actual* transgression. To be sure, Milton notes, citing Ovid, that "*Mars sees her* [sinless temptation]: *seeing desires her* [the sinful will to do evil]; *desiring enjoys her* [actual sin]." But *Mars* is the pseudonym of an already fallen angel, in whom the "law of sin" reigns triumphant. *His* culpable desire is the original sin that enables his actual transgression. For unfallen Eve, however, desire is not sin (cannot be); disobedient action is.

Diane McColley mobilizes the evidence of Thomas Aquinas to certify that the "'very moment' of [Eve's] fall and the proof of her responsibility for it, is the monologue [745–79] during which she joins her consent to the Serpent's guile."[71] But dramatic monologues are not disallowed in the unfallen human cosmos of *Paradise Lost*: only touching and tasting the forbidden fruit are mortally sinful; as Donne aptly puts it, "Nothing else is."[72] I will not essay detailed exegesis of Eve's monologue. Against an army of opponents, however, I flatly assert that, while no less suffused with misapprehension than Satan's temptation is replete with guile, the woman's musings are absolutely sinless.[73] My argument rests on three premises, the third of which I will reserve for discussion later: (1) to Milton the gap between deception and transgression is more "wondrous" than that separating chaos from cosmos (2.1025–30)—*no bridge can span it;* and (2) at the conclusion of her sinless soliloquy Eve wonders, "what hinders then / To reach, and feed at once both body and mind?" (778–79). Like Pilate, who asks Jesus "What is truth?" (John 18:38), Eve does not pause to consider the answer to her own interrogation—God's "interdiction" (8.334). *But she could pause, for she is even yet sinless.*

Thus, just prior to the monologue, either Eve's "desire" or the "fruit" itself (or both) are "Inclinable now grown to touch or taste" (9.741–42), but prelapsarian inclination is not sin—touching the fruit is. This point is driven home after the fall, when Milton's God, the best casuist in the cosmos, comments on the meaning of *Inclinable* in a witty

71. *Milton's Eve*, 157, 205.

72. "The Sunne Rising," in *Donne: Poetical Works*, ed. Herbert J. C. Grierson.

73. One need only contrast the diction of Eve's first postlapsarian monologue (795–833) with that of lines 745–79 to infer that she is as yet sinless. To fallen (satanic) Eve God is (periphrastically) "Our great forbidder, safe [!] with all his spies [= angels!] / About him" (815–16). Such blasphemy is entirely absent from her only unfallen soliloquy. The *Christian Doctrine* says that "man was to be condemned both for trusting Satan and for not trusting God" (*YP* 6:383) but does not specify *the point* at which distrust is condemnable. That point—Eve's Rubicon—occurs when deliberative distrust becomes volitional apostasy—when she touches the fruit.

punning exoneration of himself from complicity in Eve's transgression, and of the woman's will from insufficiency, even at this late juncture, to abort Satan's fraudulent temptation. Eve sins only after (but not because) she believes

> lies
> Against [her] maker; no decree of mine [for God does not
>   decree sin, he merely announces it]
> Concurring to necessitate [her] fall,
> Or *touch* [!] with lightest moment of impulse
> H[er] free will, to *her own inclining left*
> In even scale.
> (10.42–47; emphasis mine)

This is a most discriminating casuistical exercise. "God left free the will," Adam sententiously asserts (9.351), and so he did: if Eve's "desire" is "Inclinable now . . . to touch or taste," her will is still absolutely free to rein in (sinless) desire, altogether sufficient to the heroic task before her: deceptive temptation (the sphere of intellect) will soon end, and the moment of willed decision fast approaches. *Now* the will of Eve is mobilized and "to her own inclining left / *In even scale.*" The woman is equipoised between sufficiency to stand and freedom to fall. Does she incline to eat? Of course! This is indeed the matter of her sin, but it is also the very ingredient of her virtue. Thus Thomas Pierce:

> If before [Eve] sinned, she was not *inclinable* to *sin,* how then did she *sin*? was it without or against her *inclination*? If her sin was voluntary, and not committed of necessity, . . . she had an *inclination* to which she yielded, and *thereby* sinned. And which if she had *resisted,* shee had not falne, but been *victorious.* Her *meere inclination* to sin was not her sin; for if it were, she sinned before she *sinned* . . . which would imply a contradiction.[74]

The word *Inclinable* at *Paradise Lost* 9.742, which appears to the untrained eye to suggest sinful propensity (as opposed to sinless tendency) to sin is in fact a philosophical synonym for the more explicit disclaimer *yet sinless: voluntas inclinat, non necessitat.* Even at this twelfth hour Eve is free, not to penetrate satanic deceit (no created intellect can), but to say what Thomas Browne insists she would have said were she not already fallen into sinful deception: "If to know good and evil be our advantage, although we have Free-will unto both, we desire to perform but one; We know 'tis good to obey the commandment of God, but evil if we transgress it" (p. 18). Eve knows the command: she has twice uttered it only moments ago (651–54, 659–63), and she will utter it a third time—repeating Genesis 2:17 verbatim—a mere nineteen lines before transgressing: "In the day we

74. *The Divine Philanthropie Defended,* 2d series, 24.

eat of this fair fruit, our doom is, *we shall die*" (762–63; emphasis mine). This tripling of Genesis 3:2–3 is itself powerful evidence of her continuing rectitude. Her as yet unfallen will "can [still] disengage itself from the pressures that seek to influence it."[75] Unwittingly deceived by Satan, Eve forgets to remember "The high injunction" (10.13) *at her moment of decision*, and she falls—but not until she touches the fruit.

Diane McColley believes that "for Eve to *begin* falling *before encountering the Serpent*" makes God the author of sin,[76] but her own analysis, which posits a fall into sinful soliloquy, is no less prejudicial to God (and Eve) than those of far more rigorous disciples of Augustine and Aquinas: *any attempt to anteriorize the woman's transgression invites an infinite regress that inevitably yields the antitheodicial oxymoron "prelapsarian postlapsarianism."* One does not "begin" to fall as if sin were a process: strictly speaking, in relation to original sin the word *falling* is an ethical solecism. Only temptation can occur along an ethically indifferent wavelike continuum: it is the not-yet of sin, sin's arrow threaded in the bent bow of its occasion; sin, on the other hand, is the same sort of "foule and *sudden* corruption" that Milton deplores in *Of Reformation*,[77] a discrete and discontinuous phenomenon analogous in the realm of volition to the all-at-onceness of intuition in the realm of cognition. Augustine rightly calls it a "spontaneous falling away"[78]—he mistakes its moment in a hapless yearning for anteriority. Fallen Eve, on the other hand, whom I take to be a better teacher than Augustine or Aquinas, confesses that "The serpent me beguiled and I did eat" (10.162). A misogynistic tradition found specious extenuation in this brief summation of a 249-line temptation-transgression sequence (9.532–781).[79] Reiterating his chauvinist predecessors, Thomas Browne calls Eve's simple words "not only a very feeble excuse, but an erroneous translating of her own offence upon another; Extenuating her sin from that which was an aggravation, that is, to excuse the Fact at all, much more upon the suggestion of a beast, which was before in the strictest terms prohibited by her God" (p. 23). But Milton endorses Eve's account (10.159–61), as does God, who says nothing whatever about it: his articulate silence comprises a (for once) powerful *argumentum ex silentio*.[80] The *and* of *Paradise Lost* 10.162 is

75. Fish, *Surprised by Sin*, 232, n. 1.
76. *Milton's Eve*, 182, n. 4; emphasis mine.
77. *YP* 3.1.
78. *City of God*, 387.
79. One need, however, only contrast Genesis 3:12 with verse 13 to see that Eve is telling the truth, the whole truth (as far as she knows it), and nothing but the truth. It is perhaps woman's finest moment in the Old Testament.
80. Compare Messiah's rejection of Adam's guilty extenuation at 144–56. His silent approbation of Eve anticipates Adam's silence at 12.624–25: both God and man are "well pleased" (12.625) with her penitent submission.

truly paratactic, as opposed to the hypotactic implications of its deutero-Pauline analogue ("the woman was deceived and [therefore] became a transgressor"). *The serpent me beguiled* specifies the direct object
(*me*) of a sinless deception, while *I did eat* discontinuously accuses the
sinful subject (*I*) of an actual transgression. Fallen penitent Eve knows
when and *how* she sinned better than many of her critics do!

Excursus on the Fall of Lucifer

I will conclude this section by considering the third premise of my
tautological argument that Eve is sinless until she actually sins: the a
fortiori witness of unfallen Lucifer. Unlike Eve he is "Self-tempted
[i.e., by an ontological equal]," but like her he is "self-depraved"
(3.130). If I can show that no Augustinian "evil will" precedes *his* "evil
act" (*The City of God*, 387), the anteriorizing of Eve's fall from grace will
have been exposed (I hope beyond contradiction) as deutero-Pauline
antitheodicial murmurings disguised as elegant casuistry.

What inaugurates Lucifer's sin? I will broach an inquiry into this
issue by meditating on the challenge posed, for the difficulty of it all
lies ultimately in the simplicity of sin's being. To Edward Said, the
exegete of our many contingent beginnings, the great mystery of *Paradise Lost* is just this riddle of satanic origination. How account for
Lucifer's "beginning on his own to move away from God even before
the poem opens[?]: there can be no more irreducible beginning than
that."[81] Said nevertheless wrongly implies that angelic sin, since it has
a point of inception, must also have a middle (which it does not, as I
shall argue). To grasp its nature we must modify Said's definition of
origination: *sin's beginning is also its end, the first and only step in the
intentional production of disobedience* (p. 5, with apologies).

Said is right in one respect, though—that angelic transgression is irreducible. Its beginning is darkly comparable to the absoluteness of
God's "bright essence increate" (3.6), but unlike God's unoriginated
light, sin's original darkness is created and plainly visible. If it is also indeed irreducible, why must critics locate it in a prior moment of conception? Would Milton, *the* poet of the genesis of all created things,[82] fail to
isolate the precise temporal origin of Luciferean transgression?

81. *Beginnings: Intention and Method*, 60.
82. Except *the details* of three originations: the creation of the Son of God, of the
"heaven of heavens, and [of] all the powers therein" (3.390). In the *Christian Doctrine*
Milton calls "a fool" "anyone who asks what God did before the creation of the World"
(*YP* 6:299). He seems to mean the terrestrial universe by "World," but he goes on to
discuss the creation of "THINGS INVISIBLE," including Heaven and the angels (311–15).
Moreover, on 203ff. he discusses the literal generation of the Son and his metaphoric
exaltation to Messiahship. *Paradise Lost*, however, takes the first three beginnings for
granted; its point of (chronological) departure is the anointing of Messiah, and it and all
subsequent originations are considered in lucid detail.

Said playfully anteriorizes the moment of first sin, reducing it (i.e., leading it back) to some *arche* prior to the (apparently) absolute beginning of *Paradise Lost* itself. He is right, of course: since Milton's is an in medias res epic, Lucifer's transgression may justly (and wittily) be said to begin before the poem begins: it is indeed hard to imagine "a more irreducible beginning than *that*." But John Guillory can: what Said posits in serious jest, this critic asserts in deadly (antitheodicial) earnest: recapitulating centos of commentary, he locates sin "at the moment of the [*sic*] Messiah's exaltation," at which point "the loss of God as Lucifer's object choice is *immediate* and *irrevocable*."[83] William Kerrigan imagines an even more archaic beginning: he boldly extrapolates (from Lucifer's createdness) a regressive chain that finally encounters God himself as "the source of evil as well as good." Kerrigan hypothesizes this paradox to "prove" that "a rational theodicy that begins with a moral dualism *and* a strict monotheism must eventually collapse." After the cave-in, he offers his own oxymoronic version of Milton's supposedly *ir*rational theodicy: "*to be the source of evil is not to be evil*."[84]

Kerrigan is a formidable critic, and I do not wish to minimize the difficulty of the task at hand. Can the concepts *good, evil, rationality, theodicy, dualism,* and *monotheism* be made peacefully to coexist? Milton thinks so (2.378–86, 747–67, 6.262–77). Georgia Christopher, positing an extreme voluntarism vis-à-vis the issue of angelic rebellion, argues that "Milton comes no nearer to explaining the Fall [of Lucifer] than his predecessors did."[85] Similarly, for John S. Diekhoff, "how an angel falls into sin is a mystery."[86] But are they right? Let us trust not the critics but the teller and his tale; let us listen to the voice of the Great Master.

He cautions us in *The Argument* to Book 5 to expect the articulation of certain casuistical distinctions between sinless temptation and sinful transgression: Raphael's narrative begins from the enemy's "first revolt in heaven [sinful transgression], *and the occasion thereof* [sinless temptation]; how he drew his legions after him to the parts of the north [innocent seduction], and there incited them to rebel [blameless suggestion] with him [sinful disobedience for Lucifer once he actually rebels], persuading all [angels culpable at the moment they become consental accessories to Satan] but only Abdiel a seraph [sinlessly seduced]" (emphasis mine). The exegetical challenge is to specify the instant when temptation ceases and sin begins. Lucifer's ethical chal-

83. *Poetic Authority,* 115.
84. *The Sacred Complex,* 99–101. However, God created Hell as an evil (2.622–23), but not as a *moral* evil: the place is morally good, the reprobate angels' "fit habitation" (6.876).
85. *Milton and the Science,* 90.
86. *Milton's "Paradise Lost": A Commentary on the Argument,* 28.

lenge, like his cohorts' after him, Adam's and Eve's after them, and ours in the postlapsarian world, is "to apprehend and consider vice with all her baits and seeming pleasures, and yet abstain, and yet distinguish, and yet prefer that which is truly better."[87] When does this angel cease merely to *apprehend, consider,* and *distinguish* sin and instead join his consent to the rebellion he is sinlessly premeditating? When does seduction give way to transgression? What is the moment of Lucifer's sin?

He feels "Deep malice . . . and disdain" (5.666) at the installation of Messiah, but although that line (666) is the number of the beast of Revelation 13:17–18, Lucifer is not yet bestial: the "sense of injured Merit" (1.98) is not a crime. Just as Adam is not yet sinfully "foiled" by the "inward . . . feel" of prelapsarian uxoriousness (8.608), Lucifer is not a rebel for "conceiving" (5.666) rebellion. Analogously, unfallen Mammon, "the least erected spirit that fell / From heaven," is forever *about to fall,* "for even in heaven his looks and thoughts / Were always downward bent," greedy for "trodden gold." But his lust of the eye and mind is sinless, for he too enjoys the "vision beatific" of the elect (1.679–84).[88] If Gabriel's flyting in Book 4 is not exaggerated, Lucifer is a sinless "hypocrite" who "fawned, and cringed, and servilely adored" God long before he becomes a sinful rebel: the "*hope* / To dispossess" the Deity (4.957–61; emphasis mine) is not a crime. In the prelapsarian cosmos one does not desire sin, one commits it: Adam is "Led on, *yet sinless, with desire* to know" (7.61; emphasis mine). The act of sin, on the other hand, occurs in a timeless *now:* "sin, *not time, first* wrought the change" (9.70; emphasis mine) that issues eventually in the uprooting of Paradise itself (11.829–35). These and many more passages import the fact that in *Paradise Lost,* a wandering appetite and an aspiring mind are not sinful—not yet.

As for Lucifer, when his "lust hath conceived, it bringeth forth sin" (James 1:15), but she is not yet sin till she be brought forth. God decrees the headship of Messiah and commands "All knees in heaven" to "bow" and "confess him Lord" (5.606–8). To transgress is to refuse

<hr>

87. *Areopagitica,* in *YP* 2:514–15.

88. Summers, *The Muse's Method,* 29, is justly puzzled at Mammon's prelapsarian values: " 'Avarice' is difficult to ennoble, but Milton seems to hint, almost perversely, that Mammon . . . possessed something remarkably close to it even when he was in Heaven." The difficulty dissolves when one realizes that the angel's propensity to fall is the sinless guarantor of his upright freedom. Whereas Thomas Aquinas thinks their vision of God was accorded to the angels only after they withstood Luciferean temptation, and that it constituted them as unalterably elect (*Summa Theologica* 1.62.4–9), Milton deploys *God's* vision of them before the great test (5.611–15; compare 3.60–62) and insists that they remain free to fall at any subsequent point (5.535–40). These divagations from the tradition are consistent with Milton's location of angelic transgression at a point far later than Augustine, Aquinas, and others thought possible.

this, and *this only*. Put another way, only "Affecting Godhead" (3.206) is sinful in Milton's prelapsarian cosmos, for men and angels alike. As Camille Slights has argued, prior to his debate with Abdiel, Lucifer "has *not yet* decided to dedicate himself to evil"—even if "his pride and envy have initiated the transformation."[89] They have occasioned it rather, for Luciferean sin is not a process. He has "resolved / . . . to dislodge" (5.668–69) and has even tempted Beelzebub (673–96);[90] God knows that he "*intends* to erect his throne / Equal to" Messiah's, and that "he hath *in his thought* to try" Messiah's power (725–28; emphasis mine). But there is no sin until the throne is erected, or (what amounts to the same thing) until Lucifer rebaptizes his "palace" (760) as "The Mountain of the Congregation" (766), thereupon and thereby "Affecting *all* equality with God" (763; emphasis mine). This is Lucifer's sin.[91] It occurs "not long after" (762) the rebel assembles his troops at "the limits of the north" (755), but only after the assembly convenes.

When does Lucifer's sin occur? Although in his temptation speech (772–802) he proposes repudiating "knee-tribute" (782), *he does not yet claim all equality* with God, merely equality of freedom: "if not equal all [true], yet free [true], / Equally free [true]" (791–92; compare 794–97). This indisputable claim ("for orders and degrees / Jar not with liberty" [792–93]) issues not from the Devil, but from an unfallen angel (he is "great Lucifer" still [760]), *and its "argument blasphemous"* (809) *is isomorphic with sinless Eve's prelapsarian soliloquy* (9.745–79). Whereas Desmond Hamlet thinks Lucifer's orthodox analysis of volitional equality's compatibility with ontological subordination escapes "inadvertently" from an already-fallen angel,[92] the sinful perversion of this casuistical distinction—embodied, for example, in postlapsarian Eve's self-serving question, "inferior who is free?" (9.825)—has yet to occur to the seraph bright. Even Abdiel (809–48) does not label Lucifer's "*argument*" *sinful;* instead he asserts the justice of the divine decree (813–18). Abdiel comprehends the metaphorical begetting of the Son as Messiah on the Plains of Heaven in terms that resemble the exaltation of the "subjected plain" (12.640) surrounding an emblematic hill in Marvell's topographical lyric:

> See then how courteous the hill [= Messiah] ascends,
> And all the way it rises bends [= 5.829–30];

89. *The Casuistical Tradition in Shakespeare, Donne, Herbert, and Milton,* 252.

90. Beelzebub is first identified as such at 1.79–81, and by Milton; justly so, for in Book 5 he is not yet fallen, and in Book 6 he has not yet gotten his postlapsarian name.

91. Because upon rechristening the palace he fully parodies the exaltation of the Son (764–66 = 596–99 and 603–6). Just as the Son is rebaptized as Messiah (603–4 = 662–64), Lucifer is rebaptized as Satan—but *not yet.*

92. *One Greater Man: Justice and Damnation in "Paradise Lost,"* 112.

> Nor for it self the height does gain,
> But only strives to raise the Plain [= Milton's angels,
> 841–45].[93]

Hence the angel can certify the exaltation of the Son not by "a leap of faith," but by logic, experience, and desire: "by experience taught we know how good, / And of our good, and of our dignity / How provident [God] is" (826–28).[94]

Having made manifest the benevolence of God's decree, Abdiel now zeroes in on the crucial issue of equality, clarifying Luciferean uncertainty *by denying what Lucifer has not yet even asserted*, namely, that the angels are ontologically equal to Messiah. Abdiel interrogates his tempter, probing to discern whether his intentions are in fact sinful:

> Thy self though great and glorious *dost thou* count,
> Or all angelic nature joined in one,
> Equal to him begotten Son, by whom
> As by his Word the mighty Father made
> All things, even thee, and all the spirits of heaven
> By him created in their bright degrees.
>
> (833–38; emphasis mine)

This is a question ("dost thou[?]")[95]—not a statement of the facts—and its answer is NO! Not yet. Lucifer, I repeat, has thus far claimed only to be equally free, an issue Abdiel nowhere disputes (how could he?). The tempter is not yet a sinner; Abdiel therefore urges his leader to "appease" God "While pardon may be found in time besought" (846–48). Milton's God will not, however, "relent / And publish grace" (2.237–38) to a sinful angel—he must else "revoke the high decree" (3.126 = 5.602) that, "unrevoked" (5.602), "Ordain[s] damnation . . . without end" (615) for those who enact (as opposed to those who merely conceive) rebellion against Messiah. Consequently the creature whom Abdiel advises to "Cease then this impious rage" (5.845) has not yet sinned—he is not *yet* Satan.

In scorning Abdiel's advice, however (853–71), Lucifer finally be-

---

93. "Upon the Hill and Grove at Bill-borow," 21–24, in *The Poems and Letters of Andrew Marvell*, 3d ed., ed. H. M. Margoliouth.

94. Christopher, *Milton and the Science*, 93, disingenuously suppresses lines 826–48 to support the argument that "the decree cannot be certified by logic, *experience, or desire*" (emphasis mine). What, forsooth, are we to make of Abdiel's "by *experience* taught"? The decree, like everything else in *Paradise Lost*, is rational, not inscrutable. Milton's God has no Calvinist secret will.

95. Albert C. Labriola turns the question into a statement by deleting line 833 from his discussion to press the thesis that the exaltation of the Son makes the collective body of unfallen angels *equal* to Messiah. Labriola is right, however, that the exaltation is an incarnation (5.609–11 = 828–31 = 841–45 = 6.777–80). See his " 'Thy Humiliation Shall Exalt': The Christology of *Paradise Lost*."

comes a sinful "Apostate" (852); unlike the other rebels, who only much later "among the sons of Eve / Got them new names" (1.364–65), he is *"thence* in heaven called Satan" (5.821; emphasis mine; compare 1.81–82). "[N]ot so waked Satan," Raphael anachronistically tells Adam at the outset of his narrative, momentarily implying that Lucifer has sinned at the exaltation of the Son. But the affable angel at once clarifies his position: "so call him *now*" (5.657–58; emphasis mine), for *then* the "archangel" was not yet fallen, however "false" (694) he may have already been.[96]

What is the moment of Lucifer's sin? Its fountain who shall tell? Abdiel can and does; in fact, he originates it (the moment, not the sin). This faithful angel is the good tempter who proximately triggers Luciferean rebellion and fall; the begetting of Messiah (600–606) is merely its distant occasion. Fallen Satan distorts these originative phenomena when he claims that God

> his regal state
> Put forth at full [a lie; compare 3.372–82], but still his
> strength concealed [a truth-sounding prevarication:
> 6.853–55],
> Which tempted our attempt [false], and wrought our fall
> [absolutely false].
>
> (2.640–42)

Satan exaggerates the exaltation of the Son into an impossible unac-commodated epiphany of God the Father and confounds his temp-tation with his transgression, alleging that the former caused ("wrought") the latter. But in fact only temptation is conceived when Messiah is promoted to the "right hand" (5.606) of God. Temptation alone develops apace through 260 lines of Book 5; but the phe-nomenon of sin is all-at-once. *Do* you claim ontological equality with God? Abdiel asks (833–38). How *can* you, since he "made / Thee what thou art" (823–24)? The matter of sin turns on one question only: who made whom? Lucifer, however, has not yet even conceived this ques-tion, the wrong answer to which is mortally sinful; but thanks to Abdiel he conceives it now. Thomas Aquinas believes that Lucifer was good "in the first instant" of his creation but that a moment later, "in the second" instant, he fell.[97] Milton adopts the angelic doctor's con-cept of instantaneousness, but he locates sin's moment much later

96. No unfallen angel calls Satan *Satan* in *Paradise Lost* until Gabriel names him at 4.878. He may *be* Satan in Heaven from the moment he rebels, but the elect spirits do not know this until much later. The two Raphaelian anachronisms at 5.743 and 756 do not vitiate my point: this angel once refers inappropriately even to himself (at 6.363). From this point of view Raphael is a slightly less than perfect raconteur.

97. *Summa Theologica* 1.63.6; compare Dante, *Paradiso* 29.49–63.

than Aquinas does. Not at his own "suggestion" (3.129), but at the innocent instancing of Abdiel, one of his own kind, does Lucifer at once beget and bring forth sin. Comparable to eternity's *nunc stans*, sin has the unique ontology of a *nunc occidens*. In a timeless Thomistic moment Lucifer willfully embraces the dark sinless thought of "Affecting *all* equality with God" (763), which he can do only by denying the concept of subordination implicit in the paternal begetting of Messiah. "Now that you mention it," Lucifer says (in effect) to Abdiel, "I, *Satan*, *do* claim to be equal to God the Father; for unlike Messiah, whom God twice begat,[98] and by whom (*you* say) God begat *me*, I begat myself":

> We know no time when we were not as now;
> Know none before us [true and sinless], *self-begot* [*alia*
>   *iacta est!*], self-raised
> By our own quickening power [sinful in word], when fatal course
> Had circled his full orb, *the birth mature* [*ecce culpa!*]
> Of this our native heaven, ethereal sons.
>
> (859–63; emphasis mine)

This is sin's moment. Since by decree God begets the Son as Messiah ("begotten Son," 835), and since "by his Word, the mighty Father" begets (836) Lucifer, the only way this rebel can sin by "trust[ing] to have equalled the most high" (1.40) is to deny the hierarchical implications of just these originative begettings. This he does—how else?—by the spoken word, parodying the creative efficacy of both Father and Son by decreeing himself "self-begot." His denial of origins originates both Satan and his sin. This is Lucifer's crime, as Abdiel at once recognizes; he therefore declares that "other decrees / Against [Satan] are gone forth without recall" (884–85). By repudiating his creaturely contingency, Lucifer becomes sin-full in deed, a once-and-for-all metamorphosis whose moment Abdiel now specifies: "O alienate from God, O spirit accurst, / Forsaken of all good; *I see* thy fall / Determined" (877–79; emphasis mine). What Abdiel sees—in a discrete flash of "darkness visible" (1.63)—is the discontinuous conception and birth of Sin herself, visibly brought forth in a parthenogenetic ("*self*-depraved" [3.130]) cephalic parturition that parodies and confirms Satan's sinfully blasphemous claim to have begotten and delivered himself as a "birth mature" (5.862). As Abdiel discerns—by the witness of the eye—the only "mature" offspring that the Devil can beget is a full-grown sinful daughter. Although fallen Satan cannot recall either his own creation (5.856–58) or that of Sin, *she* has not forgotten whence she sprung:

---

98. Literally, at a time unspecified (3.383–89); metaphorically, as Messiah, at a specified moment (5.603–6).

> In heaven, . . . *at the assembly,* and *in sight*
> Of all the seraphim with thee combined
> In bold conspiracy against heaven's king,
> *All on a sudden* miserable pain
> *Surprised thee,* dim thine eyes, and dizzy swum
> In darkness, while thy head flames thick and fast
> Threw forth, till on the left side opening wide,
> Likest to thee in shape and countenance bright,
> *Then* [not now!] shining heavenly fair, a goddess armed
> Out of thy head I sprung: *amazement* seized
> All the host of heaven.
> (2.749-59; emphasis mine)

For Milton, Lucifer's rebellion is long-deliberating and choosing late: Sin herself isolates the moment of her own origination.[99] Lucifer becomes Satan "at the assembly"—not a moment sooner. What God creates "in a moment" (7.154) Sin destroys at a moment's notice. She indeed is born "*All* on a sudden"—the whole of her—which is why she "Surprise[s]" the sinner, angelic or human (8.547 = 2.753), however protracted and premeditated his or her antecedent temptation may be. To pre*meditate* is not to default, for "Evil *into the mind* of God [i.e., angel] or man / May come and go" unblamed (5.117-18; emphasis mine). The conception of Sin, on the other hand, is coextensive with the moment of sinful consent and at once issues in an actual parturition.

These theodicial distinctions apply equally to Satan's cohorts, whose transgressions are a riddle beyond Abdiel's ken. He claims to see the Devil's

> fall
> Determined [true], and thy hapless crew involved [true
>   at *some* point]
> In this perfidious fraud, contagion spread
> Both of thy crime and punishment [absolutely false].
> (878-81)

Unfallen Abdiel is for once himself deceived:[100] in prelapsarian life one does not catch sin from another as if it were a smallpox; one commits it—self-depraved—by willed disobedience. Like many an exegete after him, the seraph confuses satanic temptation with angelic transgression: whereas Satan's original sin is coextensive with the final stages of his cohorts' long temptation, *their* sin occurs when they actually involve themselves in his "perfidious fraud." They might in-

99. She has no reason to lie and proves her veracity at 2.767-81 by denying that the War in Heaven was in any sense a "dubious battle" (1.104).
100. Unless he remains amidst the company of the unfallen angels until they too transgress. 5.888-907 make this most unlikely, however.

deed have done so simultaneously with the birth of their leader's daughter, but Sin testifies to the contrary:

> Out of thy head I sprung: amazement seized
> All the host of heaven; back they recoiled afraid
> At first and called me Sin, and for a sign
> Portentous held me; but familiar grown,
> I pleased, and with attractive graces won
> The most averse, thee chiefly, who full oft
> Thy self in me thy perfect image viewing
> Becamest enamoured.
>
> (758–65)

After his fall Satan lustfully repeats his original sin (he "Becamest enamoured"), for in postlapsarian life, to desire Sin is already to transgress: which of us has not cast the sinful dart of fancied adultery (Matthew 5:28)? As for "the host of heaven," on the other hand, suspicious "amazement seized" "*All*" of them—Abdiel too—at the "open and discoverable apparition" (Thomas Browne) of Sin; "All" admirably "recoiled afraid / At first and called [her] Sin." They are not deceived, and their instincts about Sin are as praiseworthy as Eve's instinctive repudiation of her dream at 5.28–93. Moreover, whereas Eve, beguiled by the artificer of fraud, unwittingly denominates sin wisdom,[101] the as-yet-unfallen angels know exactly what she is—she is Sin.

Sin is also a "sign." What does she signify? Not sin, clearly, for that is what she *is*. Maureen Quilligan, amply qualified to "spell" allegory's dark conceits, nevertheless despairs of unravelling Sin's significance: "She is a character who is, in ways too numerous and closely layered to spell out, a sign."[102] But Sin's primary onomastics are transparent: *she signifies the commandment "noli me tangere!"* Satan's daughter is to the angels, really and apparently, "The only sign of [their] obedience left / Among so many signs of power and rule" (4.428–29).[103] She is therefore "Portentous," as the unfallen angels recognize. But they disregard her significance, preferring now, at *their* moment of decision, to commit themselves to what she is. Their choice is easy contrasted to Eve's, for they are about to transgress with their eyes wide open; nevertheless, they soon incline to Sin: she is "familiar grown"; she "pleases"; she is "attractive" to the eye; the unfallen angels yearn (sinlessly) for her "graces." At some subsequent moment, however, they fall. Sin claims to have "won / The most averse"—which is

---

101. Thus anticipating the mistaken onomastics of Hesiod's *Theogony*. See my " 'Real or Allegoric': The Ontology of Sin and Death in *Paradise Lost*."

102. *Milton's Spenser*, 92.

103. This fact is explained in detail in the *Christian Doctrine* (*YP* 6:352).

imprecise, for she does not "win" Abdiel.[104] She does not "win" the others either, as if they were mere pawns in some nightmarish Cole-ridgean throw-of-the-dice. These angels are not "won"; they are "*Self-lost*" (7.154; emphasis mine) at the fateful *nunc occidens* when their sinless "*a*vers[ion]" gives way to consensual *per*version—when they join their leader by embracing his incarnate daughter "actual[ly]," if not "in body" (10.587).

And what of Eve? Can we locate the *nunc occidens* of this prelap-sarian woman? Does she sin when, a split-second before she touches the "fruit divine" (9.776), she thus transforms "the invisible / Glory of him that made" her (1.369–70) into a mere vegetable and—what is more—into a medicinal "cure of all" her supposed woes (9.776)? Decidedly not. For she is as yet merely deceived into believing these mistruths: the daughter of Adam who calls the serpent "author unsuspect, / Friendly to man, far from deceit or guile" (771–72) sin-lessly resembles the daughter of Satan who correctly denominates him "my father, . . . my author"; and like Sin, Eve is about to "obey" (2.864–65) her tempter. But whereas the Devil authorizes Sin's trans-gression and is responsible for it, he does not author Eve's; only the woman can do so, but Eve has not yet committed the "Bold deed" (921) to which Adam will later refer; she has yet to touch the fruit.

What is the moment of Eve's sin? In the mind of God no temporal space intervenes between his deliberative and executive acts (7.154–55, 176–79), but he remains free to change his mutable mind and abort what he proposes to execute. It is the same with God's unfallen femi-nine image. In the transgressions of both angels and men, a more or less extended space of intellectual premeditation, which we call temp-tation, is followed by an abrupt hiatus, within which (but not during which) the irreversible agency of the will predominates. Volition does not *deliberate* in *time*; it *chooses* in a *moment*. Thomas Hobbes, an unlikely ally on whom to call as I meditate the moment of Eve's sin, provides the vocabulary requisite to the distinctions I must draw:

> I conceive that in all *deliberations*, that is to say, in an alternate *succession* of contrary *appetites*, the last is that which we call the will, & is im-mediately next before the doing of the action, or next before the doing of it becomes impossible. All other *appetites* to do, and to quit, that come upon a man during his deliberations, are called *Intentions*, & *Inclinations*, but not *Wills*, there being but *one* will, which also in this case may be called the *last* will, though the *Intentions* change often.[105]

---

104. Since, however, Abdiel has probably left the assembly immediately after Sin's birth, she may be accurate even in this all-inclusive statement. Milton is *very* precise.
105. *Of Liberty and Necessity,* 68–69.

Hobbes wrongly implies that "the last [deliberation] . . . is that which we call the WILL," for deliberation is merely intellective; the will alone is volitional: one does not decide to sin, one chooses to. Henry Lawrence clarifies this point: "between the temptation of the Divell, and sin, there ever mediates . . . cogitation or thought, *in which the temptation properly and formally lyes*, so as hee may be an effectual cause of temptation but not of sin, for hee may necessitate a man to feel temptation, but not to consent to it."[106] The satanic presentation of potentially culpable data begins in *Paradise Lost* at 9.532 and ends at line 732. At this point the "cogitation . . . in which [Eve's] temptation properly and formally lyes" is initiated; the woman's soliloquy thus sinlessly "mediates" between diabolical suggestion and sinful consent. Whatever its content, the monologue and the actions that follow it at line 780–81a are absolutely innocent. Lawrence, a better casuist than Thomas Hobbes, understands that no deliberation can comprise an act of volition.

Hobbes does understand, however, that the "last" deliberation "is immediately next before the doing of the action": the space between final judgment (which is final only because it is last) and willed execution (the domain of free will) is spatial, not temporal. It is a free space, unencumbered by deliberative acts. Therefore, we must posit no Hobbesian point after which "the doing of the action" (or the not doing of it) "becomes impossible"—not, at any rate, *until the action itself is done.* What Hobbes calls the "last will" is indeed the "one will" and, unlike a decision to sin (which is reversible—one can forever change one's mind), free volition comprises an irrevocable choice, even for God (he cannot alter his will immutable). Unfallen Adam, analyzing Eve's sin, understands this truth: "past who can recall, or done undo? / Not God omnipotent, nor fate" (926–27). What is done is done; but not yet.

What is the moment of Eve's sin? Stanley Fish, more eager even than Adam to probe her fall, nevertheless anteriorizes its moment: "The only *feeling* incompatible with innocence is the I-must-eat-the-apple feeling [not true!]; and even here the psychic decision [a sinless judgment] and the physical commission of the deed [this is sin indeed!] must follow before innocence is lost [exactly!]."[107] Fish is struggling to maintain Eve's innocence until the moment she (actually) loses it, but he fails to sustain the crucial distinction between sinless *inclination* and sinful *commission.* To feel that one must eat is still to deliberate: one may incline forever, but one chooses to eat only when one eats. At some level Fish intuits this distinction, which is why, having allowed himself the oxymoron *sinful feeling,* he then corrects

106. *An History of Angells,* 73.
107. *Surprised by Sin,* 228, n. 1.

himself, invoking the *sinful deed* that at once despoils Eve of prelapsarian innocence, right reason, and free will.

When does Eve sin? Before lapsing himself, Adam locates the moment of her fall when he asks "how hast thou yielded to transgress / The strict forbiddance, how to violate / The sacred fruit forbidden!" (9.902–4). Soon thereafter, however, in a sinless extenuation of his own imminent lapse, he anteriorizes Eve's, calling her "adventurous" for "only coveting to eye / That sacred fruit [sinless], sacred to abstinence [true], / Much more to taste it under ban to touch" (923–25). But just as Mammon can sinlessly covet Heaven's "trodden gold" (1.682), Eve is perfectly free to yearn for the "sacred fruit"; if she is "adventurous" for doing so (and she is), she is no more culpable than Milton himself, who "intends" to pursue his "adventurous song / Above the Aonian mount" (13–15). *Unfallen Adam, about to transgress, is the grandfather of such exegetes as Augustine and Aquinas who speciously anteriorize the fall of Eve.* This is why Milton has Satan-in-the-serpent describe a magic tree whose "branches would require / [Eve's] *utmost* reach or Adam's" (9.590–91; emphasis mine): because the fruit is difficult of access, there is no chance of its being touched without a firm choice; the serpent Eve beguiled, but she did touch, sinning then, and only then.

What is the precise moment of Eve's sin? As the fatal "hour of noon dr[aws] on," Milton mobilizes the triune biblical motivation for her fall (735–43 = Genesis 3:6). These data, pitifully inadequate to demystify the scriptural tragedy, comprise the penultimate link in Milton's extraordinary exfoliation of the process of human temptation in *Paradise Lost.* Deployed at this late hour they make Eve's sin plausible, *but they do not make her sin.* William Kerrigan reproduces a relevant Ramist diagram (devised by William Perkins) on the possible relations between flesh and spirit in human volition; see Table 1.[108]

Table 1: Perkins' Diagram

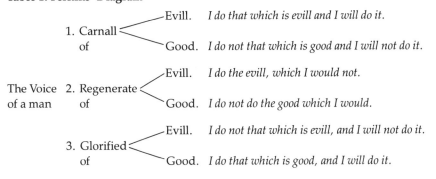

108. Kerrigan, *The Sacred Complex,* 17.

But in his *Two Treatises* Perkins neglects to include one voice, the potentially righteous wilderness outcry of prelapsarian Eve. This woman faces the cruelest temptation imposed on any unfallen creature in *Paradise Lost*. Her sinless deception nevertheless even now has "the power to wring a permutation from the voice of [her] volition that William Perkins, like [many a misogynist] before [and after] him, did not consider possible: *I do the good which I would not; I do not do the evil which I would*."[109] Adam's wife fails to utter the cry, but not because she is already fallen. Her actual sin—which is to say, her sin—occurs "on a sudden" (9.900 = 2.752); not when Eve innocently conceives rebellion (9.647–54 at the earliest); not when she inclines to it (742); not when she soliloquizes (745–79); not even when "she determines to eat the apple";[110] but when, after contemplating the "fruit divine [sinless deception], / Fair to the eye [true], inviting to the taste [all too true], / Of virtue to make wise [false but blameless]" (776–78), "her rash hand in evil hour / Forth reaching to the fruit [*still* sinless], she plucked [*now* sinful], she ate [yet *more* sinful]" (780–81).

At this moment the woman's sin is begotten and born: witness the cosmic labor pangs that accompany her meal (782–85). Deceived will-she nill-she into believing that the forbidden fruit "Gave elocution to the mute" serpent (748), who she falsely believes "hath eaten and lives, / And knows and speaks, and reasons and discerns" (764–65), Eve falls from innocent deception into culpable transgression, mortally violating God's "rigid interdiction" (8.334)—but not until she touches "the tree / Of interdicted knowledge" (5.51–52).

Milton thus proves, thanks to Uriel but in spite of deutero-Paul and his misogynous disciples, that the letter of I Timothy 2:11–15 is both true and plausible, however odious its misogynistic spirit may be: the woman was deceived and subsequently became a transgressor.

III. ADAM WAS NOT DECEIVED

Adam falls deceived by an external agent, Satan.
—**Arnold Stein**, *Answerable Style*

And what of her husband? We know from I Timothy that "the woman was deceived" but "Adam was not deceived." This biblical distinction is far from neutral, as the Greek New Testament suggests. Whereas at Genesis 3:13 Eve uses the simplex verb *epatesen* to minimize the degree of her deception and to mute the causal nexus between it and transgression ("The serpent *simply* beguiled me, and *then I* ate"), deutero-Paul uses the perfective compound *exepatesen* (as

109. Ibid., 21.
110. Fresch, "Milton's Eve," 88.

does Paul himself at 2 Corinthians 11:13) to announce her fall into sinful deceit. But Timothy reverts to the simplex Old Testament form to deny that the man was beguiled. The effect of these subtle morphological choices is to suggest that whereas "the woman was *completely* deceived," "Adam was *not at all* deceived." If, moreover, as I have argued, the Bible teaches that Eve transgressed *because* she was beguiled, its relentless linguistic dichotomizing of deception and its opposite implies as well the truth of this ethical tautology's contrapositive: Adam was not deceived; therefore *he did not transgress*. This is admittedly an overreading, but only by a little: deutero-Paul is so unconcerned with the fall of the man that the epistle never even mentions it, a biblical black (w)hole enfolding layers of institutional misogyny. The text focuses instead on Eve's sin as the true root of all our woe, exculpating her spouse with the chauvinist disclaimer "Adam was not deceived."

Milton once again corroborates his source's literal truth while repudiating its misogynistic spirit: in one of the harshest judgments rendered in *Paradise Lost*, outraged at the enormity of Adam's transgression, the poet writes: "he scrupled not to eat [sinful] / Against his better knowledge, not deceived [more sinful], / But fondly [i.e., foolishly] overcome with female charm [still more sinful]" (9.997–99). I am no numerologist, but is not line 999 the number of the beast fallen on its head? If the fool saith in his heart, "There is no God," Adam is just such a fool when, "submitting to what *seemed* remediless" (919; emphasis mine), he neither divorces fallen Eve nor turns to God for advice on how to respond to her transparently deceitful invitation that he join her in sin (856–85). Instead, "passion sway[ing] / [His] judgment" (8.635–36), he "Eat[s] his fill" (9.1005)—at which point Adam must also digest certain self-incriminating words that he has not long since admonishingly directed to his wife:

> But God left free the will, for what obeys
> Reason, is free, and reason he made right,
> But bid her well beware, and still erect,
> Lest by some fair appearing good [= fallen Eve] surprised
> She dictate false, and misinform the will
> To do what God expressly hath forbid.
>
> (351–56)

These lines, suffused with prevenient irony, approximate an etiology of Adam's fall. Though not at all beguiled by any "fair appearing good" (for he at once perceives "The fatal trespass done by Eve" [889]), Adam is indeed "surprised" at her "sudden" (900) sinful metamorphosis: "amazed, / Astonied [he] stood and blank, while horror chill / Ran through his veins" (889–91). This is a shock of eventually fatal recognition, for unlike Eve (but like the unfallen angels), Adam is suspiciously amazed at this discoverable apparition. Consequently he cannot retroactively invoke the excuse of prior deceit to mitigate his trespass—not justly, at any rate, for he is "not deceived" by Eve's seductive temptation.

Given Adam's visceral disorientation at being surprised by his wife's sin, his penetrating assessment of its causes and consequences is itself nothing short of astonishing. He grasps at once that

> Some cursed fraud
> Of enemy hath beguiled thee, yet unknown,
> And me with thee hath ruined, for with thee
> Certain my resolution is to die.
>
> (904–7)

Although unable to posit the Satan-serpent identity ("for in the wily snake, / Whatever sleights none would suspicious mark"), Adam knows for sure what continues to elude Eve—that "*Some*" satanic deceit has "beguiled" her. But then, in a specious first attempt at self-deception, he rashly blurs the crucial distinction between sinless deceit and sinful transgression, implying that the former ipso facto causes the latter, and that moreover the beguiling of Eve is about to cause his own demise ("Some cursed fraud . . . / . . . me with thee hath ruined"). Fraud, as I have argued, occasions but cannot cause sin, and Adam, already sin-full in intention ("Certain my resolution is to die") though not yet a sinner, makes straight seem intricate, to (sinless) self-extenuation swift.

Nevertheless he is not deceived. He understands that Satan has occasioned Eve's sin and fully realizes that she is doomed:

> O fair*est* of creation, last *and best*
> Of all God's works, creature in whom excell*ed*
> *Whatever can to sight or thought be form*
> Holy, *divine*, good, amiable, or sweet!
> How art thou lost, how on a sudden lost,
> Defaced, deflowered, and now to death devote?
>
> (896–901; emphasis mine)

Admittedly, nearly all of the italicized words are erroneous, for Adam, who has been disabused by Raphael of incipient uxoriousness (8.561–94), knows that Eve is neither "divine," "fairest," nor "best / Of all God's works": he is already mobilizing rationalizations to join her in sin and therefore exaggerates her ontological status. This is more (and mere) self-deception, however, because, in a discriminating deployment of the preterite participle, Adam also comprehends that his now-sinful wife only *formerly* "excelled" in virtue: excellent prelapsarian Eve has become a fallen woman indeed, a vicious has-been "now to death devote." Wary Adam is not deceived.

In fact the unfallen man is never deceived by anyone else in *Paradise Lost*, a state of affairs Milton engineers to preserve the deutero-Pauline literal discrimination of his transgression from Eve's. Self-deception, however, not merely enters but invades his psyche from the moment he consensually conceives deep malice and disdain, "For [after the fall] understanding ruled not, and the will / Heard not her lore" (9.1127–28). To the evidence already adduced I add the following from Book 10: whereas the tortured dialectic of conviction's deadly sting requires Adam to "absolute" God "after all disputes" (828–29) from complicity in his crime, it by no means eliminates his habit of deflecting blame on other (innocent) parties: "with the serpent meeting," Eve was

> Fooled and beguiled, by him thou [true enough], I by
>   thee [false],
> To trust thee from my side, imagined wise,
> Constant, mature, proof against all assaults [utterly
>   false!].
>   (879–82)

These are self-extenuating lies (compare 9.251–375). Although Adam is not charging that Eve deceived him into transgressing—only that she fooled him into prematurely dismissing her from his presence. This is merely the weak form of the much stronger assertion that *her* "Desire of wandering" has caused *his* fall (9.1136–42), which is itself propaedeutic to Adam's even more exaggerated claim, made in the presence of God himself, that Eve beguiled him into eating the forbidden fruit:

> The woman whom thou madest to be my help [true],
> And gavest me as thy perfect gift [true, but Eve is not
>   immutable], so good [true],
> So fit [true], so acceptable [true], so divine [false],
> That from her hand I could suspect no ill [false],
> And what she did, whatever in itself,
> Her doing seemed to justify the deed [entirely false];
> She gave me of the tree and I did eat [true].
>   (10.137–43)[111]

The only simple verity in these allegations is the last line, and even it is shot through with extenuation, for its hidden message is "The

---

111. This passage is a specious rehash of 8.528–59, the uxoriousness of which Raphael works hard to extirpate (561–94). Adam is lying, and he knows it. McColley, *Milton's Eve*, 27, superbly analyzes the passage.

[woman] me beguiled and [therefore] I did eat." Adam is trying desperately to insist that his crime is at worst equivalent to Eve's, *and his unwitting strategy is to reverse selected protocols of I Timothy 2:11–15* by alleging that whereas he "was . . . deceived [by the woman and became a transgressor], . . . the woman was deceived [by Satan] and became a [greater] transgressor." The attempt fails, miserably so, as God's censorious rejoinder (145–56) makes resoundingly clear. Adam has "resign[ed his] manhood" (148) to his fallen wife in sinful servile "subjection" (153). In the event, therefore, the deutero-Pauline source whose misogyny Milton disavows is once again redeemed at the literal level: Adam was not deceived.

IV. ADAM BECAME A GREATER TRANSGRESSOR

'Twas not for eating, God did Eve accuse, But that she did not Sathan's tempts refuse; Not that the crime by woman was began, But as she gave occasion to the man: She first was snared in the Devils wile, And thus deceiv'd strove others to beguile: Poor Adam to his knowledge did transgress, So did not Eve, *which makes her sin the less.*
                    —Henricus Cornelius Agrippa, *The Glory of a Woman*

Since Milton's Adam is "render[ed] . . . inexcusable" (Book 5, Argument) by falling undeceived, it may appear to follow that the deception of Eve partially extenuates her trespass. To repeat a brief remark of Thomas Browne, he speculates that "the condition of [her] Sex, and posteriority of Cremation [= creation], might somewhat extenuate the Error of the Woman" (p. 18). Browne presumably means that innate female propensity to be deceived, coupled with (and perhaps caused by) Eve's derivative and secondary parturition, might help to account for (and forgive) the ease with which Satan sinfully beguiled her. This is an interesting (and atypical) divagation from I Timothy, for the Bible condemns Eve's propensity and invokes her "posteriority" only to certify the inferiority of her daughters.

Milton, however, disagrees with Browne on the issue of extenuation. Because it is not synonymous with her fall (which it merely occasions), Eve's deception cannot excuse her mortal transgression: the beguiling of Uriel both dooms her to be fooled by Satan and renders her inexcusable for subsequent disobedience. Had the angel been instructed to deny safe passage earthward to stripling cherubs (or anyone else), he would have steadfastly refused to assist Satan thither, *however impenetrable his disguise, however noble his alleged motives.* Uriel's job is not to discern satanic fraud (a mission impossible) but to execute divine injunctions.

So is Eve's. Fallen, guilty, and self-extenuating, she speciously tells Adam that deception made her fall and would have made him fall too:

> hadst thou been there,
> Or here the attempt, thou couldst not have discerned
> Fraud in the serpent, speaking as he spake;
> No ground of enmity between us known,
> Why he should mean me ill, or seek to harm.
>
> (9.1148–52)

Eve's analysis is entirely correct but also totally irrelevant to the issue of culpability. Only God's intellectual discernment could penetrate Satan's disguise, but the power to do so is beside the point.[112] That is why Milton, no longer sympathetically identifying with "innocent frail man" (4.11), can reassess the falls of both Adam and Eve with juridical objectivity: they were

> Complete to have discovered and repulsed
> Whatever wiles of foe [= Satan] or seeming friend
>   [= hypocritical inspirited serpent].
> For still they knew, *and ought to have still*
>   *remember'd*
> The high injunction not to taste that fruit,
> *Whoever tempted;* which they not obeying,
> Incurred, what could they less, the penalty,
> And manifold in sin, deserved to fall.
>
> (10.10–16; emphasis mine)

Neither Adam nor Eve can plead ignorance of the law, which has been pounded into their exceptional heads if not written in the fleshly tablets of their hearts (for example, 4.419–35). They can offer not a scintilla of extenuating circumstance, for neither satanic deception nor feminine seduction (but rather damnable amnesia) has caused their original sin.

But for Milton, in a startling reversal of deutero-Paul, *fallen Eve is less culpable than fallen Adam.* The fact of her deception cannot minimize her trespass in the direction of exoneration, but it can and does mitigate her blameworthiness relative to Adam's and the angels', for they fall undeceived. Any casuist worthy of the name (and Milton was one) would immediately recognize the illogic of the New Testament counterargument, for the seriousness of a sin is directly proportional to the knowledge with which it is willfully committed. Since both Adam and Eve "still . . . knew, and ought to have still remembered" the prohibition against the fruit, both sin mortally by disregarding it. But Eve's knowledge of *the* relevant ethical circumstance (that is, that satanic deceit is the near occasion of her sin) is inevitably deficient: *she does not*

---

112. Uriel again: man's job is not to penetrate disguises but to obey God's commandment. Fowler's note to the contrary (*John Milton: "Paradise Lost,"* 504) is wide of the mark.

even know that she is undergoing temptation, whereas Adam recognizes at once that his wife is a deceitful seductress. The woman was deceived, but *Adam* was *not* deceived. This misogynistic scriptural distinction, which Milton deploys poetically to motivate the fall on the horizontal temporal axis of plot verisimilitude, operates simultaneously to redeem biblical misogyny on the vertical atemporal axis of hierarchical culpability. In yet another powerful confirmation of I Timothy's literal facticity, Milton shows that whereas Eve "was deceived and became a transgressor," Adam "was not deceived . . . and became a [greater] transgressor."

Who sinned more, the undeceived man or the deceived woman? The answer is self-evident in I Timothy, wherein the only relevant and fully incriminating circumstance is deception itself. But the Bible leaves related questions unanswered and indeed unasked; prominent among them is the issue of what motivated Adam's fall, a mystery slighted by Genesis and ignored by deutero-Paul, who suppresses the very fact that he transgressed in the foul but fecund womb of institutional misogyny. *That* Adam sinned, and *why* he sinned, are, however, issues reborn in the Middle Ages and beyond, and along with them the corollary question, settled so decisively in the New Testament, of whether Eve in fact erred more grievously than her undeceived husband. The authority of deutero-Paul weighed heavily indeed upon the souls of the three exegetes whose commentaries I am about to discuss: but their stumbling efforts to advance beyond (or at least to justify) the naked misogyny of the New Testament by sorting out the tangled web of male-female responsibility for original sin will foreground Milton's continuing triumph over the chauvinist etiologies of his ancient source.

I begin with Saint Augustine. In *The City of God* 14 ("Of the fall of the first man") he motivates the lapse of Adam in an original but not an unexpected way:

> we cannot believe that Adam was deceived, and supposed the devil's word to be truth, and therefore transgressed God's law, but that he by the drawings of kindred yielded to the woman, the husband to the wife, the one human being to the other human being [citing I Timothy 2:14]. . . . the woman accepted as true what the serpent told her, but the man could not bear to be severed from his only companion, even though this involved a partnership in sin.[113]

Augustine simply imposes on Timothy a rationale for Adam's disobedience—the same powerfully romantic "link of nature" (9.914) that Milton exploits. Fallen Eve calls Adam's sinful apotheosis of social

---

113. *City of God,* 386.

intercourse a "glorious trial of exceeding love" (961), and Milton critics seem to have agreed: C. S. Lewis concludes that Adam's "sin is, of course, intended to be a less ignoble sin than [Eve's]";[114] for J. M. Evans "there is no denying Adam's nobility when he decides to die with [Eve]";[115] John Reichert introduces an amazing end-justifies-the-means distinction to conclude, in a vicious turn of the hermeneutic circle, that "Adam does the wrong thing for good reasons. The reasons do not make the act right, nor does the act make the reasons base";[116] and Alastair Fowler, following this chain of unreason to its inevitable chauvinist terminus, triumphantly announces that Adam's "disobedience surpasses the virtue of most fallen men."[117] Never mind that Milton calls it "compliance bad" (994): these male critics have been reading Augustine.

They have not been reading Milton, however. As Adam is about to sin, his situation is analogous to that of Satan and his legions. He too is a father "amazed" (9.889 = 2.758) at the "sudden" (9.900 = 2.752) eruption of sin in a "Daughter" (9.291 = 2.817) "subduct[ed]" (10.536) from his "left side" (8.465 = 2.755). Just as the angels "recoiled" (2.759) at an open and discoverable apparition—at the incarnate "fatal trespass done by [Satan]" (9.889)—Adam experiences "horror chill" and muscular enervation at discovering Eve's crime (888–90). Both Sin and Eve are evil daughters, as Satan and his cohorts on the one hand, and undeceived Adam on the other, well know. If Sin is a "sign / Portentous" (2.760–61), signifying what the unfallen angels must not consent to touch, and if the tree of knowledge is the same thing to unfallen Eve, the fallen woman occupies precisely this slot with respect to her husband. In *Areopagitica* Milton writes that "God . . . left [Adam] free, *set before him a provoking object, ever almost in his eyes;* herein consisted his merit, herein the right of his reward, the praise of his abstinence" (*YP* 2:527; emphasis mine). But the tree of knowledge is not "ever almost in his eyes"; Eve is. Since, moreover, Adam is not deceived as to the supposed potency of the forbidden fruit, it can hardly serve to test his obedience.[118] In itself, the "charge" not to touch the tree will always be "easy" for him (4.421), an "easy prohibition" (433). Fallen Eve is thus brilliantly deployed as his "provoking object." When she transgresses, Milton declares that "nature from her seat / Sighing, through all her works gave signs of woe" (9.782–83). The prototype for

114. *A Preface to "Paradise Lost,"* 126.
115. *"Paradise Lost" and the Genesis Tradition,* 285.
116. *"Against His Better Knowledge: A Case for Adam,"* 98.
117. *John Milton: "Paradise Lost,"* 491.
118. Adam sins when—and only when—he eats the fruit, but he will not eat it for knowledge's sake, but only to stay with Eve. His sinless motive is different from Eve's, his sinful act the same, his sin greater than hers.

this terrestrial manifestation of the pathetic fallacy is the appearance of Sin as a sign and her horrified shout at the birth of "Death; / Hell trembled at the hideous name, and *sighed* / From *all* her caves, and back resounded Death" (787–89; emphasis mine). Adam likewise hears the mournful sigh of mother earth (845–46) and sees Eve's "fall / Determined" (5.878–79) shortly after encountering her. Although after her creation he calls them "one flesh, one heart, *one soul*" (8.499; emphasis mine), after her fall he says only that "we are one, / One flesh" (9.958–59). Man and woman are no longer unanimous, as Adam well knows. This earth-born woman, then, is Adam's sign; like the serpent, she is herself a "specious object by the foe suborned" (9.361); like Sin she is "a serpent armed / With mortal sting" (2.652–53 = 10.867); and like the interdicted tree, she signifies *noli me tangere*.

Adam knows all this and more. Joseph Summers correctly accuses him of failing "to turn to God" for assistance in his moment of truth.[119] But I would go further: Adam ought (and he knows it) to repudiate his wife with such words as spew forth from Satan when he encounters Sin at the gates of Hell: "I know thee not, nor ever saw till now / Sight more detestable than . . . thee" (2.744–45). But not so. Like the angels before him, Adam "Becamest enamoured" (2.765 = 9.909–16) at the sight of "so fair" a creature (2.748 = 9.896)—even though, like the angels, he is about to name her sin (9.896–916 = 2.760). Like Satan, Adam finds the "shape and countenance bright" (2.756) of his wife's "heavenly form" (10.872) irresistibly "attractive" (2.762). Although Sin and fallen Eve are in fact "Crooked" and "*sinister*" (10.885–86; emphasis mine), both Satan and Adam—the former correctly, the latter inexcusably—persist in seeing the object of their "affections" as their "perfect image" (2.764 = for example, 5.95). Therefore, like the angels, who eventually become "pleased" (2.762) with Sin, Adam recapitulates their transgression when "he scrupled not to eat," "fondly overcome with female charm" (9.997–99). Not that Eve is isomorphic with Sin: "for [Adam] ordained / A help," she *becomes* his "snare" (11.164–65; emphasis mine). Fallen Eve is not Sin (not by a long shot), but she is now sin-full.[120] She has become what Tertullian so misogynistically implies woman to have been *ab ovo*: "the

119. *The Muse's Method*, 175.
120. Against feminists like Sandra Gilbert who offer the sinister (i.e., left-sided) birth parallel as evidence that Milton is a misogynist. But Eve is born from Adam's left side only so her embryonic rib may be bathed in "Cordial [i.e, from the *heart* of Adam] spirits warm" (8.466). She is thus contrasted to Sin until she falls. Milton's similes almost always discriminate tenor from vehicle; theodicy demands as much from the poet, and he demands as much from readers. See Gilbert's "Patriarchal Poetry and Women Readers: Reflections on Milton's Bogey" and my rebuttal, "Milton's Bogey."

devil's gateway."[121] Adam knowingly, and with malice aforethought, embraces this adopted daughter of the archfiend "Against his better knowledge" (998), yet Milton's Augustinian male critics would have us excuse this sort of "Casual fruition" (4.767) as illustrious evidence.

So would at least one woman, Katherine M. Rogers. Determined to prove Milton a misogynist, she cites *The City of God* as referring "to Eve's responsibility for the Fall" and as "exonerating Adam as much as possible," a ploy Rogers thinks Milton repeats when he "gilds Adam's sin with amiable weakness."[122] And indeed, at first glance, Augustine's *socialis necessitudo* theory does seem to add Carthaginean insult to New Testament injury, extenuating gregarious Adam at the considerable expense of a wife who believed lies against her maker. Augustine, however, continues:

> the man could not bear to be severed from his only companion. . . . *He was not on this account less culpable, but sinned with his eyes open.* And so the apostle does not say, "He did not sin," but "He was not deceived." For he shows that he sinned when he says, "By one man sin entered into the world," and immediately after more distinctly, "In the likeness of Adam's transgression" [Romans 5:12]. But he meant that those are deceived who do not judge that which they do to be sin [i.e., Eve]; but [Adam] knew. Otherwise how were it true "Adam was not deceived"?[123]

This is poor exegesis but superb casuistry. Augustine cannot find evidence of male transgression in I Timothy 2:11–15—there isn't any—but he knows from Genesis that Adam did in fact sin. He therefore glosses Timothy (which he thinks Saint Paul to have written) with supposedly corroborative evidence from Romans 5:12. Profoundly aware of, and presumably disturbed by, the chauvinist proclivity of his proof-text, as well as by its evident incompatibility with Romans 5:12, Augustine imposes extramural Pauline commentary on deutero-Paul to support his opinion that Adam "was not . . . less culpable, but sinned with his eyes open." Had the critics cited in my previous paragraph followed him to this hard-won conclusion (or had they read Section III above), they might have reassessed their interpretations of Adam's fall as a compelling piece of "Illustrious evidence" (9.962)—the deluded opinion of fallen Eve.

But whereas Augustine denies the (possible) deutero-Pauline implication that Adam did not transgress at all, he does not settle the question of the seriousness of her husband's offense relative to Eve's: "he was not . . . less culpable." Than his wife? Than he would have

---

121. *On the Apparel of Women*, in *Ante-Nicene Fathers IV*, 19.
122. *The Troublesome Helpmate: A History of Misogyny in Literature*, 20.
123. *City of God*, 386–87; emphasis mine.

been had he been deceived? Was Adam in fact *more* culpable than Eve? Augustine does not say, preferring to rest in a (deliberate?) ambiguity that awaited further clarification in the later Middle Ages. I turn therefore now to the less-than-illustrious evidence of Thomas Aquinas. In the *Summa Theologica* he repeats Augustine's version of why Adam sinned, but only to place far the greater blame for original sin where I Timothy 2:11–15 deposits it all: on the already overburdened shoulders of hapless Eve:

> as regards the species of pride, the woman sinned more grievously, for three reasons. First, because she was more puffed up than the man. For the woman believed in the serpent's persuasive words. . . . On the other hand, the man did not believe [them] to be true. . . . —Secondly, the woman not only herself sinned, but suggested sin to the man; *wherefore she sinned against both God and her neighbor.* —Thirdly, the man's sin was diminished by the fact that [citing Augustine] he consented to the sin out of a certain friendly good will, on account of which a man sometimes will offend God rather than make an enemy of his friend. . . . It is therefore evident that the woman's sin was more grievous than the man's.[124]

Aquinas does not cite Timothy, but he evidently treats Augustine as a palimpsest disguising the biblical prototype of Thomas's own blatant (if sophisticated) misogyny. Augustinian ambiguity is entirely absent from his triune denunciation of Eve: although Adam erred (as Aquinas reluctantly concedes), he was seduced into rebellion by a wicked wife, who became a more grievous transgressor than he.

Milton absolutely rejects this notion. I will take up in reverse his responses to Aquinas's threefold bill of particulars. As to the third point, that the man's sin was diminished by his love of Eve, Milton dispenses with this nonsense by having similar sentiments issue from the mouth of unregenerate Adam. Eve has just finished berating him for permitting her separation that fateful morning, speciously alleging that had he not dismissed her, neither she nor he had fallen (1155–61). To which Adam, now "incensed," responds in kind:

> Is this the love, is this the recompense
> Of mine to thee, ingrateful Eve, expressed
> Immutable when thou wert lost, not I,
> Who might have lived and joyed immortal bliss,
> Yet willingly chose rather death with thee.
>
> (1162–67)

This *sounds* good, but in fact the only "recompense" (1162 = 994) Eve ever promises or gives Adam for allegedly loving his neighbor as

---

124. *Summa Theologica* 2.2.163.4; emphasis mine.

himself is the forbidden fruit (990–97). Eve merely delivers what he "willingly chose"—death—which he incurs not (as she, Augustine, and Aquinas think) "for her sake" (993), but in self-aggrandizing pursuit of carnal gratification. As Irene Samuel has argued, Adam's "sole concern is to keep Eve; she is his, not to be taken from him, his possession."[125] Adam characterizes his transgression in just such terms of amicable benevolence ("friendly good will") as Aquinas certifies as bona fide and (partly) exculpatory; but far from ennobling him, in *Paradise Lost* the blasphemous notion that *greater love than this hath no man than that he lay down his life for his wife* indicts Adam as an unreliable self-extenuating exegete.

Turning now to Thomas's second point—that Eve sinned twice, "against both God and her neighbor"—she did, of course, but it is a strange casuistry that takes the measure of sin's gravity by the merely quantitative calculus of simple addition. To Milton, the man's single apostasy—perpetrated with eyes wide open—vastly exceeds Eve's reiterated trespasses. The poet implies as much in Book 10, in a passage inversely proportional (ethically speaking) to Adam's Thomistic extenuation. If an unregenerate *peccator* will underestimate his trespass in the name of guilty extenuation, a regenerate *peccatrix* will overestimate hers in the name of penitent conviction. Thus Eve:

> both have sinned, *but thou*
> *Against God only, I against God and thee*
> And to the place of judgment will return,
> There with my cries importune heaven, that all
> The sentence from thy head removed may light
> On me, sole cause to thee of all this woe,
> Me me only just object of his ire.
> (10.930–36; emphasis mine)

This is the spirit incarnate of I Timothy and the very letter of Thomas Aquinas ("she sinned against both God and her neighbor" = 10.930–31), but its fallen logic will not withstand scrutiny: only a radical feminist, such as Katherine Rogers, could allege that "Eve humbly—and rightly, we must infer—accepts full responsibility for the Fall."[126]

Regenerate Eve gets the last (scrupulous) word in *Paradise Lost* ("All by me is lost" [12.621]), but her judgment there is no more accurate than her misinterpretation of Adam's "own last reasoning words" (9.379) at the conclusion of the separation scene, in which, like her fallen Doppelgänger, she gets the "last" (erroneous) word (377). Her

---

125. "*Paradise Lost* as Mimesis," 27–28.
126. *The Troublesome Helpmate*, 156.

self-incriminating indictment at 10.930–36 is likewise mistaken. Much later, *Adamus recidivus*, forever extenuating, will seek to confirm Eve's opinion, discerning "the tenor of man's woe [= 10.935] / From woman to begin"; but the archangel Michael peremptorily repudiates this specious grievance: "From man's effeminate slackness [woe] begins" (11.632–33).[127] Delete the angel's censoriousness, and his words apply equally to Eve's regenerate scrupulosity. Although contrite hyperbole is not altogether unwarranted in an accessory to genocide, even Adam, deeply moved by his wife's sorrowful confession, concedes its excess, acknowledges that he occasioned her fall, and (*mirabile dictu!*) offers to extenuate *it* (after the fashion of Thomas Browne) as coextensive with her "frailty and infirmer sex" (10.947–57). This attitudinal reversal has its own interest, but my present concern is with how Milton heaps Thomas Aquinas's devilish insinuations back upon his own misogynous head—and *through the retributive offices of the very woman whose reputation he has besmirched*. It is as fine an instance of poetic justice as exists in literature: the poet traces the *Summa*'s misogyny to a repetition, in Thomas's finite mind, of his general mother's excessive self-loathing.

As to Aquinas's first point—that "the woman believed in the serpent's persuasive words" whereas "the man did not"—this is true but irrelevant (in its Thomistic context) to the issue of their relative culpability; first, because the serpent never tempts Adam; and second, because if he had, the man too would have failed to discern fraud in the beast, whose satanic "sleights none would suspicion mark" (9.92). I am not implying that Adam would have fallen at Satan's suggestion (though that he in fact transgresses undeceived at the instancing of an ontological equal confirms that he might have); but beyond dispute he would have been *beguiled* by the Devil,[128] as was Uriel.

Ever eager to split theological hairs, Aquinas advances deutero-Pauline misogyny by discerning in Augustinian exegesis reasons not implausible to exonerate Adam at Eve's expense. His efforts did not, however, survive quite unscathed into the Renaissance. Thomas Browne retreats a piece—though perhaps not a far piece—from Thomas Aquinas in his own witty epigrammatic adjudication of who sinned more, the woman or the man. Finessing the New Testament "deceived–not deceived" distinction by suppressing it, Browne also ignores Adam's Augustinian "friendly good will" and its correlative

127. As Barbara Lewalski has aptly put it, "Michael . . . gives such misogynist platitudes short shrift" ("Milton on Women—Yet Once More," 12).
128. Had Satan approached Adam with a sequence of sly insinuations, he too would have fallen into deception unaware. Burden, *Logical Epic,* 81, thinks otherwise, but he ignores the evidence of Uriel.

Thomistic extenuations. These hopeful deletions suggest intent to rehabilitate hapless Eve but, alas, not so. Where Aquinas expands Timothy and Augustine to clarify misogyny's trinitarian rationale, Browne contracts Aquinas to obfuscate its ethical irrationality. This medical doctor zeroes in on point two of the angelic doctor's affidavit against Eve—that "she suggested sin to the man": "whether the transgression of Eve seducing, did not exceed that of Adam seduced; or whether the resistibility of His Reason, did not equivalence the facility of her Seduction; we shall refer it to the Schoolman" (p. 20). I will analyze this amazing passage by dealing seriatim with the two *whethers* it hypothesizes.

If Browne is not mobilizing specific responses to Timothy and Augustine, he certainly has scholastic Thomas ("*the* Schoolman") right at his slippery fingertips. Browne is gunning for Eve: that is why he nowhere mentions the fact of her apostasy from God. Far from seeking to exonerate her by suppressing this credulous greater offense, Browne is rather setting the woman up for additional abuse by unfairly comparing her *lesser* "transgression," that "of Eve seducing [Adam]" (the crime against her neighbor), to her husband's single offense against God ("the transgression . . . of Adam seduced"). This comparison may sound like potential compassion—especially if one considers that a writer such as Thomas Jackson could conclude that "Eve was more deeply in the transgression than the man, because she seduced him to eat of the forbidden fruit, as the serpent had done her."[129] For Jackson the mere fact that Adam did not tempt anyone else implies Eve's greater culpability (never mind that she herself was not only seduced but deceived). Browne, on the other hand, does not appear to foreclose the question of relative culpability at the outset. He does not appear to, but this is only a deceptive ploy. For, astonishingly, Browne poises *Eve's marital infidelity* against *Adam's apostasy* to speculate "whether" the former "did not exceed" the latter, tipping justice's scales against the woman. He dare not propose this outrageous comparison of apples to oranges as an apodictic truth, so he merely hypothesizes it; and he even intimates the opposite notion, invisibly insinuated into the twisted syntax of a hypothetical *whether* and an equivocal *did not:* perhaps Eve's sin did not exceed Adam's after all? Perhaps not, but it probably did: why else would Browne refer not directly to what Adam did but elliptically to what he suffered (*that of Adam seduced*)? This periphrasis reduces the man's original sin to a demonstrative pronoun (*that*) and demotes man himself to the passive participial victim (Adam *seduced*) of his actively aggressive temptress

---

129. *A Treatise on the Primeval Estate of the First Man,* in *Works,* 10:56.

(Eve *seducing*). Browne is gunning for the woman, make no mistake about it.

His intentions are evident, moreover, from his use of capitalization ("*His* Reason" versus "*her* Seduction") and from the scholastic form in which he pursues the very question (itself a Thomistic parody) of relative culpability. Schematically put, Browne asks whether x (Eve's sin) exceeded y (Adam's sin); since this is followed by the adversative conjunction *or*, we naturally await symmetrical consideration of the opposite hypothesis, namely, whether y exceeded x. But not so: the thought that Adam outsinned Eve never violates Thomas Browne's patriarchal mind. At best he concedes the possibility that the two transgressors shared equal culpability.

At least I think he does.

Abandoning entirely the x and y with which he began (and the concept of excess that he predicated of these terms), Browne next interjects three new elements into the logical proportionality he is so disproportionately unfolding. The question now is whether "the resistibility of [Adam's] Reason did not equivalence" (that is, "strike a balance with": the scales are still poised) "the facility of [Eve's] Seduction." The writer speculates that the man's superior intellect endowed him with a power to resist temptation (which Browne might more aptly have called *free will*, since reason also is choice) equal to (but by no means greater than) the (irresistible?) "facility" with which the woman tuned her seductive proem. For all its talk of "equivalence," however, this hypothesis again inclines decisively to Eve's disadvantage. In the Bible (Genesis 3:6, 17) the woman simply gives the fruit to the man, who takes it after simply hearkening unto her voice. (Why he eats is shrouded in mystery, which is what gave Augustine his entree into the question.) These scriptural lacunae leave open the question of just how much "resistibility" the man possessed. But are we to believe with Browne that perhaps—or perhaps not—onomastic Adam, who named the animals (2:19–20), had at best brains *just* sufficient to ward off the temptress? Where did Eve acquire seductive skills comparable to her husband's yet unfallen integrity? Was she all *that* crafty? Was she not rather—in *Paradise Lost* if not in Genesis—an open and discoverable apparition? If, moreover, Adam was not deceived, how indeed did he succumb so facilely to a mere woman, however seductive?

These questions have answers, of course, but Browne does not stop to ask them, preferring merely to assert—or rather to conjecture—that Adam might possibly have been equal to the occasion of his temptation, and that his and Eve's transgressions might be equivalent if—*and only if*—he had a cerebrum proportional to her charms. Eager to establish the woman's decisive instrumentality in her husband's fall,

Browne never even concedes that Adam's weakened (because female and fallen) adversary was herself seduced—and deceived—by a power greater than she. Instead he relies on semantic legerdemain to postulate allegedly reciprocal equivalences between vaguely defined analogates that obfuscate the very issue he sets out ostensibly to clarify. Lost (by misogynistic design) in errant mazes of casuistry, finding no end therein (indeed how could he?), the good doctor concludes exactly where he began—with "the Schoolman" whose interminable hairsplitting *questions* he has so brilliantly mimicked and to whose dubious cogitations he remands the whole perplexed question of who sinned more, the man or the woman.

Milton, on the other hand, refers the question to the final, definitive appellate judge: a school-divine named God, who invokes his own casuistical sleight-of-hand to transubstantiate institutionalized deutero-Pauline misogyny into a pretext (and moreover a pre-text) for prevenient grace: for if the woman was deceived and became a transgressor, the man, who was not deceived, became a (greater) transgressor. *Yet the man will be saved through the woman.*

V. Some Niceties I Confess There Are Which Extenuate

The angel was the author of his own crime, but the man was deceived by a trick. Also the greater was the angel's glory, so much the greater was his downfall: but the frailer was the man's nature, so much the easier was his pardon.

—**Alcuin,** *Interrogationes et Responsiones in Genesim*

I begin once more with Thomas Browne, whose *Pseudodoxia Epidemica* rehearses most of the relevant theological data to infer mostly erroneous casuistical conclusions. The issue is one we broached at the outset, whether the serpent had a human face: "the assumption of humane shape," Browne writes, "had proved a disadvantage unto Sathan, . . . leaving some excuse unto the woman, which afterward the man took up with lesser reason [Genesis 3:17]; that is, to have been deceived by another like her self" (p. 344). The argument goes something like this: since Eve was deceived by an inferior (i.e., by a mere brute serpent), she had no excuse, for she ought to have penetrated such an open and discoverable apparition. Browne excoriates fallen Eve for deploying just this tactic at Genesis 3:13 (p. 23). But had she been deceived by a human-visaged snake she could have pleaded nolo contendere and have escaped perhaps with a verdict of voluntary manslaughter: for in *that* case her adversary would have been not an inferior, but one of her own kind (the serpent Browne disqualifies was Eve's spitting image—it had "a Virgin's head").

If Browne judges Eve's deception to be more culpable because an inferior effected it, others felt deception to be more truly deceptive under just these circumstances. Centuries before Browne, John Chrysostom, addressing not ethics but the issue of verisimilitude, observed in his *Homilies on the Epistles of Paul:*

> The woman said, *The serpent beguiled me.* But the man did not say, The woman deceived me, but, she gave me of the tree. . . . Now it is not the same thing to be deceived by a fellow creature, one of the same kind, as by an inferior and subordinate animal. This [that is, deception by a subordinate] is *truly* to be deceived. Compared therefore with the woman, he is spoken of as not deceived. For she was beguiled by an inferior and subject, he by an equal.[130]

Like Browne, Chrysostom is trying to preserve certain crucial deutero-Pauline distinctions. Adam was undeceived, at least comparatively speaking (a notion to which I shall return), notwithstanding that Eve sought to beguile him. Why was he not fooled? For Chrysostom, however one adjudicates the question of comparative responsibility, the psychological fact remains that deception may be more authentically accomplished by a subordinate than at the instancing of an equal—the former "is *truly* to be deceived." This distinction accounts for the plot exigency that Eve was deceived while her husband was not deceived; but it is difficult to square it with Browne's casuistical opinion that deception by an inferior is more blamable (because more easily rebuffed) than deception by a peer.

Of course Chrysostom had no interest in achieving rapprochement with Thomas Browne—any more than Browne sought consistency with himself. His own line of casuistical reasoning (that deception by a human-visaged snake would have been less culpable in Eve's case) is itself impossible to reconcile with his insistence, vis-à-vis plot verisimilitude, that Eve could not have been deceived at all by such an animal; but I am less concerned with Browne's consistency than with his theodicial arguments, whose implications I shall explore momentarily.

Browne, however, continues: Adam too tried Eve's ploy (at Genesis 3:12), alleging that she deceived him. He "took up" this "excuse," but "with lesser reason" than Eve. Why *lesser*? Was he not deceived by another like himself? Decidedly not! The man was not deceived at all. Moreover, he was not even seduced *by another like himself,* for Eve, a secondary and derivative creation—a spare part in fact—is (Browne thinks) patently inferior to the man. Here at last misogyny begins to expose its pseudo-casuistical duplicity: Adam had less reason than Eve to plead extenuation (not that she had any), because whereas she

---

130. *Homily on Timothy,* ix; in *Homilies on the Epistles of Paul,* xii.

was deceived by an inferior, he was merely seduced by one. To preserve Adam's masculine headship, Browne must logically deny him even an angstrom of excuse. Whereas Eve might possibly refer to *her* inferiority ("the condition of Sex, and posteriority of Cremation," etc.), and whereas she was deceived, the fall "was very strange and inexcusable in the Man," who "was the wisest of all men since": he *knew* better ("a naked offer proved sufficient unto him," p. 18) and—what is worse—he compounded his trespass after the fact, blaming God for giving him the woman who gave him the fruit, "making the fountain of good, the contriver of evil, and the forbidder of the crime an abettor of the fact prohibited" (pp. 22–23).

What are we to make of all this? Browne's strategy is to deduce (from an unstated major premise) inferences consistent with his conviction in faith that neither the man nor the woman had any excuse for committing original sin. *If and only if you are deceived by another like yourself, may you plead for "minoration of [your] offences"* (p. 23). Neither Adam nor Eve can meet *both* these conditions ([1] deception and [2] deception by a peer), so both are rendered inexcusable. This is Browne's conclusion, and Milton agrees with it. But there is more: Eve has half a Brownean excuse to offer (she was deceived), whereas her husband has none (*he* was *not* deceived): *therefore Adam's transgression exceeded hers in gravity*.

Others before Browne had raised the horrible specter of deception as a mitigating casuistical circumstance, but only to reject it for misogyny's sake. Thomas Aquinas, conceding that in one respect only—that "Adam was more perfect than the woman"—was his sin "the more grievous than hers," proceeds rather to excoriate Eve on other, more palpable grounds. As is his custom, Aquinas begins by creating a straw man for rebuttal:

> *Objection* I. It seems that Adam's sin was more grievous than Eve's. For it is written [citing I Timothy 2:14] . . . and so it would seem that the woman sinned through ignorance, but the man through assured knowledge. Now the latter is the graver sin [citing Luke 12:47–48] . . . Therefore Adam's sin was more grievous than Eve's.[131]

This is precisely Milton's position, the inescapable consequence of I Timothy itself. But Aquinas escapes all right, just as deutero-Paul does, compelled by misogyny to repudiate his own logic:

> *Reply Obj. I.* The woman was deceived because she was first of all puffed up with pride. Wherefore *her ignorance did not excuse, but aggravated her sin,* in so far as it was the cause of her being puffed up with still greater pride. (*Summa Theologica* 2.2.163.4; emphasis mine)

131. *Summa Theologica* 2.2.163.4

In order to "justify" this chauvinist bigotry Aquinas must, as I have shown, anteriorize the moment of sin, locating it prior to Eve's initial susceptibility to deceit: "Though the woman was deceived before she sinned in deed, still it was not till she had already sinned by interior pride" (*Summa Theologica* 1.94.4); hence "ignorance . . . aggravated her sin."

This is, I submit, bad theology and worse misogyny, expropriated from deutero-Paul and transmitted virtually intact to Thomas Browne, who could not (any more than Aquinas) draw the plain inference to which his own premises fairly deliver him over—that deception mitigates Eve's sin relative to Adam's. Ever the misogynist, Browne retreats to safer ground, speculating (for example), "Whether there was not in Eve as great injustice in deceiving her husband [who was nevertheless not deceived], as imprudence in being deceived herself" (p. 20). For although this doctor may have had the moral courage to advance beyond Timothy and Aquinas by (perhaps) recognizing (with Augustine) that if Adam was seduced by Eve "the fall was very strange and inexcusable" in him, Browne was too mesmerized by the mighty wings outspread of his predecessors' chauvinist etiologies to more than recapitulate most of the misogynist polarities they bequeathed to him.

John Milton was mesmerized by no one. Did he get the idea from Browne, or had he perhaps read John Yates's analysis of the fall? In his commentary Yates writes, apropos of whether Adam was in fact present at Eve's temptation,

> it is probable, that Adam stood by all the time of the disputation, and *therefore his sin was the greater,* that he rebuked not the Serpent [Abdiel!], and rescued his wife from all such suggestions: or if he was absent, (whereof the text makes not mention) *then should he show himself a weaker vessel then his wife, who had all the bad Angels* (in one crafty beast) *to set vpon her; whereas hee had onlely one weake woman in his purest integrity to ouerthrow him* . . . .[132]

Excepting only his opinion that Adam was probably present at Eve's seduction, Yates's is exactly the theodicial position Milton develops in *Paradise Lost:* whereas Eve was (sinlessly) deceived into (sinful) transgression—and not indeed by an inferior serpent, but "by all the bad Angels" "constrained / Into a beast, and mixed with bestial slime" (9.164–65)—Adam was not deceived, for "hee had onlely one weake woman . . . to ouerthrow him"; "therefore his sin was the greater." Whether Milton derived these notions from Yates (which I doubt), or whether he developed them independently after decades of inspired

132. *A Modell of Divinitie, Catechistically composed,* 178; emphasis mine.

meditation on I Timothy and its misogynistic tradition (which I do not for a moment doubt), in *Paradise Lost* he transforms the deutero-Pauline concept of deceit by an inferior into a sublime premise similar to (but far more radical than) those of John Yates and Thomas Browne: *if and only if you are deceived by an ontological superior may you plead for prevenient grace abounding and regain a paradise within*:

> The first sort by their own suggestion fell,
> Self-tempted, self-depraved: man falls deceived
> By the other first: man therefore shall find grace,
> The other none: in mercy and justice both,
> Through heaven and earth, so shall my glory excel,
> But mercy first and last shall brightest shine.
>
> (3.129–34)

Stanley Fish, deliberately blurring casuistical distinctions that Milton sought all his life to preserve, finds the just-cited lines to be logically untenable, ethically arbitrary, and downright coy:

> The implication in the syntax is that grace is *due* man because his error is someone else's responsibility: man therefore shall find grace. But this is deliberate teasing, if not on God's part, then on Milton's. *The "therefore" is not logical but arbitrary;* Satan's presence in the garden is not really an extenuating circumstance; God merely chooses to make it the basis of an action that proceeds solely from his good will. . . . *We want very much to read "deserve"* [says who?] *instead of "find" grace,* and do so until the word "mercy" reminds us that grace is *gratuitous,* cannot be earned and certainly not *deserved.*[133]

There *is* something arbitrary about God's decree: he arbitrarily (i.e., freely) chooses to ransom sinners who deserve damnation (10.1–16). But there is nothing arbitrary (i.e., capricious) about the *rationale* God deploys to account for and otherwise explain his reasons for graciously (not gratuitously) saving Eve. God's *therefore* is absolutely logical. His decree of predestinated redemption is no more inscrutable than the exaltation of the Son; but Fish obscures its sublime rationality by "discovering" the concept of obligation (*due, deserve*) where Milton discerns only fittingness. Fallen Eve finds a grace she cannot even seek, because she knows she does not deserve a pardon. But it is fitting and proper for God to forgive her be*cause* (the causal nexus is crucial) she falls deceived by Satan. Her sinless errors are entirely *his* responsibility (witness Uriel). "Satan's presence" does not exonerate Eve, but it "mitigate[s]" (10.76) her sin relative to those of the undeceived angels. Divine forgiveness indeed proceeds "solely from [God's] good will," but in *Paradise Lost* the will of God is "Founded in reason, loyal, just,

133. *Surprised by Sin,* 215, n. 1; emphasis mine.

and pure" (4.755), not troublesomely disguised—as if he were ashamed of it—amidst logically disjunctive adverbial *therefores*. Fish's analysis, the brilliant question-begging concomitant of his determination to "find" in Milton's epic discontinuities that he has put there himself, recapitulates, in a far subtler tone, the specious casuistry of such exegetes as Thomas Browne.

For, in fact, six lines from *Paradise Lost* fully redeem both fallen Eve and deutero-Pauline misogyny; they also fully compensate whatever hint of tyrannical self-defensiveness may be (erroneously) thought to infect God's just-completed specification of "Ingrate" (3.97 = 5.811) angels and men as "authors to themselves" of their own transgressions, "Both what they judge and what they choose" (122–23): for although *God* "had no influence on [the] fault" (118) of his creatures, *Satan* in fact deceived Eve. This circumstance does not extenuate her mortal trespass, but it provides a compelling pretext for offering her prevenient grace.

Thomas Browne, I have suggested, mobilizes all the relevant data but usually pursues it to the wrong conclusions. *If* Eve had "been deceived by another like herself," even that would have left "*some* excuse unto" her. But in fact a power greater than herself occasioned her lapse. Browne knows this to have been the case, but once again he dodges its ineluctable correlative, minimizing the contribution of the Father of Lies and insisting that his deceit was "an open and discoverable [serpentine] apparition." Eve was admittedly deceived by a superior, but he was a mere serpent in appearance; his disguise thus compounds rather than mitigates her offense, as indeed it does for I Timothy, Thomas Aquinas, and a host of others. But where his predecessors misogynistically condemn beguiled Eve, Milton lovingly redeems her, *on account of her deception*. Since, as I have argued, Satan's stratagem is for Milton hidden and impenetrable, chock full of "deceit and lies" (5.243), the fact weighs heavily in the direction of mitigation. This is why, this is indeed the only reason why—in "the strife / Of mercy and justice in [God's] face discerned"—the Father "purposed not to doom frail [Eve] / So strictly, but much more to pity inclined"; "through [Satan's] malice fallen" (400–407), she experiences an infusion of supererogatory grace that she is powerless even to request (230–33): "[Eve] falls deceived / By [Satan] first: [Eve] *therefore* shall find grace." This proto-feminist soteriology would have made the stubborn blood of deutero-Paul congeal as ice more hardened after thaw!

And what of Adam? To unravel the [il]logic of *his* redemption, we must pause first to consider the fate of the fallen angels. "The first sort [i.e., Satan and his legions] by their own suggestion fell, / Self-tempted, self-depraved." As we have seen, at the "suggestion" of Abdiel (5.809–48) Lucifer himself conceives and bears sin parthenogenetically (5.853–85; 2.746–61): tempted by a good angel but seduced by himself, he is therefore irrevocably "Cast out from God and blessed vision" (613). His cohorts, moreover, share his fate; for if "with lies / [Satan] Drew after him the third part of heaven's host" (709–10)—in which respect their temptation resembles Eve's—they too were nevertheless "Self-tempted" (i.e., intramurally, from within "the angelic species,"[134] by one of their own kind) and "self-depraved" (as all free creatures must be). For Thomas Browne, ironically enough, this fact would have weighed in their favor ("to have been deceived by another like [themselves]")—except that the bad angels do not fall into deception unaware. Although "unwary" Beelzebub (5.695) anticipates "Unwary" Eve (10.947), fallen Satan himself confirms that he merely "seduced" "the spirits beneath" (4.83) into "perfidious fraud" (5.880) without leading them into deception. They sin with their eyes wide open, as the counterexample of Abdiel (803–907) makes abundantly clear. *This servant of God is to the unfallen angels what Adam might have been to unfallen Eve had he witnessed Satan's deceptive temptation of her.* Abdiel exposes Lucifer's transparent fraud before the angels sin, thereby eliminating the circumstantial mitigation of deception. This is why *Paradise Lost* consistently affirms that "Subtle he needs must be, who could seduce [not *deceive*] / Angels" (9.307–8). Adam, who speaks the just-cited words, has fully internalized the exemplary parable of Abdiel.

The absence of an Abdiel-like warning voice further mitigates Eve's transgression (she falls *deceived* by a *bad* angel); but Abdiel also renders Adam inexcusable, because the seraph is precisely the model whom the first man ought to have emulated upon encountering fallen Eve. Given the good angel's exemplary rebuttal of transparent Luciferean fraud, the woman becomes to her husband what Satan is to the as-yet-unfallen angels: a seductress but not a (successfully) deceptive one. Like the angels, therefore, Adam "fell, / Self-tempted [i.e., at the 'suggestion' of Eve, one of his own kind], self-depraved"; on the analogy with the fallen angels, then, *he ought not to find grace:* "Die he or justice must" (3.210).

Nevertheless in *Paradise Lost* justice is, with respect to fallen Adam, merely "the sharp right profile of Mercy";[135] and (unlike the

134. In the felicitous phrasing of Fowler, *John Milton: "Paradise Lost,"* 150. The contrary opinion of E. F. Daniels, in "Milton's Fallen Angels—Self Corrupted or Seduced," will not withstand scrutiny. All creatures in *Paradise Lost* are seduced by another creature; all fall self-corrupted; but *only Eve is deceived.*
135. Jon S. Lawry, *The Shadow of Heaven: Matter and Stance in Milton's Poetry,* 160.

serpent) mercy has a fully human face—the penitent face of sinful Eve. She "falls deceived by the other *first*," while Adam falls undeceived by her *second*. He ought to die but lives to repent because the woman was deceived *and therefore* became a *lesser* transgressor. When Adam comes around to convicting himself of sin in Book 10, he adjudges himself "To Satan only like both crime and doom" (841). This is an exaggeration, but not by much: for Adam indeed deserves to be "like in punishment, / As in [Satan's] crime" (544–45). But a merciful God forgives his satanic transgression by blurring the distinction between Eve's being deceived and his being not deceived.

Milton may have derived support from John Calvin for his benevolent conjunction of what deutero-Paul had so emphatically divided. In his *Commentaries upon Genesis* Calvin prepares the ground for a corrective to New Testament misogyny by dissenting from the Augustinian argument that Adam fell merely at the instancing of an alluring spouse:

> because Moses simply relates that he ate the fruit at the hands of his wife, the opinion has been commonly received, that he was rather captivated with her allurements than persuaded by Satan's impostures. For this purpose the declaration of Paul is adduced, "Adam was not deceived, but the woman" (I Timothy 2:14). *But Paul in that place,* as he is teaching that the origin of evil is from the woman, *only speaks comparatively.* Indeed, it was not only for the sake of complying with the wishes of his wife that he transgressed the law laid down for him; but being drawn [i.e., seduced] by her into fatal ambition, *he became partaker of the same defection with her.* And truly Paul elsewhere states that sin came not by the woman, but by Adam himself (Romans 5:12). Then, the reproof which soon afterwards follows, "Behold, Adam [*sic*] is as one of us" [Genesis 3:22] clearly proves that he also foolishly coveted more then was lawful, *and gave greater credit to the flatteries of the devil,* than to the sacred word of God.[136]

Without a doubt Calvin has *The City of God* at hand as he puts pen to paper. He recapitulates Augustine point for point, thought following thought, the spirit leading: there is the same need to motivate Adam's fall in the absence of arresting Old Testament evidence; the same concern to rationalize deutero-Paul on the score that the man was not deceived; partial confirmation of Augustine's social compulsion theory; and citation of the precise Pauline text (Romans 5:12) that Augustine impresses to confirm that Adam did in fact transgress, I Timothy notwithstanding. But what a different spirit leads Calvin to the radical conclusion that Adam was deceived! Where Augustine "cannot believe that . . . [the man] supposed the devil's word to be the

136. *Commentaries upon Genesis,* trans. J. King, 1:152.

truth," Calvin cannot *but* believe that he "gave greater credit to the flatteries of the devil, than to the sacred word of God." This is a far cry from the New Testament.

So resolved is Calvin to promulgate his transmogrification that he alleges deutero-Paul to have spoken of Eve's deception "only . . . comparatively"—which is to say, "Adam was less deceived than Eve, but not therefore *un*deceived." Nothing in Timothy warrants this hairsplitting exegesis, which proceeds rather from the desire to clarify Augustinian ambiguity (Adam "was not . . . less culpable [than Eve?]") by implying that only if the man was less deceived than the woman and *yet* believed lies against his maker, could Paul rightly say that "sin came not by the woman, but by Adam himself." Calvin is struggling to reconcile the contradiction between I Timothy (where Eve originates man's woe) and Romans (where Adam does) by imputing the more heinous transgression of the woman to the man. Neither Eve nor Adam gains in the bargain, but Pauline and deutero-Pauline theology is made consistent with itself.

Milton engineers much the same maneuver, but he rejects Calvin's casuistically indefensible conviction that a fall into deception does not mitigate original sin. Where Augustine construes Timothy literally ("Adam was not deceived") to infer a social motive for the man's undeceived transgression, and where Calvin adjusts the deutero-Pauline letter to provide an ethical rationale—rooted in the concept of shared deception—for answering in the affirmative the question "whether the transgression . . . of Adam seduced . . . did not equivalence . . . [Eve's] Seduction [by Satan]," Milton, in an inspired stroke of antimisogynist genius, combines the New Testament letter with a purely superficial expropriation of Calvin (minus the Calvinist deception ethic) to orchestrate the salvation of Adam:

> The first sort [Adam] by [Eve's] suggestion fell,
> Self- [i.e., intramurally] tempted, self-depraved: man
>   [Eve and Adam!] falls deceived
> By the other [Satan] first: man [Eve *and* Adam!] shall
>   find grace . . . .

God's prestidigitation hinges on the equivocal word *man,* which allows the Deity to predicate deception of Adam; not substantively, as Calvin does, but purely nominally, by an arbitrary divine fiat: Eve falls deceived—therefore *Adam* shall find grace! This casual casuistry is indeed "the basis of an action that proceeds solely from [God's] good will";[137] it does not compute in the realm of ethics, but it accomplishes a devastating critique of pure ethics in the transcendent realms of

137. Fish, *Surprised by Sin,* 215, n. 1.

prevenient grace and inspired poetry: *before dividing the falls of man and woman in the name of theodicial justice, Milton must unite them in the name of theodicial mercy,* which "first and last shall brightest shine" if God has his way. This is a far cry indeed from I Timothy 2:11–15: "Some niceties I confess there are which extenuate" Adam's transgression (Browne, p. 20).

VI. Beati Quorum Tecta Sunt Peccata!

> . . . that uxorious king, whose heart though large
> Beguiled by fair idolatresses, fell
> To idols foul.
> —*Paradise Lost*

The inclusion of Adam in the deception of Eve at 3.129–34 is repeated elsewhere in *Paradise Lost.* To redeem the man, Milton must theologically cover up his heinous undeceived transgression. Christ indeed provides a robe of righteousness (10.211–23) for both Adam and Eve, selected from the treasury of *vestimenta honoris* that an atoning sacrifice remands to his forgiving custody; but fallen Eve—or rather the fact of her deception—is Adam's first human mediatrix. Milton mercifully deploys pivotal ambiguities suggesting that both the woman and her husband were beguiled. If Satan "deceived / The mother of mankind" (1.35–36), he also (by a simple ellipsis) "deceived . . . mankind," female and male alike. The Devil himself contributes to this blurring of etiological distinctions (though not indeed to facilitate Adam's redemption): he hopes "by fraud or guile" (2.646) to seduce not Eve but "A generation" of men (653). In Book 4 he determines to defraud *both* Adam and Eve (514–27), though in the event he of course deceives the woman alone. And when he returns to Pandaemonium in the "permissive glory" and "false glitter" (10.451–52) of his supposedly triumphant Odyssean *nostos,* this liar concocts a biased recension of his deceptive mundane transactions. He "found / The new created world," and "therein man":

> *him by fraud* I have seduced
> From his creator, and the more to increase
> Your wonder, with an apple; he thereat
> Offended, worth your laughter, hath given up
> Both his beloved *man* and all this world.
> (480–89; emphasis mine)

All was for an apple, an apple that *he* (that is, *Adam*) took. The song, however, is partial: ever the self-aggrandizer, Satan is obfuscating the fact that he deceived only Eve; "*Man* I deceived," he insists (496;

emphasis mine). But his melody ironically suspends the doom of Adam by affirming that he too was led into deception unaware.

God similarly condescends to verbal ambiguities to accuse Adam of falling deceived—but, unlike Satan, preveniently, for redemption's sake, before he announces deception's ameliorative rationale:

> [Satan nears] the new created world,
> And *man* there placed, with purpose to assay
> If *him* by force [i.e., Eve's dream] he can destroy, or worse,
> By some false guile pervert; and shall pervert
> For *man* [Eve only] will hearken to his glozing lies,
> And easily transgress the sole command,
> Sole pledge of *his* obedience: so will fall
> *He* [Eve *and* Adam] and *his* faithless progeny: whose fault?
> Whose but *his* own? Ingrate, *he* had of me
> All *he* could have; I made *him* just and right,
> Sufficient to have stood though free to fall.
> (3.89–99; emphasis mine)

This passage is the locus classicus for much misplaced vilification of Milton's God. Most defenses of it turn on proving the justice of God's justice, but this is a futile and unnecessary route by which to engineer an apologia for the Deity:[138] the passage readily accommodates itself to a pious interpretation in the context of the trope of deception in *Paradise Lost*. Georgia Christopher believes that the "explicit doctrine" of these lines "is not only the center of coherence in Milton's poetry [true], but a source of poetic energy as well [exactly!]." But she paradoxically locates the origin of dogma's power in the supposed "extraliterary properties [of] God's 'word.'"[139] On the contrary: whereas God appears bent (defensively, they say) on clearing "his own justice and wisdom from all imputation," his equivocal semantics literarily "declare his purpose of grace towards" Adam (Book 3, Argument) before God announces this redemptive purpose at 3.129–34. The Father's judgment can easily be distinguished into mercy, thanks to English's incapacity to distinguish generic *man* (Greek *anthropos*, Latin *homo*) from human *male* (Greek *aner*, Latin *vir*). These distinctions enable the author of I Timothy to promote misogyny by exonerating Adam,[140] but language enables Milton's God merely to redeem Adam,

138. The best attempt to defend God's justice is Dennis Danielson's *Milton's Good God: A Study in Literary Theodicy*. There is no need to do so, however, since justice is usually the sharp right profile of mercy in *Paradise Lost*. See also Chapter Three, passim.

139. *Milton and the Science*, 20–21.

140. Adam, the individual *aner*, was not beguiled, but the woman (Eve as representative of her entire gender) was. The woman, in her capacity as Adam's helpmeet, nev-

not to excuse him: he confounds the man's transgression in Eve's deception, for in fact *she*, not *he*, "will hearken to Satan's glozing lies." What sounds suspiciously like pharisaic legalism is merely (and lovingly) a mercy actually present in God's bare-boned words before the Word of God enfleshes them at 3.144–66 and (especially) 227–65.

In confirming the Father's gracious decree that "man falls deceived / . . . man therefore shall find grace," Messiah reiterates the paternal confusion of tongues that enables grace to abound:

> For should *man* finally be lost, should *man*
> Thy creature late so loved, thy youngest *son*
> Fall circumvented thus *by fraud*, though joined
> With *his* own *folly*?
>
> (150–53; emphasis mine)

This is an exercise in deliberate soteriological obfuscation: Eve is entirely absent from the lexical surface of the Son's rhetorical interrogation, her "Fall . . . by fraud" having been hoodwinked for the sake of redeeming God's "youngest *son*," by which phrase Messiah can mean Adam alone. And although the distinction between *fraud* and *folly* may appear momentarily to put asunder what God hath joined together, separating Eve's deceit from Adam's more culpable offense ("*fondly* overcome with female charm*," 9.999), this opposition collapses upon further inspection. If Eve falls by fraud, she also aggravates sinless deception with "foul distrust, and breach / Disloyal on the part of man" (9.6–7)—on *her* part, that is, for she foolishly apostasizes by disobediently acting upon Satan's blasphemous prevarications. Messiah is thus actually distinguishing not Eve's fraud from Adam's folly (in fact he posits them as "joined," 152), but the deceit that occasions both their sins from the perfidy that constitutes them.

Similar ambiguities occupy the Father in Book 10 when he denies the unfallen angels' complicity in the fall of man:

> I told ye then [3.92–134] [Satan] should prevail and speed
> On his bad errand, *man* should be seduced
> And flattered out of all, believing lies
> Against *his* maker.
>
> (40–43; emphasis mine)

This sounds exactly like John Calvin (Adam "gave greater credit to the flatteries of the devil, than to the sacred word of God"), but the literal

---

ertheless induced him to sin. She (not Eve, but woman) shall nevertheless be saved through childbearing, if *they* (Greek plural: all women, *all* of whom inherit Eve's sinful propensity to deception) remain in faith. Romans 5:12, much harder on Adam, says that by one man (*aner*, not *anthropos*) sin entered into the world. This judgment is impossible to harmonize with I Timothy 2:11–15; nor is it necessary to if the Epistle to Timothy is understood as deutero-Pauline.

sense of these words is deutero-Pauline, Augustinian, and Thomistic: Eve alone believes "that God had forbidden them to eat of the tree, lest they should become like to Him" (*Summa Theologica* 2.2.163.4), whereas the man "sinned with his eyes open" (*City of God,* 387). But God deceitfully includes Adam's transgression in his wife's, giving postlapsarian persuasive heft to his prelapsarian argument that "*man falls deceived* / . . . ; *man therefore shall find grace.*"

Stella Revard—striving to rescue Eve's dignity by the stratagem of regarding her transgression as culpably equivalent to Adam's (from which premise, working backwards, she infers Eve's prelapsarian independent responsibility, and thence her equivalent "Sufficien[cy] to have stood" [3.99])—asks plaintively, "Does any voice in *Paradise Lost* urge us in assessing the fall to view one of the human couple as more to blame than the other?"[141] My response is, "Virtually every voice *but* those of the Father and his 'omnific Word' (7.217) *commands* that we assign greater blame to Adam." And even here, at 3.129–34, certain relevant deutero-Pauline distinctions survive Milton's rehabilitative category confusion. In I Timothy the subjugation of woman is doubly verified, not only by the nature of Eve's fall but also by the "posteriority of [her] Cremation." "For Adam was formed *as the first,* then Eve." The Greek text uses the predicate adjective *protos,* not the adverbial form of the word: not only was the man created before Eve, his anteriority confers hierarchical priority on him as well (as it does in Genesis 2). But in *Paradise Lost* Milton significantly redeploys the Pauline adjective as an adverb: "[Eve] falls deceived / By the other *first*" (3.131). *The priority of her transgression mercifully counteracts the jurisprudential antiextenuating fact of Adam's created priority.* His ontological anteriority, implying that he is not the weaker vessel, would deny him prevenient grace were he to have fallen first. Adam is not deceived; thank God he falls *second,* for to sin both *un*deceived and *first* would doom him (but not Eve) to the fate of Satan. Consistent with his other deutero-Pauline transformations, Milton reevaluates even the biblical logic of priority, discovering in Timothy's misogynistic *protos* a redemptive adverb with which to save sinful Adam, given the "posteriority of [*his*] Transgression." "[Eve] falls deceived / By the other first; [Adam] therefore shall find grace": "Beati quorum tecta sunt peccata!" ("Blessed are they whose sins are covered!"; Dante, *Purgatorio,* from Psalm 32).

VII. ADAM WAS DECEIVED AND BECAME A TRANSGRESSOR

Then the LORD God said to the [man], "What is this that you have done?" The [man] said, "The serpent beguiled me, and I ate."

—Genesis 3:13

141. "Eve and the Doctrine," 69.

So the man was beguiled after all—at least in the benevolent fiction that God articulates to deconstruct Milton's carefully wrought hypotaxis of the otherwise irreducible deutero-Pauline fact that "Adam was not deceived." But if God thus unmakes the poet's plot in order to redeem fallen *aner,* the poet must—in a reciprocal compensatory gesture—unmake his own plot to show that, if Adam is (soteriologically speaking) deceived no less than Eve, he also, *no less than she,* believed lies against his maker ("nor was godhead from [*his*] thought," 9.790):[142] in the end Calvin was (in fiction) correct. Milton prepares for this metamorphosis as early as Book 4, when he advises the sleeping couple, "Sleep on / Blest pair; and O yet happiest if ye seek / No happier state, and know to know no more" (773–75). In the factual plot of *Paradise Lost* this admonition pertains to Eve alone, but in the theodicial fiction, pride of intellect must be applied nominally to Adam to balance his nominal incorporation in the deception of his wife. This theological reciprocity explains at once the otherwise puzzling circumstance that Adam, who in fact falls only for Augustinian societal motives, retroactively accuses himself of having "sought / Forbidden knowledge by forbidden means" (12.278–79). He arrives at this remarkable pass as a regenerate complement to Eve's scrupulous self-accusation at 10.930–36. *Old* Adam—supping full of extenuation's deadly poison—says he was "Fooled and beguiled" (880) in order spuriously to affiliate himself with Eve's sinless deception. *New* Adam—chastened and subdued by his wife's penitence (958–59), and awaiting redemption *through the seed of the woman* (12.376–82)—is only too happy to affiliate himself with her sinful transgression:

> Greatly instructed I shall hence depart,
> Greatly in peace of thought, and have my fill
> Of knowledge, which this vessel can contain;
> Beyond which was my folly to aspire.
>
> (557–60)

Articulating a personal theology of his own, Adam humbly appropriates his wife's transgression, a fully penitent gesture corresponding precisely to God's deceptive obfuscation of Eve's deception for Adam's redemption's sake: "The serpent beguiled me, and I ate."

VIII. Yet Man Will Be Saved through the Woman

And a sweet melody ran through the luminous air; wherefore good zeal made me reprove Eve's daring, that, there where earth and heaven were

142. Milton writes, in the *Christian Doctrine,* "Each was sacreligious and deceitful, cunningly aspiring to divinity although thoroughly unworthy of it, proud and arrogant" (*YP* 6:384).

obedient, a woman, alone and but then formed, did not bear to remain
under any veil, under which, if she had been devout, I should have tasted
those ineffable delights before, and for a longer time.
—Dante, Purgatorio 29 (translated by Charles S. Singleton)

[Milton's] assertion that man has "despotic power" [*SA*, 102] over woman
places him among the more rigorous interpreters of St. Paul.
—Katharine M. Rogers, The Troublesome Helpmate

But it might well be argued that in his actual presentation of Adam and Eve
Milton gives Eve the advantage in moral and spiritual qualities.
—Helen Gardner, A Reading of "Paradise Lost"

> Restored by [Eve], vile as I am, to place
> Of new acceptance.
—Paradise Lost

Catharine F. Seigel, arguing that Milton is a misogynist, claims
that *Paradise Lost* 10 "crystallize[s]" the poet's "unkindest treatment of
women." To verify this opinion, Seigel must argue that "Milton never
intended Eve to be the fine catalyst for the reconciliation" transacted at
lines 909–65ff. She alleges that "Adam takes the initial step"—which
she considers synonymous with "the positive action"—in reestablish-
ing a cordial relationship with his wife.[143]

Seigel is not alone in this pernicious opinion. Georgia Christopher, who certainly does not subscribe to the view that Milton hated
women, has argued the importance (to the renovation of Adam) of the
hopeful anagnorisis accomplished in his halting soteriological interpretation of the protevangelium (10.1026–37). Christopher calls this
"great interpretive leap" a discontinuous "*instant de passage* from despair to faith."[144] But the only human discontinuity in *Paradise Lost* is
the fall of man, and even it is only theologically (not exegetically)
detachable from the temptations that occasion it. It would require
separate study, however, to prove that Adam's delayed understanding
of the biblical curse on the serpent (10.175–81 = Genesis 3:14–15)—the
curse itself comprising yet another manifestation of the sharp right
profile of God's mercy—is actually the predictable outcome of a con-
geries of far-fetched but recoverable antecedent causes. My present
concern is to refute Christopher's isolation of the protevangelium (at
Eve's expense) as the *sole* decisive catalyst in Adam's rebirth. For if
"Prevenient grace descending" (11.3) is the cause of regeneration (and
it is), its phenomenology necessitates concomitant psychological inter-
ventions, including the truly pivotal mediation of fallen woman.

143. "The Reconciliation in Book X of *Paradise Lost*," 261–62.
144. *Milton and the Science,* 167.

First among the postlapsarian instruments of rehabilitation[145] is God's indictment of Adam (10.145–56): the rigor of its justice requires the man (after long delay) to exculpate God from complicity in his offense (828–33). But the self-extenuating misogynist continues to blame Eve (867–908), notwithstanding that the seriality of the judgment has treated him far less kindly than she: Messiah first curses the quite innocent serpent (163–80),[146] then (briefly and matter-of-factly) sinful Eve (193–96), and finally (at length) more sinful Adam (198–208). *The last shall be worst in the realm of retribution, but the worst is first in guilty extenuation.* This is why Satan, the most grievous sinner in cosmic history, not only "excuse[s the] Devilish deeds" (4.394) he is about to essay, but quite literally forgets his aboriginal transgression (2.737–47). In Book 10 Adam resembles the Father of Lies; to rectify his unregenerate amnesia God takes advantage of the benevolent intervention of Eve, a fact Georgia Christopher stubbornly underestimates. Adopting a specious hermeneutic dichotomy, she proposes to show that, because the protevangelium alone triggers a regenerate literary experience in Adam, Eve's antecedent conciliatory gestures "seem as much an expression of her own need as of gratuitous love," "may have no bearing on Adam's salvation," and play only "an inadvertent role" in turning his attention to the protevangelium.[147] Eve certainly exhibits inadvertency with respect to jogging her husband's memory; but Milton's recasting of I Timothy 2:11–15 requires him to deploy her as *the* human mediatrix of prevenient grace. Eve intervenes not adventitiously, but deliberately and selflessly; and only her scrupulous self-accusation roots out the degenerate unreason whereby Adam has, up to this point, persisted in "calibrating the *crassa peccata*"[148] of his already regenerate spouse.

When Eve draws "nigh" her "afflicted" (10.863–64) husband to assuage his despair, he rejects the gesture before she completes a sentence:

> Out of my sight, thou serpent, that name best
> Befits thee with him leagued, thy self as false
> And hateful; nothing wants, but that thy shape,
> Like his, and colour serpentine may show
> Thy inward fraud, to warn all creatures from thee

145. Raphael serves as the *prelapsarian* instrument of prevenient grace. See Chapter Three, passim.
146. He also curses the most guilty party—Satan—in the same breath. The last shall be first!
147. *Milton and the Science,* 165, 171. She makes the same point in an earlier version of this argument: "The Verbal Gate to Paradise: Adam's 'Literary Experience' in Book X of *Paradise Lost.*"
148. Christopher, *Milton and the Science,* 164.

> Henceforth; lest that too heavenly form, pretended
> To hellish falsehood, snare them.
>
> (867–73)

These vicious words are shot through with sinful extenuation: unlike her counterpart in *Samson Agonistes*, Eve is even now what she has always been—an open and discoverable apparition—and although Adam compulsively rejects her candor as a deceitful subterfuge, he is not deceived. Moreover *his misogyny approximates what he ought to have said to Eve in Book 9 when he was as yet sinless.* After venting his spleen for another thirty-five lines (874–908), Adam "from her turned" (909). *This is precisely what he ought to have done when Eve offered him the forbidden fruit.* It follows axiomatically that this sinful man is as yet psychologically impotent to respond to an unmediated infusion of prevenient grace. The Bible insists, as does Milton, that no *peccator* can make peace with God while he continues to abhor his neighbor. Adam therefore cannot distinguish the judgment of the *Word* (Genesis 3:14–15) into mercy until Eve "soften[s his] stony heart / To pray, repent, and bring obedience due" (3.189–90)—not with equivocal scriptural conundrums, but with plain and perspicuous "Soft words" (10.865 = 3.189) of regenerate conviction.

Refusing to be put off by her husband's outraged aversion, Eve "at his feet / Fell humble, and . . . besought his peace " (10.909–13). We must wind back the clock to comprehend this gesture, for the woman who manages it is she who "Persisted, yet submiss, though last" (9.377)—to quite different effect—at the conclusion of the separation scene. There Eve was adamantly adventuresome and rashly overconfident; here she is sorrowfully "Immovable till peace obtained from fault / Acknowledged and deplored" (10.938–39). On both occasions she is "submissive" (10.942 = 9.377)—*submiss* embodying the preternatural mystery of prelapsarian oxymoron, and *submissive* suggesting the natural concomitant of postlapsarian contrition. Though Eve "*unweeting* ha[s] offended, / Unhappily *deceived*" (10.916–17; emphasis mine)—a crime mitigated, as I have argued, by the circumstances of deception that literally surround it in these lines (compare 332–36)—she offers to atone for Adam's greater offense by vicarious substitution (10.930–36 = 3.234–41). This is the woman whose "love sincere" (915) Georgia Christopher and Catharine F. Seigel cannot credit.

What is Milton's view of it? He tells us, in propria persona, that Eve's contrite confession "in Adam wrought / Commiseration; *soon his heart relented*" (10.939–40; emphasis mine) and "his anger all he lost" (945). Although in the judgment Messiah "warned / [Adam of his] sinful state, and to appease betimes / The incensed Deity" (3.185–87), the sinner—who remains as yet trapped one-sidedly in a "hostility" that remained "perfectly reciprocal"[149] throughout Book 9—must first do unto his neighbor what he cannot yet even imagine that God might do unto him. Thanks to Eve it happens now, the softening of his hard heart: *Eve* opens Adam to the grace abounding that will "clear [his] senses dark, / What may suffice" (3.188–89) to unriddle a soteriology cryptically embedded in the curse on the serpent.

Eve alone facilitates this crucial exegesis. She undoes the amnesia that has caused the fall and has imprisoned Adam in sinful extenuation by reminding him of the protevangelium. We learn later that, at the moment of its utterance, the curse on the serpent was "then *not minded in dismay*" (11.156; emphasis mine). Adam is, however, "disarmed" (10.945) of this disabling affect by his penitent wife, who argues for reconciliation by herself remembering "the place of judgment" (932), "the sentence" (934) of God, and the protevangelium itself:

> Between us two let there be peace, both joining,
> As joined in injuries, one enmity
> Against a foe by doom express assigned us,
> That cruel serpent.
>
> (924–27 = Genesis 3:15)

These human words are the near occasion of Adam's allegedly "sudden grasp of the oracular" Word of God,[150] just as the man's subsequent plan to return to the place of judgment in search of divine clemency (1086–92) is occasioned by—and in fact repeats—Eve's initial offer to make this pilgrimage herself (932–36). Adam arrives at these determinations not all on a sudden—only sin is sudden in *Paradise Lost*—but by exercising his "more attentive mind / Labouring" (1011–12); and to what does he attend if not to the intimations of salvation provided by Eve? It requires staunch faith or subtle dialectics to assert, as Georgia Christopher does, that Adam's "calling to mind with heed / Part of our sentence, that [Eve's] seed shall bruise / The serpent's head" (1030–32) occurs "fortuitously."[151]

Christopher is not innocent of the evidence I have just discussed, but she relentlessly underestimates it to salvage an interpretation of the reconciliation scene that recapitulates the institutional misogyny of I Timothy 2:11–15.[152] But why purchase so doubtful a reading at so inflated a cost? The answer lies in this scholar's conviction that to trace Adam's rebirth to the regenerate promptings of Eve is "historically

149. Ibid.
150. Ibid., 171.
151. Ibid., 166.
152. Ibid., 171.

improbable": since Protestant reformers "make the point that 'saving' grace occurs when one responds to divine words, not when one responds to other people,"[153] Christopher deduces, on the assumption that Milton agrees with his predecessors, that Adam's salvation cannot involve a decisive push from Eve. But the poet thought it not beneath his dignity to disregard, apropos of the trope of deception, Tertullian, Thomas Browne, Chaucer's Nun's Priest, deutero-Paul, Peter Comestor, William Perkins, Edmund Spenser, Thomas Aquinas, Saint Augustine, John Donne, Thomas Jackson, John Chrysostom, and Dante. Would he nevertheless hesitate to depart from Martin Luther and John Calvin on the protocols of prevenient grace?

Milton was beholden to no man, was captive to no tradition. In the *Christian Doctrine* he asserts, with respect to questions of systematic theology, that "*all* previous writers have failed"; he never depends "on the belief or judgment of others in religious questions": "I devote my attention to Holy Scripture alone. I follow no other heresy or sect. I had not even studied any of the so-called heretical writers, when the blunders of those who are styled orthodox, and their *unthinking distortions of the sense of scripture,* first taught me to agree with their opponents whenever these agreed with the Bible."[154] These are not the words of one held hostage to historical precedent—or to the Bible either: this great and good poet did not hesitate to create deliberate "distortions of the sense" of I Timothy 2:11–15. If, as William Kerrigan has argued, Milton "did not require inspiration to write a legalistic theodicy,"[155] he did not require patronizing conformity to human opinion to do so either. But in fact *Paradise Lost* is not legalistic; thanks to the ministrations of a feminine "celestial patroness" (9.21), Milton's "unpremeditated verse" (25) can "justify the ways of" deutero-Paul (1.26) to woman. Every line of the epic's "great argument" (24) reflects zealous determination to eliminate misogyny from this seminal New Testament text. The last stage in Milton's rehabilitation of his source *requires* (I use the term advisedly) deployment of Eve as the instrument of Adam's regeneration. Her benevolent self-accusation exposes the last of deutero-Paul's chauvinist etiologies ("Yet woman will be saved through bearing children"), thus consummating the poet's commanding demonstration that, if the spirit of I Timothy killeth (which it does),

153. The phrase "historically improbable" appears in Christopher's reply (titled "Adam and Eve in *Paradise Lost*") to Jeanne Clayton Hunter's rebuttal of her *PMLA* article. Christopher concludes, "To be sure, Adam does not ride into Grace on Eve's coattails" (116). But *he must;* the logic of Milton's reconstruction of I Timothy 2:11–15 demands just this denouement.

154. *YP* 6:118, 123–24; emphasis mine.

155. *The Sacred Complex,* 99.

the core of its problematic letter giveth life: *Adam was not deceived [and became a transgressor], but the woman was deceived and became a [lesser] transgressor. Yet [man] will be saved through [Eve].*

It remains now to demonstrate the truth of this premise with respect to the postlapsarian world of *Samson Agonistes,* wherein a fallen son of Adam is brought to regeneration by the inadvertent ministrations of a fallen daughter of Eve.

3

Regeneration
The Role of Raphael
in *Paradise Lost*
and *Samson Agonistes*

> How fresh, oh Lord, how sweet and clean
> Are thy returns! even as the flowers in spring;
> To which, besides their own demean,
> The late-past frosts tributes of pleasure bring.
> Grief melts away,
> Like snow in May,
> As if there were no such cold thing.
> **—George Herbert, "The Flowers"**

Mary Ann Radzinowicz has recently argued that "the fullest response to Milton's poetry . . . comes from interpreting its meaning in relation to its evolution within the corpus of his works."[1] As the title of this chapter implies, I endorse Radzinowicz's belief in the centrality to Milton studies of author-contextual criticism, upon whose assumptions I rely in the following comparative study of regeneration in *Paradise Lost* and *Samson Agonistes*.[2] I also accept, along with the vast majority of Milton scholars, the traditional chronology according to which *Samson* is the last-composed of Milton's poems.[3] Chronology aside, however, my intention to read the tragedy in the light shed upon it by the epic is the more plausible given the fact, as Joseph Wittreich has observed, that "even if [*Paradise Lost, Paradise Regained*, and *Samson Agonistes*] were not composed sequentially, they were pub-

1. *Toward "Samson Agonistes": The Growth of Milton's Mind*, xix.
2. All citations of Milton's poetry in Chapter Three will be to *John Milton: Complete Poems and Major Prose*, ed. Merritt Y. Hughes.
3. In my view, the definitive case for the traditional chronology has been made by Radzinowicz, among others. See *Toward "Samson Agonistes*," Appendix E, "The Date of Composition of *Samson Agonistes*," 387–407.

lished that way," and so (presumably) were intended to be read in the order of publication.[4] In the *Christian Doctrine* Milton writes, apropos of scriptural exegesis, that "difficult texts . . . must be explained by many clearer passages which resemble them; for clear things are not elucidated by obscure things but obscure by clear."[5] Exactly this relationship appertains between *Samson Agonistes* and *Paradise Lost:* since the God of the play is so much a *deus absconditus* as to have been omitted from the dramatis personae, and since the play lacks "normative characters,"[6] and since there is "no narrator authorized by God to guide our human response"[7] to the exfoliation of its plot, its meanings are sometimes more elusive than those of *Paradise Lost,* wherein the ways of God are often enough rendered less than inscrutable by the definitive analyses of the epic bard. If both epic and tragedy proceed from essentially the same poetic and religious sensibility, the more leisurely exposition of the former ought to provide a telling context in which to resolve doubts and ambiguities in the latter.

To be specific, I will argue that, excepting differences necessitated by the formal demands of genre, the descent of Raphael in *Paradise Lost* is precisely analogous to the marriage of Samson to the Woman of Timna in *Samson Agonistes.* Both angel and woman are embodiments of prevenient grace sent by the Deity to initiate the regeneration of fallen man before he has fallen. Both therefore corroborate Anthony Low's assertion that "secretly guiding and shaping the action [of *Samson*] is the hidden providence of God."[8] Unlike the fall of a sparrow, there is special providence in the falls of Adam and Samson: through the mediation of Raphael and the Timnite, Milton's God preveniently renders these sinners inexcusable for sins they have yet to contemplate committing. He thereby lovingly hastens their regeneration by enabling them to internalize that conviction of guilt without which spiritual renovation cannot occur.

Before developing this thesis, I think it best to elaborate on the two methodological hypotheses that will comprise my exegetical approach in this chapter. First, I assume, given the sequential publication of *Paradise Lost* and *Samson Agonistes,* that Milton expects us to approach the tragedy from the normative perspective of fall and regeneration enumerated in the diffuse epic. It is, however, theoretically possible that he regards *Samson* as a revisionary critique of *Paradise Lost,* or that both poems are to be judged against the ethical and aesthetic axioms of

---

4. *Visionary Poetics: Milton's Tradition and His Legacy,* 191.
5. *Christian Doctrine* 1.4, in *YP* 6:181.
6. Edward Tayler, "Milton's *Samson:* The Form of a Christian Tragedy," 317.
7. William Kerrigan, *The Prophetic Milton,* 203.
8. *The Blaze of Noon: A Reading of "Samson Agonistes,"* 63.

Paradise Regained, which Milton deliberately interposed between them. Arthur E. Barker has said of the brief epic and the tragedy that "in some sense we are involved with the last two items in a trilogy," but his probing analysis fails to specify whether and how the poems are "properly sequential."[9] Both Balachandra Rajan and Mary Ann Radzinowicz have discerned that *Samson* is a fitting sequel to *Paradise Regained,* but neither addresses the appropriateness of using *Paradise Lost* as a scholium upon the drama.[10] Joseph Wittreich has attempted to read all three poems as mutually illuminating, but his conclusions as to their interrelatedness differ radically from mine. According to Wittreich, *Paradise Lost*

> serves as a gateway into the brief epic and the tragedy; yet these poems are much more than recapitulations of the diffuse epic, and certainly they are not redactions of one another's visions. In no case does the perspective of one poem duplicate that of the other: the diffuse epic is a focusing of orthodoxies that *Paradise Regained* proceeds to demolish; the brief epic is a formulation of a new system of religion, more perfect and enduring than the one it supersedes. . . . having shown how the paradise within may be achieved, [it] is complemented by a tragedy that shows how it may be lost, and the effects of its being lost.[11]

For Wittreich indeed "*Paradise Regained* finds its demonic parody in *Samson Agonistes,* Milton's tragedy showing not a man freeing other men from the cycles of history but a 'hero' binding men down to them."[12] The brief epic thus negatively illuminates both its predecessor and its sequel—especially the latter, wherein one finds recapitulated neither the redemptive paradigm of Christ in the wilderness nor the regenerative experiences of Adam and Eve in the Garden. Given these considerations, what (if anything) justifies my assumption that *Samson* should be read in the supposedly definitive context of *Paradise Lost?*

The assumption derives support from my second methodological hypothesis, namely, that the diffuse epic and the biblical tragedy are poetically and spiritually homologous, standing as twin monuments to Milton's unchanging mind. If they are of a piece, then the fall and regeneration of Adam ought to be repeated chapter and verse in the career of Samson, and *Paradise Lost* ought in many ways to clarify what is obscure in *Samson Agonistes.* But are the poems isomorphic? I recognize the pitfalls of beginning with this assumption, so my analysis will

9. "Calm Regained through Passion Spent: The Conclusions of the Miltonic Effort," 13–16.
10. Rajan, "'To Which Is Added *Samson Agonistes*—,'" 98; Radzinowicz, *Toward "Samson Agonistes,"* 284.
11. *Visionary Poetics,* 208–9.
12. Ibid., 207.

try assiduously to validate it by examining both poems in search of exemplary homologues. Here I will pause only to comment on the striking and suggestive analogy between Genesis and Judges that Milton draws in *Paradise Lost* as Adam and Eve arise after their first postlapsarian coitus:

> So rose the *Danite* strong
> *Herculean Samson* from the Harlot-lap
> Of *Philistean Dalilah*, and wak'd
> Shorn of his strength. They destitute and bare
> Of all thir virtue.
>
> (9.1059–63)

Apart from the fact that the Dalila of *Samson Agonistes* is married to Samson, whereas here she prostitutes herself to him, this passage suggests that in Milton's mind, Adam and Samson are alike in punishment as in their crime—and perhaps also in the dialectic of their regeneration, as I shall argue. At the very least, the hint of congruence between epic and drama asserted in Milton's simile is surely worth tracking to its inmost cell. Among the immediate dividends of doing so will be the opportunity to understand how *Samson* can at once adhere to the formal generic norms of Greek tragedy as Aristotle understood them, and yet redefine the moral parameters of tragic experience, thereby to eliminate the self-extenuating I-am-a-man-more-sinned-against-than-sinning propensities latent in Aristotle's definition of tragic *hamartia* as involving "the sort of man who is not conspicuous for virtue and justice, and whose fall into misery is not due to vice and depravity, but rather to some error."[13] In addition, this approach allows for the regeneration of the tragic hero, in fact his categorical restoration to divine favor, so that one's final response to a completed tragic action can resemble Manoa's asseveration, at the end of *Samson Agonistes*, that

> Nothing is here for tears, nothing to wail
> Or knock the breast, no weakness, no contempt,
> Dispraise, or blame, nothing but well and fair,
> And what may quiet us in a death so noble.[14]
>
> (1721–24)

Irene Samuel has argued eloquently against Manoa's position by conjoining the Aristotelian bias of the prefatory note to *Samson Agonistes* with the definition in the *Poetics* of *hamartia* to assert that "Milton

---

13. Aristotle, *Poetics* 13, in *Aristotle, Horace, Longinus: Classical Literary Criticism*, trans. T. S. Dorsch.
14. But is Manoa right? See *Lycidas*, lines 165–85, *Paradise Lost* 12.645–49, and Revelation 7:17 and 21:4 for corroboration.

called [his drama] a tragedy, not a martyr play; its subject cannot be Samson restored to divine favor."[15] The possibility remains, however, that Milton's indebtedness to Aristotle, to the Greek tragedians, and to their Renaissance commentators extends only to formal features, such as the presence of a Chorus, the measure of the verse, and observance of the three unities. Matters such as these constitute the primary concern of the prefatory epistle, and here as elsewhere Milton cites the opinion of David Paraeus that no less joyful a book than Revelation itself, given its "solemn scenes and acts" interspersed "with a seven-fold chorus of hallelujahs and harping symphonies," deserves on these structural grounds alone to be called "a high and stately trag-edy."[16] It is, moreover, probable that Milton wishes his reader to un-derstand tragedy conceptually (as opposed to formally) in precisely the terms in which he couches it in *Paradise Lost*. There, as he reluc-tantly essays to narrate the fall of man, the poet offers a view of the tragic entailing, contra Aristotle, the case of one whose misfortune comes about through "vice and depravity"; there, Milton's Christian tragic notes recount not Hellenic *hamartia* but

> foul distrust, and breach
> Disloyal on the part of Man, revolt,
> And disobedience: On the part of Heav'n
> Now alienated, distance and distaste,
> Anger and just rebuke, and judgment giv'n.[17]
> (9.6–10)

If, as I believe, *Paradise Lost* and *Samson Agonistes* are conceptually complementary, then the tragic fall of the Danite will recapitulate the tragic Adamic paradigm, and the regeneration of Samson may pro-ceed, on the analogy with the restoration of Adam, without any oxy-moronic violation of the norms of tragic experience as Milton (not Aristotle) conceived of them.

My point in thus entering into questions of generic definition is to engage my reader's sympathy toward the prima facie plausibility of supposing *Samson Agonistes* to be in some sense a repetitive codicil to *Paradise Lost*. If the epic's explicitness can alert us to Milton's prefer-ring, in typical departure from the predilections of the Greeks, to

15. "*Samson Agonistes* as Tragedy," 239.

16. *The Reason of Church Government Urged Against Prelaty, YP* 1:815; repeated thus in the prefatory epistle to *Samson Agonistes*: "Paraeus, commenting on the *Revelation*, divides the whole Book as a Tragedy, into Acts distinguisht each by a Chorus of Heav-enly Harpings and Song between."

17. *Paradise Regained* more explicitly rejects Aristotle's sentimentalized definition of tragedy: according to Christ (*PR* 4.310–12), the Greek tragedians are "Ignorant . . . / . . . how man fell / Degraded by himself" (the true Miltonic definition of tragic *hamartia*).

write a tragedy of regeneration,[18] it can just as likely contribute to the adjudication of other disputes about the meaning of *Samson Agonistes*. If the diffuse epic can make us see that the possibility of Samson's regeneration is not a priori outlawed by Milton's definition of tragedy, *Paradise Lost* can also offer compelling external evidence that such regeneration is in fact accomplished in the play. The issue is more than a quibble, for much recent criticism has sought to depreciate the traditional view that Samson finishes his career as the reinstated faithful champion of God. To the already-cited testimony of Joseph Wittreich and Irene Samuel may be added the witness of other twentieth-century commentators for whom *Samson Agonistes*, in Wittreich's words, criticizes "men and civilizations that have repeatedly reverted to the ways represented by Samson from which Jesus, as an example, provided them with a release."[19] The most extreme statement of this revisionist position is perhaps that of John Carey, for whom the climax of the play "is indeed morally disgusting": Samson's "last bloody act of vengeance, which the surface voice of the drama invites us to applaud, is condemned, at a deeper level, by the progression of imagery." To Carey, far from achieving spiritual regeneration, "the weak-minded, vengeful hero" is reduced "to the level of Dalila and the Philistines."[20] The purveyors of this and similar views tend to deny the essential rationality of *Samson Agonistes*, whose catastrophe—even if they applaud it—seems to them inscrutably bizarre. Almost two decades ago Stanley Fish argued that although Milton's God is just, "we cannot infer his benevolence or validate his justice from the known facts" of the play;[21] more recently Lawrence W. Hyman has found us forced by the absence of viable alternatives to rely on the admittedly inadequate Choral explanation of the plot's significance;[22] and John C. Ulreich, Jr., has maintained that "neither the action of [*Samson*] nor its argument is fully coherent on its own terms," for "letter [i.e., action] and spirit [i.e., argument] remain irreconcilably opposed to one another."[23]

In opposition to the revisionist readings of Wittreich, Carey, and Samuel, and to the fideistic or skeptical hermeneutics of Fish, Hyman,

18. Of the thirty-four extant Greek tragedies, only Sophocles' *Oedipus at Colonus* might genuinely be called a "tragedy of regeneration."

19. *Visionary Poetics*, 207.

20. Introduction to *Samson Agonistes*, in *The Poems of John Milton*, ed. John Carey and Alastair Fowler, 335–43. The present chapter was completed before the appearance of Wittreich's *Interpreting Samson Agonistes*, which argues for an unregenerate Samson. I have addressed this argument in a review, "On Reading Joseph Wittreich: A Review Essay."

21. "Question and Answer in *Samson Agonistes*," 263.

22. "The 'true experience' of *Samson Agonistes*," 91–92.

23. " 'This Great Deliverer': *Samson Agonistes* as Parable," 81–82.

and Ulreich, I shall argue that Samson is indeed a regenerate hero and that the Chorus of *Samson Agonistes,* no less than the narrator of *Paradise Lost,* accurately avers that "Just are the ways of God, / And justifiable to Men" (293–94 = *PL* 1.26). My thesis is not new but my evidence is, for much of it will come from *Paradise Lost.* I shall begin with a discussion of certain problems in the descent of Raphael arising in the main from the foreknown fact that the angel's admonitions to Adam and Eve will be ignored; solution of these problems will be found by contrasting Raphael to his Hesiodic, Homeric, and Virgilian literary forebears and by showing how God, given his divine prescience and the special providence whereby he decrees the predestined redemption of Adam, sends the archangel to him to facilitate his regeneration before he falls. I shall then turn to *Samson Agonistes.* After comparing it with certain analogues in Judges 13:16, knowledge of which helps the reader discern the providential hand of God lovingly manipulating the play's bewildering succession of Miltonic ironies, I shall study the Woman of Timna, whose career must be understood as the repetition on a finer tone of the restorative descent of Raphael. In the event, blessed angel and heathen woman will prove, just as we saw Eve do in Chapter Two, that "the ways of [Milton's] God are just and merciful," while "the ways of the poet are particularly merciful . . . his greatest pity [being] reserved for the discovery that chastened remorse may be among the purest and least ambivalent responses to life of which the individual is capable."[24]

I

The circumstances of Raphael's descent from Heaven are these: Satan has tempted Eve in a dream that has distressed her, but from the painful effects of which Adam has been able quickly to restore her. After lengthy morning orisons, our father and mother have hastened to their garden work and, so occupied, have become the focus of divine attention: "Them thus imploy'd beheld / With pity Heav'n's high King, and to him call'd / *Raphael,* the sociable Spirit" (*PL* 5.219–21). Out of celestial condescension God sends the archangel on a mission whose protocols repay the closest scrutiny:

> *Raphael,* said hee, thou hear'st what stir on Earth
> *Satan* from Hell scap't through the darksome Gulf
> Hath rais'd in Paradise, and how disturb'd
> This night the human pair, how he designs
> In them at once to ruin all mankind.
> Go therefore, half this day as friend with friend

24. Radzinowicz, *Toward "Samson Agonistes,"* 187.

> Converse with *Adam*, in what Bow'r or shade
> Thou find'st him from the heat of Noon retir'd,
> To respite his day-labor with repast,
> Or with repose.[25]
>
> (224–33)

In language reminiscent of the conciliar prediction by which he has already announced the fall of man to the assembled angels (3.86–128), God enjoins Raphael to

> advise [Adam] of his happy state,
> Happiness in his power left free to will,
> Left to his own free Will, his Will though free,
> Yet mutable; whence warn him to beware
> He swerve not too secure: tell him withal
> His danger, and from whom, what enemy
> Late fall'n himself from Heaven, is plotting now
> The fall of others from like state of bliss.
>
> (234–41)

Faithful angel that he is, Raphael will execute these orders to the last jot and tittle. His motive is obedience: "nor delay'd the winged Saint / After his charge receiv'd" (247–48).[26] God's motive is *"to render Man inexcusable"* (Book 5, Argument) for a crime he has as yet scarcely thought of perpetrating: "this let him know, / Lest wilfully transgressing he pretend / Surprisal, unadmonisht, unforewarn'd" (243–45). The proximate consequence of the mission (and hence its apparent rationale) will be to clear God's *"own Justice and Wisdom from all imputation,"* he *"having created Man free and able enough to have withstood his Tempter"* (Book 3, Argument): "So spake th' Eternal Father," Milton concludes, "and fulfill'd / All Justice" (5.246–47).

Now, as I see it, and as the literature on the subject amply attests, at least the following objections can be raised to Raphael's journey: (1) it seems redundant, Adam having already been warned by God himself to "swerve not too secure"; it is a mission either (2) impossible or (3) beside the point, God's unerring prescience of Adam's fall having assured that Raphael's admonitions, however vehemently reiterated, will be ignored; and (4) it is allegedly conceived in "pity" but in reality executed in "Justice," a "Justice" moreover so odious that Thomas

---

25. Recent studies of the mission (that is, of *Paradise Lost* 5.219–450) have emphasized its biblical analogues, especially vis-à-vis the meal Adam and Eve serve Raphael. The work of her predecessors is conveniently summarized by Beverley Sherry, "Not by Bread Alone: The Communication of Adam and Raphael." The fullest treatment I know of the protocols of the visit is by Thomas Greene, whose work I cite in my next note.

26. Echoing, among others, *Iliad* 2.166–67 and *Aeneid* 4.238–39. Many classical analogues to the descent of Raphael have been studied by Thomas Greene, *The Descent from Heaven: A Study in Epic Continuity*.

Greene has concluded, in a searching criticism of the role of Raphael in *Paradise Lost*, that "when it is scrutinized, God's generosity in dispatching [the angel] turns out to be not at all a true magnanimity but a petty legalistic self-righteousness."[27]

The first two of these objections are easily disposed of. As to the first, even if Adam has already been told by God that he will die if he eats the forbidden fruit (4.419–32), and even if he knows already of his free estate (5.548–49), this knowledge is, in Adam's innocence, of purely "academic" interest, so to speak: witness his naive reference to the "easy charge" (4.421) and his incredulous question "can we want obedience then / To [God], or possibly his love desert[?]" (5.514–15). Raphael's mission is designed in part to persuade Adam of the real and present danger of disobedience—and of Satan: the angel is to "*admonish him . . . of his enemy near at hand; who he is, and why his enemy*" (Book 5, Argument). So his descent is not redundant. As to the second difficulty, although there may be certain missions impossible in *Paradise Lost*, Raphael's is not one of them;[28] as commissioned, he communicates, in language accommodated to Adam's human understanding, matters of fact, principles of philosophy, and specific warnings, all of which our father readily comprehends.

As to Raphael's "Venial discourse" (9.5) being beside the point, God having long since "*fore*[*told*] *the success of Satan in perverting mankind*" (Book 3, Argument), this is a more weighty objection. For although God enjoins Adam at his creation not to eat the fruit of the Tree of Knowledge, and though Raphael cautions Adam to beware by the example of Satan, a warning he twice reiterates, and though Satan cannot "deceive" the archangel Uriel "once warn'd" (4.124–25), nevertheless, Adam will certainly repudiate Raphael's advice and "easily transgress the sole Command" (3.94). Given these foreknown facts, the angel's mission would appear to be an exercise in futility.

That it is futile seems even more evident when one considers the descent of Raphael in the context of its classical prototypes. The mission corresponds to a part of the epic repertoire studied by Thomas Greene and (more recently) by Francis C. Blessington.[29] Among relevant analogues, Greene cites the descent of Hermes in the 5th *Odyssey*, the suasive purpose of which is to convince Calypso to facilitate the captive Odysseus's return to Ithaca, and the appearance of Mercury to

27. *Descent from Heaven*, 409.

28. Many allegedly impossible missions in the epic have been studied by Boyd M. Berry, who comments, in *Process of Speech: Puritan Religious Writings and "Paradise Lost,"* 179, "Milton's God repeatedly sends his creatures on missions which are strategically impossible and eventuate in no conclusion." He mentions Raphael's trip to Hell (8.229–46) as "one such impossible mission."

29. Blessington, *"Paradise Lost" and the Classical Epic*, 25–34, 47–48.

Aeneas in the 4th *Aeneid*, wherein he twice enjoins Aeneas to free himself from uxorious bondage to Queen Dido. Greene finds the Virgilian exemplar a particularly apt Miltonic source because of the ethical urgency with which it is suffused: Mercury's descent, like Raphael's, takes the form of a categorical imperative, the god demanding "that the self be made an *imperium*."[30] Common to both Homeric and Virgilian usage, however, is the foreknown fact that the divine admonitions will speedily be heeded, whereas in *Paradise Lost* the reverse is true. Sensing perhaps the latent absurdity of Raphael issuing warnings that both he and God foreknow will be ignored, Greene is persuaded finally to deny the legislative motive of his mission: the angel "is dispatched neither to prod nor to encourage nor to punish," he writes, "but to explain, almost indeed to lecture."[31] Greene's denial of the mission's admonitory rationale is ultimately unconvincing, but is not our only alternative to dismiss Raphael's injunctions as patently futile?

So at any rate they have seemed to a number of Milton scholars. The vague sense of dissatisfaction with Raphael that Arthur E. Barker expressed when he wrote that the angel "learns much in his effort to respond adequately to his call"[32] becomes a firm if temperate judgment of failure in a later essay: the angel's "somewhat Platonized and uncertain account of past history should prepare Adam (and Eve) for the trial to come," Barker writes, "but somehow fails of doing so adequately."[33] And Thomas Greene's attempt to rationalize by denial has been seconded recently by Robert Crosman: "the pretext of Raphael's visit to warn Adam is *perceived* by us as a pretext," he claims, because "Adam can't be helped to resist the Fall but only to repair its effects afterwards."[34] In the final analysis these criticisms may reflect their authors' grasp of the properly legislative role generally assigned to prophetic utterances in the later Renaissance: "after Tasso," Joseph Wittreich writes, "legislative responsibility becomes increasingly more of an obsession to the poet, especially after epic joins with prophecy. . . . Like the epic poet the prophet may recount history; but his purpose is less to record it than to bring it to an apotheosis."[35] In the matter of Raphael's prophetic utterances, however, both he and the reader foreknow that their presumed world-transforming functions will be vitiated, Adamic apotheosis being contingent upon an obedience (5.493–505) that will be honored only in the breach. Ought not

30. *Descent from Heaven*, 57–58, 99.
31. Ibid., 405.
32. "Structural and Doctrinal Pattern in Milton's Later Poems," 187.
33. "Calm Regained through Passion Spent," 12–13.
34. *Reading "Paradise Lost,"* 137.
35. *Visionary Poetics*, 34.

therefore Raphael (and Milton) to have preferred a blameless silence before the futile office of hopeless admonition?

Yes, assuredly—*if* one endorses the parsimonious assumption that the reiterated warnings of *Paradise Lost* ought to have been motivated by the hope (if not the certainty) that they would be heeded. Although a moment's reflection will suffice to lay bare the illogic of this misconception, the fallacy that to be adequately forewarned is ipso facto to be insuperably forearmed merits further discussion, for it is attractive enough to have insinuated itself into the impassioned plea for help that, in distant anticipation of Raphael's descent, escapes from the lips of *Paradise Lost's* narrator at the intrusion of Satan into the sacred precincts of Eden:

> O for that warning voice, which he who saw
> Th' *Apocalypse,* heard cry in Heav'n aloud,
> Then when the Dragon, put to second rout,
> Came furious down to be reveng'd on men,
> *Woe to the inhabitants on Earth*! that now,
> While time was, our first Parents had been warn'd
> The coming of thir secret foe, and scap'd
> Haply so scap'd his mortal snare.
>
> (4.1–8)

One cannot but be struck by the audacity of this prayer. If, on the one hand, in a rare suspension of narrative omniscience, Milton does not foreknow that Raphael's mission is in the offing, his supplication hovers on the edge of blasphemy, for its contrary-to-fact modality implies that God neglected "innocent frail man" (11) in the aboriginal human crisis. If, on the other hand, Milton is deliberately anticipating the descent of the archangel, his prayer seems at best disingenuous (since it implies that Raphael never came to warn Adam), and at worst a proleptic disqualification of the angel's stewardship (since Milton desiderates the voice of Revelation 12:10–13, not Raphael's). Overwhelmed with the sense of Heaven's desertion, the poet appears to conceive of adequate forewarning and the supposed infallibility of "our first Parents" as being anon twin halves of one august but tragically unrealized event, for "had" Adam and Eve "been warn'd / The coming of thir secret foe," they would have "scap'd / . . . *so*" (i.e., thereby, by means of the warning)—as if, in a complete reversal of Raphael's priorities, Milton would substitute external admonition for internal self-sufficiency as the sine qua non of human perseverance.

But, on the other hand, Milton—the prophetic Milton who, in the hallowed tradition of Isaiah and Jeremiah, published on the eve of the Restoration *The Ready and Easy Way to Establish a Free Commonwealth,* a tract whose impassioned admonitions he knew to a moral certainty would fall on deaf ears—assuredly he knew that timely warnings are often ignored. That is why he carefully wrote not "scap'd / . . . *so* scap'd" but "scap'd / *Haply* [i.e., perhaps, by chance] so scap'd": the doublet "Haply so" oxymoronically signals the absence of any relevant connection between Raphael's (or God's) admonitions and Adam's standing (or his sufficiency to have stood). Is the relationship between warning and standing casual (*Haply*) or causal (*so*)? But the question is absurd! The two events are not at all related, though they have appeared to be united. Aware of this, Raphael would not expect God's charge to him to follow the illogical pattern "Go therefore, converse with Adam, tell him of Satan, *lest he transgress*"—for the italicized words constitute a non sequitur that would indeed make the angel's mission an impossible exercise in futility. Milton takes certain risks in *Paradise Lost* 4.1–8 in order to admonish not Adam but the reader, whom he cautions not to be shocked upon learning that Raphael is sent to warn Adam not lest he willfully transgress, but "Lest willfully transgressing he pretend / Surprisal." Far from requiring, as the condition of sufficiency, the insights about Satan he acquires from Raphael, Adam need not even know of the Devil's existence.

This brings me to the final difficulty with the role of Raphael in *Paradise Lost*—that it seems motivated by a legalism less indicative of divine magnanimity than of pharisaic self-righteousness: "*God to render Man inexcusable sends* Raphael *to admonish him*" (Book 5, Argument). Given the apparently defensive rigor of the deity, Thomas Greene seems entitled to complain that "the majesty of Raphael's descent can only be appreciated if the awkwardness of its motive remains half-forgotten."[36]

Greene and others like him might nevertheless have judged Milton's God less harshly had they considered the two most relevant classical parallels to Raphael's mission. The first occurs in Hesiod's *Works and Days* when Zeus sends Hermes to punish Epimetheus's reception of the gift of fire from Prometheus: the blacksmith god Hephaistos having created Pandora, and Hermes having "into her heart . . . put lies, and wheedling words of falsehood, and a treacherous nature," Zeus sends Maia's son to present the first woman to mankind: "the Father sent the gods' fleet messenger, Hermes, to Epimetheus, bringing her, a gift, nor did Epimetheus remember to think how Prometheus had told him never to accept a gift from Olympian Zeus, but always to send it back, for fear it might prove to be an evil for mankind. He took the evil, and only perceived it when he possessed

---

36. *Descent from Heaven*, 409.

her."[37] This account bears intimately upon Milton's practice in *Paradise Lost* insofar as it is a paradigm instance in classical literature of a timely warning being issued notwithstanding the certainty that it will be ignored: just as Adam forgets to remember the high injunction (endlessly reiterated by Raphael) not to taste the forbidden fruit, so Epimetheus foolishly, absent-mindedly, and in blatant disregard of the warnings of Prometheus neglects to repudiate Pandora. But in Hesiod, Zeus *intends* that the admonitions of his enemy the fire-bringer be ignored: Pandora is a "sheer, impossible deception" (83), and the messenger god is an accessory to his father before and during the tragic fact: "to Hermes . . . [Zeus] gave instructions to put in Pandora the mind of a hussy, and a treacherous nature" (68–69). The celestial descent in the *Works and Days* is designed to ruin mankind, whose fall from grace proceeds (if I may be permitted a theological anachronism) in the harshest supralapsarian tradition of Calvinist predestination. The bottom line on the mission of Hermes is indeed that "there is no way to avoid what Zeus has intended" (105).[38]

For these reasons Milton is at great pains in *Paradise Lost* to dissociate himself from Hesiod's so-called "theodicy"—precisely to discredit the intimate Wittgensteinian family resemblance between pagan myth and Christian mystery. As Adam and his wife enter their "blissful Bower" (4.690), Milton articulates a simile that carefully distinguishes Hesiod's narrative from his own:

> Here in close recess
> With Flowers, Garlands, and sweet-smelling Herbs
> Espoused *Eve* deckt first her Nuptial Bed,
> And heav'nly Choirs the Hymenæan sung,
> What day the genial Angel to our Sire
> Brought her in naked beauty more adorn'd,
> More lovely than *Pandora*, whom the Gods
> Endow'd with all thir gifts, and O too like
> In sad event, when to the unwiser Son
> Of *Japhet* brought by *Hermes*, she ensnar'd
> Mankind with her fair looks, to be aveng'd
> On him who had stole *Jove's* authentic fire.
> (708–19)

37. *Works and Days*, 83–89, in *Hesiod*, trans. Richmond Lattimore. All citations of Hesiod will be to this edition.

38. The same paraenetic purposes are operative in Hesiod's *Theogony*, 508–616, which recounts a slightly different version of the Promethean myth. Emphasizing the punishment of the fire-stealer, Hesiod concludes: "So it is not possible to hide from the mind of Zeus, nor escape it; for not even the son of Iapetos, the gentle Prometheus, was able to elude that heavy anger, but, for all his numerous shifts, force and the mighty chain confine him" (613–16).

In this simile *"Eve," "the genial Angel,"* Adam ("our Sire"), and God are comparable to *"Pandora," "Hermes,"* Epimetheus ("the unwiser Son / Of *Japhet"*), and *"Jove"*; moreover, in both Hesiod and Milton, woman is given to man "to be aveng'd / On him [Prometheus/Satan] who had stole Jove's [Jehovah's] authentic fire."[39] But the perfection of naked Eve, who is "Virtue-proof" (5.384), far excels Pandora's in all real dignity, and Milton's God, unlike Hesiod's Zeus, intends Eve to rectify man's "single imperfection," not to destroy him (8.423–51). Milton, pace Hesiod, laments that Eve and Pandora are "O too like / In sad event"—in outcome, that is, when Adam's wife, "for thee ordain'd / A help, *became* thy snare" (11.164–65; emphasis mine) through acquired (not innate) perversity. Eve thus becomes (in a true Aristotelian peripeteia) what Pandora always is, and Adam, who, although "not deceiv'd," nevertheless permits himself to be "fondly overcome with Female charm" (9.998–99), thus becomes our true Epimetheus.[40] Milton's simile is a precise exercise in close discrimination that by implication condemns the descent of Hermes in the *Works and Days* as blasphemously prejudicial to both the goodness and greatness of God: however awkward the mission of Raphael may appear to his modern detractors, it becomes a work of genuine magnanimity when compared to the pusillanimous machinations of Hesiod's Zeus and Hermes.[41]

The mission's equanimity is likewise evinced when it is compared to a second celestial descent ignored by Greene and others—that alluded to by Zeus in the opening lines of the *Odyssey*. Odysseus is trapped on the island of Calypso, victim at once of the goddess's lust and of the implacable hatred of Poseidon, whose son Polyphemos had been blinded by Odysseus years before in self-defense. At the insistence of his benefactress Athena, who pleads Odysseus's case by appealing to fair play, Zeus promises to dispatch Hermes to secure the hero's release. First, however, the god recalls (by way of anticipatory

39. The identification of Pandora with Eve was a Renaissance commonplace. For example, see Henry Reynolds, *Mythomystes* (1632?), rpt. in Edward Tayler, *Literary Criticism of Seventeenth-Century England*, 256. That Milton censured Prometheus as a parody of Satan is implicit in his youthful poem *"In Inventorum Bombardae,"* in Prolusion 2, "On the Harmony of the Spheres," in his *Defense of the English People* (*YP* 4:1, 424–25), and in innumerable passages from *Paradise Lost*.

40. So Milton calls Adam in *The Doctrine and Discipline of Divorce* (*YP* 2:294).

41. I hasten to add that *Hesiod* does not view Zeus and Hermes in the pejorative light in which I have cast them; in the ancient world it took Aeschylus to do so—in *Prometheus Bound*. Hesiod everywhere reveres Zeus, which confirms the view of Hugh Lloyd-Jones that the primordial "Greek notion of the divine . . . differed utterly from the Jewish or Christian notion" and that only *"from a modern point of view"* the "gods are monstrously unjust. But for Homer, and for later poets also, they are perfectly within their rights" (*The Justice of Zeus*, 3–4; emphasis mine).

contrast and in order to clear his own justice) the legal circumstances surrounding the retributive murder of Aigisthos:

> The father of men and gods began to speak among them.
> In his heart he was remembering excellent Aigisthos
> Whom Agamemnon's son, far-famed Orestes, had slain.
> Thinking of that man, he made his speech to the immortals:
> "Well now, how indeed mortal men do blame the gods!
> They say it is from us evils come, yet they themselves
> By their recklessness have pains beyond their lot.
> So this Aigisthos married beyond his lot the lawful
> Wife of the son of Atreus, and killed him on his return;
> Knowing he would be destroyed, since we told him beforehand:
> We had sent sharp-eyed Hermes, the slayer of Argos,
> To tell him not to kill the man and not to woo his wife,
> Or payment would come through Orestes, descendant of Atreus,
> As soon as he came of age and longed for his own land.
> So Hermes told him, but though of good mind himself, he
>   did not
> Change Aigisthos' mind. And now he has paid for it all."[42]

If the *Odyssey* was composed after the *Works and Days*[43] its author— whoever he was—may have invented the above passage with Hesiod in mind. It certainly represents a dramatic jurisprudential advance over the crude casuistry of the Boeotian shepherd. It is also a corrective codicil to the *Iliad:* the "speech of Zeus implies a belief radically differ- ent from that found in the *Iliad*," writes Hugh Lloyd-Jones. "There the god puts evil ideas, no less than good ideas, into men's minds; that is how men's *moira*, the portion assigned them by the gods, comes to be fulfilled. When the god wishes to destroy a man, he sends Ate to take away his wits. But now Zeus denies that the gods put evil ideas into the minds of men, and even claims that they warn men against evil ideas they themselves have thought of."[44]

For these reasons, it is certain that Milton vastly preferred the *Odyssey's* theodicy to those in the *Works and Days* and the *Iliad:* he concludes his analysis "Of Predestination" in the *Christian Doctrine* by twice citing "even a heathen like Homer" to the effect that man's own free will self-corrupted is the adequate and sufficient cause of his disobedience.[45] Milton's proof-texts are, first, the observation that Odysseus's companions "lost their own lives because of their reck-

42. *Odyssey,* trans. Albert Cook, 1.28–43.
43. On which see the learned commentary of M. L. West, ed., *Hesiod: "Theogony,"* 40–48.
44. *Justice of Zeus,* 28.
45. YP 6:202.

lessness" (*Odyssey* 1.6–9) in ignoring Teiresias's and Circe's abjurations not to eat the cattle of Hyperion (*Odyssey* 11.84–117, 12.127–41), and second, Zeus's disclaimer that the gods are responsible for the destruction of Aigisthos—or indeed of any man. Milton evidently regarded the descent of Hermes in *Odyssey* 1.28–43 as a rare pagan instance of perfectly realized distributive poetic justice. As Maia's son to Aigisthos, so Raphael to Adam: Zeus/God to render Aigisthos/Adam inexcusable sends Hermes/Raphael to admonish man of his obedience. Their cautionary warnings fall on deaf ears but serve the noble purpose of "fulfill[ing] / All [distributive] Justice" (*PL* 5.246–47). Given the evident isomorphism of the two episodes, it is patently unfair to accuse Milton of awkwardly motivating the mission of Raphael: by using it to clear God's "*own Justice*" (Book 3, Argument) he is merely emulating the *Odyssey*'s justification of the ways of Zeus to Aigisthos, and no one (to my knowledge) has taken exception to the Greek narrative as an unsatisfactory theodicy characterized less by divine justice than by self-justifying paranoia and pharisaism.

In the *Odyssey*, nevertheless, the justice we encounter is rather more often retributive than distributive: Hermes "did not / Change Aigisthos' mind. *And now he has paid for it all*" (1.42–43; emphasis mine)—and witness also the gruesome vengeance exacted of the suitors of Penelope at *Odyssey* 22 and 24. Were *Paradise Lost* to recapitulate exactly the Greek archetype, the descent of Raphael would eventuate in retribution for Adam's and Eve's transgression that would make the fate of Aigisthos seem paradisiacal by comparison; for in addition to adultery and murder, our grandparents commit a plethora of offenses, including blasphemy and genocide.[46] Milton, however, never merely recapitulates his Hellenic and Roman forebears:[47] unlike Zeus vis-à-vis Aigisthos, Milton's God beholds unfallen Adam and Eve "with pity" (5.220) *and therefore* sends Raphael paradoxically to satisfy "All Justice" (247). Since Messiah has already "offer'd himself to die" in vicarious atonement of "man's offense" (3.409–10), precisely "to appease [God's] wrath, and end the strife / Of Mercy and Justice in [his] face discern'd" (406–7), and since the Father has already accepted the offer, "as is most just" (294), it is possible in *Paradise Lost* to distinguish most of God's judgments as mercies. Although divine retribution of the sort meted out to the fallen angels (5.600–15) and to incorrigibly hard-hearted men (3.198–202) is purely punitive, it is also atypical: even immediately after Adam's and Eve's fall, when Milton

46. In the *Christian Doctrine* 1.11, Milton catalogs the hideous litany of offenses included under the rubric of Original Sin (*YP* 6:383–84).

47. For recent studies of this thesis, see my " 'Real or Allegoric': The Ontology of Sin and Death in *Paradise Lost*" and "*Paradise Lost* and the Greek *Theogony*."

has led us to expect not pity but "distance and distaste, / Anger and just rebuke, and judgment giv'n" (9.9–10), we encounter instead a "gracious Judge" (10.118) who dispenses "Mercy colleague with Justice" (59) in ample fulfillment of God's earlier assurance that "Mercy first and last shall brightest shine" (3.134). The foreknown death of Messiah having repaid man's debt of retribution measure for measure (214–15), the dispensation of justice to Adam can be exclusively restorative;[48] it is therefore less justice than—as we have seen in Chapter Two—the sharp right profile of mercy.

This is nowhere more true than with respect to the role of Raphael. His mission is a work of special providence consequent to God's eternal prescience of Adam's fall and dependent upon the decision of "his Heart [not *mind*] / Omniscient" (10.6–7), through infinite pity, to ameliorate that catastrophe before it happens by predestinating Adam to salvation according to rubrics spelled out in *Christian Doctrine* 1.4:

> The principal SPECIAL DECREE of God which concerns men is called PREDESTINATION: by which GOD, BEFORE THE FOUNDATIONS OF THE WORLD WERE LAID, HAD MERCY ON THE HUMAN RACE, ALTHOUGH IT WAS GOING TO FALL OF ITS OWN ACCORD, AND, TO SHOW THE GLORY OF HIS MERCY, GRACE, AND WISDOM, PREDESTINED TO ETERNAL SALVATION, ACCORDING TO HIS PURPOSE or plan IN CHRIST, THOSE WHO WOULD IN THE FUTURE BELIEVE AND CONTINUE IN THE FAITH.[49]

Thus in *Paradise Lost* God, foreseeing that man will fall (3.92–99), "*declares his purpose of grace towards him*" (Book 3, Argument) by publishing the decree of predestination: "Man therefore shall find grace" (131). The decree entails the foreknown death of Messiah, whose willing expiation of Adam's crime (211–12) enables God's predestinating words to become flesh, so to speak: "man shall find grace," Messiah cries, "And shall grace not find means[?]" (227–28). The "means" are, first, Christ's redemptive death, but also, and most importantly in the context of the descent of Raphael, the renovation of Adam's and Eve's "lapsed powers" (176) through quite ordinary psychological processes that, in *Christian Doctrine* 1.19, Milton calls "recognition of sin, contrition, confession, abandonment of evil and conversion to good."[50] Precisely these stages occur in Book 10 of *Paradise Lost* when, in what seems a wholly natural sequence of events, Adam and Eve eventually acknowledge their mutual sinfulness, confess their mutual guilt to God, and beg his "pardon" "with tears" and "sighs" "sent from hearts contrite" (10.1101–3). We then learn (as we ought to have expected

48. I borrow the term from Desmond Hamlet, *One Greater Man: Justice and Damnation in Paradise Lost*.
49. *YP* 6:168.
50. *YP* 6:468.

after reading 3.185–90) that their rehabilitation has been mediated by "Prevenient Grace descending" that "remov'd / The stony from thir hearts" (11.3–4).[51]

The ways of regeneration in *Paradise Lost* are the key to the role of Raphael. In the matter of Adam's rehabilitation, he is the *angelus ex machina* in a renovative plot requiring three instances of visible divine intervention (the other two being by Messiah [10.47–102] and Michael [11.99–225]). Visiting unfallen Adam, Raphael *is* "Prevenient Grace descending"—"descending from the Thrones above" (5.363)—in anticipation not only of man's repentance (the ostensible function of prevenient grace) *but of his fall as well.* Shall not predestinated man find grace? And shall not grace find means? Enter Raphael. Through him Adam will "oft be warn'd / [His] sinful state" (3.185–86) before he has sinned! Or more precisely, he will be admonished of Satan's imminent intentions, so that once fallen he will be forced, so to speak, by ineluctable evidence to convict himself of grievous sin. Raphael descends, in short, to soften Adam's stony heart before it has hardened, to initiate his postlapsarian regeneration before he lapses.[52] Insofar as he is sent to render man inexcusable, his mission may appear petty, legalistic, and self-righteous; his function nevertheless is not so much to clear God's justice as to hasten Adam's repentance by telling him unequivocally that God "made him just and right, / Sufficient to have stood" (3.98–99). The "Justice" that God "fulfill'd" in dispatching Raphael is thus less fair play than a merciful work of supererogation, assuring Adam of the Original Justice of his creation and fulfilling "*All* Justice"—even that which a fallen, sinful, and self-extenuating creature might unreasonably expect—by warning him above and beyond the demands of distributive jurisprudence.[53]

Do Adam and Eve need Raphael? As our father is about to fall he is said to "*extenuat[e] the trespass*" (Book 9, Argument), and later both he and Eve engage in "mutual accusation," "neither self-condemning" (9.1187–88). Adam subsequently extenuates in the very presence of God, attributing his fall to Eve (10.125–43)—a specious allegation he

51. For contrary readings, namely, that the regenerative processes of *Paradise Lost* proceed by quantum leaps and radical equivocations that are ultimately inexplicable in human terms, see Georgia Christopher, "The Verbal Gate to Paradise: Adam's 'Literary Experience' in Book X of *Paradise Lost*," and Boyd M. Berry, *Process of Speech*, 254–67.

52. Because the announcement that prevenient grace has done its work is made ex post facto in Book 11, commentators have wrongly assumed the prevenient motions themselves to have begun only in Book 10. Arthur Barker expresses this commonplace in his essay "*Paradise Lost*: The Relevance of Regeneration," 65–67.

53. Justice does not require the descent of Raphael, for even without it Adam and Eve ought to have remembered the high injunction not to eat the fruit; even without Raphael they were sufficiently forewarned. See 10.1–16, and my "'More Theirs by Being His': Teaching Milton to Undergraduates."

reiterates in a vicious barrage of misogyny directed both at her (10.867–908) and later about her (11.632–33). He also blames God for having made him (10.743–52), for having made Eve (888–95), for having commanded an impossible obedience (750–52), and for having punished all men for his offense (822–24). Given these epidemic extenuating propensities, Milton's remark about Adam's and Eve's falling to variance with one another seems entirely apposite: "of thir vain contest appear'd no end" (9.1189).

Do Adam and Eve need Raphael? Short of a more direct act of divine intervention in the form perhaps of some irresistible grace (like that which converts Saul at Acts 9), some such intermediary as Raphael seems requisite to put an end to the vicious cycle of self-extenuating summarized above—if, that is, Adam and Eve are to be redeemed. Fallen Eve blames her satanic seduction on Adam, who erred, she argues, in permitting her that fateful morning to garden solitarily—whence, she erroneously thinks, her fall (9.1155–61). Adam's rejoinder, however ill-motivated, shows, as I suggested in Chapter Two, that shortly before Eve's transgression he did for her exactly what Raphael had done for both of them:

> I warn'd thee, I admonish'd thee, foretold
> The danger, and the lurking Enemy
> That lay in wait; beyond this had been force,
> And force upon free Will hath here no place.
>
> (1171–74)

Had Raphael been permitted to converse with Adam after the fall, he might well have spoken the same words to him. Even without them, however, his mission eventually has precisely the desired effect: thanks to Raphael, dim beginnings of *metanoia* are scattered amidst Adam's fallen ravings: "I deserv'd it" (10.726), he says, "Be it so, for I submit, [God's] doom is fair" (769). The first substantive breakthrough toward full conviction of guilt occurs, however, after Adam acknowledges the justice of his Original Sin's hereditary penalties (821–28). The admission marks the terminus not, to be sure, of Adam's regeneration, but of the infinite pity that has sought so lovingly "*to render Man inexcusable*":

> [God] after all Disputes
> Forc't I absolve: all my evasions vain
> And reasonings, though through Mazes, lead me still
> But to my own conviction: first and last
> On mee, mee only, as the source and spring
> Of all corruption, all the blame lights due.
>
> (828–33)

Raphael has thus been privileged to play a pivotal role, as the harbinger of prevenient grace, in the redemption of Adam. No wonder Milton calls him "the sociable Spirit" (5.221), and no wonder the "affable Arch-angel" (7.41) so speedily and unreluctantly (5.247–48) executes his aery purposes: his motive has been a true *imitatio Christi:* "immortal love / To mortal men, above which only shone / Filial obedience" (3.267–69). The finest commentary on his descent from Heaven was composed preveniently by the sage and serious Edmund Spenser, with whose unwitting tribute to Raphael I hasten to conclude this section:

> And is there care in heauen? and is there loue
> In heauenly spirits to these creatures bace,
> That may compassion of their euils moue?
> There is: else much more wretched were the cace
> Of men, then beasts. But O th' exceeding grace
> Of highest God, that loues his creatures so,
> And all his workes with mercy doth embrace,
> That blessed Angels, he sends to and fro,
> To serue to wicked men, to serue his wicked foe.
> How oft do they, their siluer bowers leaue,
> To come to succour vs, that succour want?
> How oft do they with golden pineons, cleaue
> The flitting skyes, like flying Pursuiuant,
> Against foule feends to aide vs millitant?
> They for vs fight, they watch and dewly ward,
> And their bright Squadrons round about vs plant,
> And all for loue, and nothing for reward:
> O why should heauenly God to men haue such regard?[54]

To resolve the dilemma posed in Spenser's concluding alexandrine, and to show also how and how universally Milton's God has "such regard" to the "wicked" sons of Adam, I turn now to the exemplary case of Samson and the Woman of Timna in *Samson Agonistes*.

II

In a convincing clarification of Christ's strategic allusion to Deuteronomy 6:16 ("Tempt not the Lord thy God") in *Paradise Regained* 4.650–61, Irene Samuel asserts, as I suggested in my Introduction, that in matters of biblical exegesis "the direction of Milton's nonconformities was never toward greater mystery, greater miracle, but rather always toward greater rationality, greater availability as a guide in living."[55] Her point is as true of *Samson Agonistes* as it is of the brief epic

54. *The Faerie Queene*, 2.8.1–2, in *Spenser: Poetical Works*, ed. J. C. Smith and E. De Sélincourt.
55. "The Regaining of Paradise," 116.

(and, as I have argued, of *Paradise Lost*). F. Michael Krouse has hedgingly averred that "one can say that Milton's interpretation of the Samson story *is ostensibly* an example of rationalistic literalism,"[56] but I will argue the far stronger hypothesis that Milton's reconstruction of Judges 13–16 is designed part and parcel to rehabilitate a highly embarrassing biblical narrative. My primary proof-text will be the poet's recasting of Samson's relation to the Woman of Timna, whom in Judges he marries at the urging of "the LORD, that he sought an occasion against the Philistines: for at that time the Philistines had dominion over Israel" (14:4). Milton's God, I shall demonstrate, has additional, nonterritorial reasons for motivating the marriage: he does so first, to make sense of Samson's subsequent marriage to Dalila, and second (on the analogy with the descent of Raphael in *Paradise Lost*), to facilitate his regeneration before he falls. *Samson Agonistes* thereby transforms a signally awkward episode in the Judges saga into yet another instance of God's loving providence, and in the process completes the work of making the Bible safe for Milton's zealously rational theodicy.

Let us begin by briefly enumerating those features of the Old Testament folk hero that required Milton to accommodate the details of his life and death to a pious interpretation; for even if the poet saw in the biblical Samson a ready-made and divinely sanctioned alter ego through whom to sublimate his personal anxieties about having gone blind, he saw little else worth emulating or commemorating in the boorish, womanizing Danite of Holy Writ. J. Blenkinsopp has summarized part of the case against Samson in a brilliant study of the saga's structure: the Judges plot "revolves around an explicitly religious theme," he writes, "that of the broken vow. . . . Samson is a *nazir*. The regulations for the Nazirite [Numbers 6:1–21] specify that he must avoid contact with a dead body, must not drink wine or *sekar* and, most important, must not allow his hair to be cut for the whole period of the vow."[57] According to Blenkinsopp, Samson's marriage to the Timnite involves a threefold rejection of his vocation: (1) his taking a Philistine wife (14:1–3) "is an implicit repudiation of the vow in intent," marriage with a Canaanite being expressly forbidden by Deuteronomy 7:1–3; (2) his eating honey from the carcass of a lion he has killed (14:5–9) involves ritual defilement by forbidden contact with the dead; and (3) his "alliance with the alien woman leads inevitably to his taking part in a marriage feast at the heart of which is a 'drinking

56. *Milton's Samson and the Christian Tradition*, 89. Krouse waffles on the matter because he wants to see *Samson Agonistes* as an allegory and its hero as a type of Christ (119–33, especially 119–24).
57. "Structure and Style in Judges 13–16," 65.

bout.' "[58] These violations are compounded (4) when Samson destroys a contingent of Philistines with the jawbone of an ass (15:9–17); (5) when he traffics with a prostitute at Gaza (16:1–3); (6) when he lusts after Dalila (16:4); and (7)—most egregiously—when he reveals to her the secret of his strength, whereupon she divests him of both his power and his Naziriteship, her shearing of Samson's locks being the symbolic equivalent of terminating his affiliation with the select group of *nazirim*. To this litany of sins may be added at least the following corollary offenses: (8) Samson obeys—without demur—the Philistines' command to entertain them at the festival of Dagon (16:25), thereby violating the Mosaic prohibitions against idolatry (Exodus 22:5 and 23:24); (9) he commits suicide when he declares, just before destroying the pagan temple, "Let me die with the Philistines" (16:30); and (10), perhaps worst of all, he expresses not an iota of remorse for any of the nine offenses just cited.

Now in spite of the biblical Samson's dubious record, the author of the Epistle to the Hebrews found him worthy of mention (along with Abel, Abraham, Moses, and others) as an Old Testament hero of faith (Hebrews 11:1–32). Perhaps for this reason Saint Jerome's Vulgate expunges from the authoritative Masoretic text the hero's suicidal valediction; perhaps for this reason the marginal glosses of the Geneva Bible—as George W. Whiting and Jackie DiSalvo have shown—exculpate Samson of all sin save revelation of his strength's secret springs; perhaps for this reason—perhaps for others—Milton likewise adjusts the biblical text in *Samson Agonistes* to eliminate the ethical inconveniences of most of Samson's behavior.[59] Reserving offenses (1), (7), and (10) for later—and fuller—discussion, I offer the following examples to illustrate the poet's rehabilitative compositional strategy: (1) as to Samson's twice ritually defiling himself, Milton nowhere mentions the incident with the dead lion, and while both the Chorus and Samson allude briefly to the proverbial ass's jawbone, they do so only to evidence the Danite's strength and his probity in assaulting Philistines (142–45, 261–64); (2) as to his becoming intoxicated at his bachelor party—if in fact Milton was aware of it—again both Samson and the Chorus affirm his perpetual abstinence;[60] (3) in the matter of the harlot of Gaza, *Samson Agonistes* never refers to this lustful episode (though the poet willingly records its immediate consequence, the strong man's prodigiously carrying the doorposts of the Gaza city gates to the

58. Ibid., 66, citing Judges 14:10.
59. See Don Cameron Allen, "The Idea as Pattern: Despair and *Samson Agonistes,*" 83; Whiting, "*Samson Agonistes* and the Geneva Bible"; and DiSalvo, " 'The Lord's Battells': *Samson Agonistes* and the Puritan Revolution," 42, 48.
60. In 541–52, Milton may or may not have understood the word *misteh*. AV has "made there a feast" (14:10), usage echoed in *SA* 1193–94.

top of a steep hill (146–50); (4) as to Samson lusting after Dalila, Milton, as I indicated earlier, transforms his promiscuity into married love; (5) in the matter of attendance at the Dagonalia, Milton's Samson—unlike his biblical prototype—*thrice* refuses to accompany the Public Officer to the spectacle (1319–47), and when at last he capitulates, he justifies doing so on impeccable casuistical grounds;[61] and (6) the problem of Samson's suicide is likewise resolved casuistically, both in the Argument (wherein a Messenger "*relat[es] the Catastrophe, what* Samson *had done to the Philistins, and by accident to himself*") and twice in the text (1586–89, 1660–68). A skeptical reader might protest one or more of these face-saving modifications, but their cumulative weight suggests a deliberate and systematic rehabilitative effort. To clinch the point, I might mention a final relevant (but apparently quite minor) Miltonic variation on a biblical theme: in Judges 15:8, having smitten many Philistines in revenge for their murder of the Woman of Timna, Samson "went down and dwelt in the top of the rock Etam." The text does not say why—perhaps Samson is merely resting, perhaps he has withdrawn, Achilles-like, to sulk over the death of his Timnite bride—but in any event he is not about his heavenly Father's business, so to speak. In *Samson Agonistes* Milton adjusts the biblical account to eliminate the implicit charge of dereliction of duty: *his* Samson

> Safe to the rock of *Etham* was retir'd,
> *Not flying,* but forecasting in what place
> To set upon [the Philistines], what advantag'd best.
> (253–55; emphasis mine)

It is as if the hero has the text of Judges at hand and seeks to set the historical record straight by filling in the inspired (but elliptical) paratactic transitions of Judges with a pious hypotactic scholium; certainly Milton at least has this purpose in mind.

The same is true with respect to Samson's marriage to the Woman of Timna. Judges 14:4 claims—awkwardly, given the xenophobic tenacity with which Deuteronomy prohibits mixed marriages—that Yahweh has arranged the union to create a subterfuge for harrying Philistines. Providentially, the stratagem works: in devastating response to his bride's betrayal of him (14:15–18), Samson slays thirty Ashkelonites (14:19), destroys Philistine crops and vineyards (15:4–5), occasions the immolation of the Timnite and her father (15:6), indulges

61. Samson's decision to go with the Officer culminates a debate with the Chorus (1348–90) that anachronistically invokes distinctions found in Renaissance textbooks of moral theology. Camille Slights has studied the influence of these "cases of conscience" on Milton's play in "A Hero of Conscience: *Samson Agonistes* and Casuistry."

in a general rampage (15:8), and dispatches "a thousand men" with "the jawbone of an ass" (15:15–17). So important is his vendetta that it requires fully a fifth of the biblical narrative (twenty-one of ninety-six verses) to recount the bloodbath triggered by Samson's marriage.

Samson Agonistes acknowledges these violent consequences, but it radically deemphasizes them: less than 8 percent of the tragedy (129.5 of 1,758 lines) alludes to Samson's retaliation, most of the references are peremptory, and one incident—that involving the three hundred foxes (15:3–5)—is omitted entirely. On the other hand, whereas Judges motivates the marriage almost offhandedly, devoting only a single verse (14:4) to supernaturalizing what would otherwise appear to be a case of lust at first sight, Milton takes relatively greater pains (fifty-two lines) to scrutinize the union's origins: he is apparently less than edified with Samson the scourge of God and more than a little anxious to reconcile his hero's Timnite interlude with the matrimonial caveats of the Mosaic code. Thus, early in the play, in response to Choral doubts (215–18), Samson justifies his marriage (219–26) "on the basis of the casuistical concept of the significance of the intention, surrounding circumstances, and probable consequences of an action."[62] Although Manoa expresses lingering ambivalence as to whether his son was prompted by "Divine impulsion" (422) to marry a gentile, which he will neither confirm nor deny,[63] Samson's account satisfies the Chorus, which repeats the rationale of Judges 14:4 (315–21) and later justifies its endorsement of the marriage (239) by invoking the dispensational prerogatives of God:

> [He] made our Laws to bind us, not himself,
> And hath full right to exempt
> Whom so it pleases him by choice
> From National obstriction, without taint
> Of sin, or legal debt;
> For with his own Laws he can best dispense.[64]
> (309–14)

In sum, there is ample warrant in the play for accepting Samson's

---

62. Ibid., 398.

63. His ambivalence is perhaps the legacy of slavish adherence to the Mosaic law; on Milton's attitude to such adherence see Samuel S. Stollman, "Milton's Dichotomy of 'Judaism' and 'Hebraism.' " Alternatively, Manoa may be egotistically unable to approve Samson's "marriage choices," which *he* "approv'd . . . not" (420–24).

64. On the soundness of this Choral justification see Stollman, "Milton's Samson and the Jewish Tradition," and especially Joan S. Bennett, "Liberty Under the Law: The Chorus and the Meaning of *Samson Agonistes*," 150–53. (The Chorus is repeating distinctions articulated by Abdiel in *PL* 5.822–25; see also *SA* 322–24, which echo *PL* 5.826–31.)

analysis of his first marriage—and no reason to fault him for the union, as at least one critic has done.[65]

On the other hand, Milton's redaction differs importantly from the Bible's in at least this respect: whereas Judges never says that Samson knew God was urging him to marry the Woman of Timna—only that his parents did *not* know—the hero of *Samson Agonistes* married her in obedient response to an inner prompting that grew daily upon him:

> The first [woman] I saw at *Timna*, and she pleas'd
> Mee, not my Parents, that I sought to wed,
> The daughter of an Infidel: they knew not
> That what I motion'd was of God; I knew
> From intimate impulse, and therefore urg'd
> The Marriage on; that by occasion hence
> I might begin *Israel's* Deliverance,
> The work to which I was divinely call'd.
>
> (219–26)

This most striking departure from Holy Scripture is a modification consistent with Milton's intention throughout *Samson Agonistes* to associate the inward light of God's Spirit with reasoned deliberation and critical self-awareness. Moreover, Samson's intuition of the divine will enables the poet to utilize the Timnite marriage—with extraordinary dramatic economy—for purposes never dreamed of by the redactors of Judges. Proximately, it motivates Samson's marriage to Dalila: the Woman of Timna "proving false," Samson explains,

> the next I took to Wife
> (O that I never had! fond wish too late)
> Was in the Vale of *Sorec*, *Dalila*,
> That specious Monster, my accomplisht snare.
> I thought it lawful from my former act,
> And the same end; still watching to oppress
> *Israel's* oppressors.
>
> (227–33)

In Judges Samson's assignation with Dalila is a private and selfish affair, lust (or perhaps love) having led him to interrupt his vocation as Israel's judge to sport with yet another gentile in the shady vineyards of Sorec. By having *his* Samson *marry* Dalila for *public political* reasons, Milton neatly eliminates the implicit censoriousness of the scriptural version. *His* Samson "interpreted intuition by analogy,"[66] and so

65. Albert C. Labriola, "Divine Urgency as a Motive for Conduct in *Samson Agonistes*," 102–3.

66. Quoting the felicitous language of Stein, *Heroic Knowledge*, 146. Stein, how-

decided to marry a second Philistine woman, "still watching to oppress / *Israel's* oppressors." What a far cry from the backsliding *nazir* of the Old Testament.

Thus it is clear—given my hypothesis that *Samson Agonistes* is a rehabilitative reconstruction of Judges—that for Milton the Timnite marriage is explained as exculpating Samson from an array of embarrassing charges ranging from lust through ritual defilement and intoxication to military desertion. But the matter is not that simple, for Milton's decision to use the first marriage to motivate the second also entails an inconvenience quite absent from the Bible: it appears to make God's original "intimate impulse" (223) responsible for Samson's fall. God causes the Timnite wedding, which causes the marriage with Dalila, which causes the hero's blindness, humiliation, and despair— the state of affairs with which *Samson Agonistes* commences. Although this sort of thinking is easily refuted as an instance of the post hoc, ergo propter hoc fallacy, and although—in contravention of *Paradise Lost* 3.120–23—it would make God the author of sin, it is so attractive an error as to pervade Milton's play, especially discussion of Samson's second bride. Early on, Samson parenthetically laments that he married her (228), as if the fact of marriage were synonymous with his downfall; much later the Chorus similarly yokes the two events when, in a veiled allusion to Dalila, it speciously describes Samson's sin as the ineluctable consequence of his wedding a Philistine (1044–45). Manoa is more explicit, alleging in a final comment that his son was as good as blind the moment he married the Woman of Timna: "The Virgins," he concludes,

> also shall on feastful days
> Visit [Samson's] Tomb with flowers, only bewailing
> His lot unfortunate in nuptial choice,
> From whence captivity and loss of eyes.
>
> (1741–44)

No wonder Manoa has earlier declared, in a rare and uncharacteristically laconic litotes, that he "cannot praise thy marriage choices, Son" (420).

Nevertheless, Samson's father has got things all wrong: in point of

---

ever, concludes that Samson sins in marrying Dalila (145–46, 172). So do Low (*The Blaze of Noon*, 133) and (if somewhat equivocatingly) John S. Hill ("Vocation and Spiritual Renovation in *Samson Agonistes*," 155–56) and (emphatically) Joan Bennett ("Liberty Under the Law," 153). Nevertheless, I stand firmly with those critics who understand Samson's second marriage as sinless per se. See Krouse, *Milton's Samson and the Christian Tradition*, 96–97; John M. Steadman, "'Faithful Champion': The Theological Basis of Milton's Hero of Faith," 17; Stollman, "Milton's Samson and the Jewish Tradition," 189–92; and (most persuasively) Slights, "*Samson Agonistes* and Casuistry," 399.

fact Samson's marriages do not necessitate his blindness—even if they have appeared to be twin halves of one lamentable and tragically realized Aristotelian peripeteia. Just as, in *Paradise Lost* 4.1–8, Milton takes certain risks to exorcise the specious assumption that to be adequately forewarned is to be insuperably forearmed, in *Samson Agonistes* he ventilates the kindred misogynistic fallacy that to marry at all is at all events to miscarry. Loving father that Manoa is, he would extenuate Samson's trespass by assigning its etiology to a union arranged by God. Yet not God either: rather than attribute such a catastrophe to the inducing motions of a providential deity, Manoa finds a more convenient scapegoat in Samson's "lot" (= Greek *moira*) "unfortunate" (= Greek *tyche*), which he thus characterizes, oxymoronically, as the foreordained outcome of some chance destiny. But Manoa has got things all wrong.

When, however, he speaks of Samson's "lot unfortunate in nuptial *choice*," Manoa approximates a partial truth, for Samson was indeed free to hear and heed or to neglect and scorn God's call to marry the Woman of Timna: to Milton the divine motions are not at all irresistible impulses. Moreover, Manoa seems vaguely to comprehend a fuller truth, namely, that Samson's first and second marriages alike are related to his malfeasance only contiguously, as its necessary but not its sufficient conditions: thus his initial stumbling analysis of his son's espousals is punctuated by a more or less coherent effort to sort out the tangled web of responsibility for them:

> I cannot praise thy marriage choices, Son [wrongly implying
>   that they caused Samson's fall],
> Rather approv'd them not [implying pique that Manoa's advice
>   fell on deaf ears]; but thou didst plead
> Divine impulsion prompting how thou might'st
> *Find some occasion* to infest our Foes [confirming Judges
>   14:4].
> I state not that [implying doubt whether God would urge such
>   disasters upon Samson]; this I am sure; our Foes
> *Found some occasion* thereby to make thee
> Thir Captive, and thir triumph; thou the sooner
> Temptation found'st, or over potent charms [wrongly
>   implying that Samson could not resist Dalila's
>   blandishments]
> To violate the sacred trust of silence
> Deposited within thee [correctly identifying his son's
>   transgression]; which to have kept
> Tacit, was in thy power; true [reluctantly conceding that
>   Samson was sufficient to have stood, though free to fall].
>   (420–30; emphasis mine)

This most interesting oscillation between the obligation to censure his suffering son and the desire to extenuate his trespasses correctly names Samson's marriages as *the occasion* of his downfall—for they comprise the fact, event, or state of affairs that made it possible—without, however, necessitating it (a distinction Manoa repeats in lines 1714–16). The concept of occasional causality rescues God from complicity in Samson's sin (just as it enables us to distinguish temptation from transgression in *Paradise Lost*), which is why Milton arranges for Manoa to invoke it—even if the old man cannot apply it consistently to the case of conscience that continues to perplex him.

The reader of *Samson Agonistes,* however, forearmed with the prescience conferred upon him by the Book of Judges, and sensitized to the subtle intricacies of special providence as incarnated in the descent of Raphael in *Paradise Lost,* can apply the concept of occasional causality more rigorously than Manoa can to render a full account of the Woman of Timna motif in the play: for if she is the distant occasion of Samson's fall, she is also the near occasion of his regeneration (just as, *mutatis mutandis*, Raphael triggers from afar the revivification of Adam and Eve). Milton's God (no less than the Bible's) urges Samson to marry the Timnite as a pretext for harrying Philistines—foreknowing, however, that given the Danite's military zeal, he will interpret the marriage as precedent-setting and so marry Dalila. God also foreknows that given the bias of Samson's free inclinations he will, having wed a second time, sin mortally by "divulg[ing] the secret gift of God" (201) to his wife. Now God could have prevented the sin, removing its near occasion (Dalila) by removing its distant occasion (the Timnite), just as he could have prevented Adam's and Eve's transgressions by eliminating from *their* world certain "specious object[s] by [Satan] suborn'd" (*PL* 9.361)—namely, fallen Eve and "the spirited sly Snake" (613) respectively. But the gracefully prevenient motions of Milton's God never violate the free agency of his rational creatures (3.120–23), however catastrophic the foreseen contingent consequences of their choices may be. God therefore urges Samson to initiate a chain of events that involves, in a first marriage, innocent publication of one secret (Samson's), but in a second, wrongful publication of another (God's). Foreseeing these contingencies, God all the while utilizes them, through the mighty wings outspread of his predestinating Spirit, to effect his hero's salvation *if only he will repent.* Shall not predestinated Samson find grace? And shall not prevenient grace find means? Enter the Woman of Timna. God sends her first, I repeat, to seek occasion against the Philistines, but second, given his prescience of the marriage's medium-range implications, to render Samson inexcusable for "publish[ing]" "God's . . . holy secret" (496–99) to Dalila.

In thus preveniently reducing to absurdity the hypothetical claim of circumstantial extenuation as regards Samson's fall, God hastens his regeneration (as he does Adam's and Eve's) by educing from him the conviction of sin that is regeneration's critical first step.

Consequently, in startling and suggestive contrast to its biblical prototype, *Samson Agonistes* can, in nine well-defined stages, rehearse the psychology of guilt and sorrow even unto superfluity: nearly every utterance of Samson is steeled with the sense of ire merited and affliction self-wrought. His opening soliloquy contains a first admission that exonerates God and identifies with astonishing precision the nature of Samson's "own default" (45),

> Who this high gift of strength committed to me,
> In what part lodg'd, how easily bereft me,
> Under the Seal of silence could not keep,
> But weakly to a woman must reveal it,
> O'ercome with importunity and tears.
> O impotence of mind, in body strong!
>
> (47–52)

The seriousness of Samson's offense is implied in the diction with which he later describes it: he has violated the "hallow'd pledge / Of all my strength" (535–36), a crime he characterizes in language reminiscent of the fall of Adam. Indeed, Samson precisely recapitulates our grand father's Original Sin: just as Adam succumbs to "effeminate slackness" (*PL* 11.634) and profanes the interdicted tree, the "Sole pledge of his obedience" (3.95), so Samson has surrendered to "foul effeminacy" (*SA* 410) and "profan'd" his hair, "The Mystery of God giv'n me under pledge / Of vow" (377–79). Apart from the inheritability of Adam's transgression, his and Samson's sins are virtually identical.

The crucial difference is that whereas conviction of guilt is wrested as it were from Adam in a tortuous self-extenuating dialectic, Samson is first and last his own harshest critic. The mere presence of the Chorus elicits from him a second confession (195–202); when it offers misogynistically to extenuate his trespass by blaming Dalila (210–12), Samson guiltily insists that "She was not the prime cause, but I myself" (234); and when Manoa alleges that the punishment of blindness does not fit his son's crime, he having merely "through frailty err[ed]" (369), Samson doggedly dissents, discerning in the conviction of sin reasons to justify God's judgments from the insulsity of his father's mortal tongue:

> Appoint not heavenly disposition, Father,
> Nothing of all these evils hath befall'n me

> But justly; I myself have brought them on,
> Sole Author I, sole cause: if aught seem vile,
> As vile hath been my folly, who have profan'd
> The mystery of God giv'n me under pledge
> Of vow, and have betray'd it to a woman,
> A *Canaanite*, my faithless enemy.
>
> (373–80)

This is a remarkable third confession: though spoken by the guilty accused, it achieves the juridical objectivity of the detached judge—in fact of Milton himself, whose rigorous analysis of the falls of Adam and Eve in *Paradise Lost* 10.1–16 applies equally well to Samson's offense:

> Meanwhile the heinous and despiteful act
> Of *Satan* done in [Sorec's Vale], and how
> Hee [through gold] had perverted [Dalila],
> Her Husband shee, to [cut his fatal locks],
> Was known in Heav'n; for what can scape the Eye
> Of God All-seeing, or deceive his Heart
> Omniscient, who in all things wise and just,
> Hinder'd not [Dalila] to attempt the mind
> Of [Samson], with strength entire, and free will arm'd,
> Complete to have discover'd and repulst
> Whatever wiles of Foe [i.e., Satan] or seeming Friend
>   [i.e., Dalila].
> For still [he] knew, and ought to have still remember'd
> The high Injunction [God's secret ne'er to tell],
> Whoever tempted; which [he] not obeying,
> Incurr'd, what could [he] less, the penalty,
> And manifold in sin, deserv'd to fall.

That the Samson we encounter even thus early in Milton's tragedy would endorse these opinions chapter and verse is evident (1) from the vaguely incremental repetition whereby, echoing God's specification of angels and men as "Authors to themselves" (*PL* 3.122) of their own sins, the blind hero calls himself "Sole Author I, sole cause" of his misery; (2) from the hint of poetic justice expressed in his conditional chiasmus, "if aught seem vile, / As vile hath been my folly"—a hint Samson quickly elaborates when he castigates his "servile mind / Rewarded well with servile punishment" (412–13); and (3) from the pitilessness with which he thrice identifies his Philistine accomplice, not indeed to lessen his offense (408–9), but rather to weigh in justice's scales the gravity of his crime: Samson has capitulated to "a woman" (bad enough), to "A *Canaanite*" (worse still), and to "my faithless enemy" (worst of all). How unlike the Ciceronian entanglements of fallen Adam, who, in a parallel situation, *and in God's very presence*, makes straight seem intricate, to extenuation swift (*PL* 10.137–43). The full measure of Adam's retreat from conviction of sin may be taken by observing, as I suggested in Chapter Two, that only his last words ("Shee gave me of the Tree, and I did eat") are both relevant and true, and even they are contaminated with self-extenuation.

Samson, on the other hand, specifies his own guilt with uncanny accuracy; for whereas Adam has forgotten the antiextenuating descent of Raphael, *he* remembers the Woman of Timna:

> This well I knew, nor was at all surpris'd,
> But warn'd by oft experience: did not she
> Of *Timna* first betray me, and reveal
> The secret wrested from me in her height
> Of Nuptial Love profest, carrying it straight
> To them who had corrupted her, my Spies,
> And Rivals? In this other was there found
> More Faith? who also in her prime of love,
> Spousal embraces, vitiated with Gold,
> Though offer'd only, by the scent conceiv'd
> Her spurious first-born; Treason against me?
> (*SA* 381–91)

The key to this passage is its opening words, which recall the charge given to Raphael in *Paradise Lost*. Just as, to render Adam inexcusable, the angel is commissioned to "warn him to beware / He swerve not too secure" (5.237–38), "Lest wilfully transgressing, he pretend / Surprisal, unadmonisht, unforewarn'd" (244–45), so in *Samson Agonistes* the Woman of Timna is sent as the unwitting prevenient instrument of God's antiextenuating purposes. The memory of his sinless capitulation to the Timnite (he told her the solution to the secret riddle propounded in Judges 14:14) forces Samson to concede the absence of extenuating circumstances in his sinful capitulation to Dalila:[67] he "was [not] at all surpris'd" at his second wife's treachery; rather, in his first marriage, he had already been "warn'd by oft experience" not to trust Philistine women (Samson's *oft* is, incidentally, a telling hyperbole, conviction of sin leading him to exaggerate the Timnite's betrayal into a multitude of deception prototypes). More than adequately forewarned, Samson ought to have been more than cavalierly forearmed against Dalila's "impuden[t]" "importunity" and unsubtle "wiles" (397–402). He knew better; he should have been more wary. Admonished by the Timnite's treachery, he ought, like Adam, to have "known thyself aright" (*PL* 10.156). Undeceived no less than our grand father,

---

67. Since Samson invented the riddle about honey coming out of the lion's mouth (*SA* 1016–17, 1064), it was within his jurisdiction to reveal it to whomever he pleased. Hence, while he erred prudentially in telling it to the Timnite Woman, he did not sin thereby. The Nazirite secret was not his to tell, however; it was God's.

he was likewise "fondly overcome" (9.999) with "feminine assaults" (*SA* 403). Rendered thus inexcusable and thus overwhelmed with the profoundest conviction of guilt, Samson had no recourse except to say, "in sign / Of sorrow unfeign'd, and humiliation meek" (*PL* 10.1103-4), "Sorrie I am, my God, sorrie I am, / That my offences course it in a ring."[68] Thanks be to the Woman of Timna that he does. For like Raphael (and Eve) apropos of Adam, she is the preveniently arranged occasion of Samson's regeneration.

Has Samson benefited from the Timnite marriage? Assuredly, for how else are we to account for the virtual absence of extenuation in his unremitting examination of conscience? I can find only a single instance—and that a doubtful one—in which he retreats from full conviction (63–64); otherwise the hero manifests a proper guilt for heinous crimes inexcusably perpetrated.[69] His conviction of guilt, occasioned by the recollection of the Timnite's admonitory treachery, enables a contrite Samson to confess his crime, to expiate it, to depart from evil, and to convert to good—following the same regenerative path negotiated by Adam and Eve in *Paradise Lost*. After Manoa (420–47) quite brutally goads his son by animadverting upon the Philistine feast at which Dagon will be glorified and God blasphemed, Samson convicts himself of sin yet a fourth (pivotal) time, in what I take to be an incipient act of perfect contrition:

> Father [Manoa? God?], I do acknowledge and confess
> That I this honor, I this pomp have brought
> To *Dagon*, and advanc'd his praises high
> Among the Heathen round; to God have brought
> Dishonor, obloquy, and op't the mouths
> Of Idolists, and Atheists; have brought scandal
> To *Israel*, diffidence of God, and doubt
> In feeble hearts, propense enough before
> To waver, or fall off and join with Idols:
> Which is my chief affliction, shame and sorrow,
> The anguish of my Soul, that suffers not
> Mine eye to harbor sleep, or thoughts to rest.
>
> (448–59)

There are no more memorable or more hopeful words than these in *Samson Agonistes*. Prodded by his nightmarish, antiextenuating recollection of the Woman of Timna, and jogged by the harsh accusations of

68. George Herbert, "Sinnes round," in *The Works of George Herbert*, ed. F. E. Hutchinson.

69. Georgia B. Christopher, however, argues in "Homeopathic Physic and Natural Renovation in *Samson Agonistes*" that Samson continues to extenuate until the appearance of Dalila, who stimulates his sense of conviction homeopathically.

a father whose reputation he has besmirched, Samson has, to cite Arnold Stein, "moved to a full facing of his crime and its consequences, which exceed the personal and so, it may seem, the personal power to expiate by punishment, or to have any human relation to, except that of a despairing recognition. The high point of moral advance, then, is the low point of psychological retreat. . . . Here we have the place marked, the point where the two lines cross. What shall we call these lines, or is there a name?"[70]

There is indeed a name—or rather two names—for this crucial conjunction of ethical progress and affective regression: Aristotle's anagnoresis (recognition or discovery) and peripeteia (reversal). The plot of *Samson Agonistes* is, as Milton's prefatory epistle puts it (echoing *Poetics* 10), "intricate" rather than "explicit"; in such plots the catastrophe is accompanied by (and ideally is effected by) either recognition ("a change from ignorance to knowledge") or reversal of fortune ("a change from one state of affairs to its opposite") or—even better, as in Sophocles' *Oedipus Tyrannos*—both (*Poetics* 11). Milton's tragedy outdoes its Hellenic predecessors by arranging for its catastrophic denouement to be the consequence of two anagnoresis-peripeteia complexes. The first—thanks be to the Woman of Timna—occurs early in this tragedy of regeneration when, in the fourth stage of a regenerative sequence, Samson recognizes *and confesses* the full hideousness of his offenses, including their farthest-reaching sinful implications.[71] His discovery is coextensive with and causes an immediate reversal of fortune, for conviction enables Samson to move beyond a purely despairing confession (of the sort that exulcerates Satan's tormented conscience in *Paradise Lost* 4.13–113) to the faintly but genuinely felt hypothesis that he can sorrowfully atone for his transgressions.

Thus in a fifth admission of guilt (following hard upon its pivotal predecessor), Samson hopes (I use the term advisedly) to "pay on my punishment; / *And expiate, if possible, my crime*" (489–90; emphasis mine). This is admittedly only the subtlest, most tenuous hint of a brighter future—a secret joy, weakly clasped in the midmost heart of guilty grief—but it is decisive, and the advice Manoa now gives—"Be penitent and for thy fault contrite" (502)—has already been enacted:

70. *Heroic Knowledge*, 153.
71. The second occurs late in the play when, imitating *Oedipus*, Milton has a Public Officer summon Samson to the Dagonalia. "In *Oedipus* . . . the Messenger who came to cheer Oedipus and relieve him of his fear about his mother did the very opposite [peripeteia] by revealing to him who he was [anagnoresis]" (*Poetics* 11); in *Samson Agonistes* the Public Officer who comes to induce Samson to entertain the Philistines does the very opposite (occasions their destruction) by revealing to him what he can do (he can sinlessly disobey the second commandment).

thanks be to his Timnite bride, Samson's sixth confession (522–40) is preceded by the vital addition "[God's] pardon I implore" (521), a gesture that repeats fallen Adam's and Eve's restorative decision to "confess / Humbly our faults, and pardon beg, with tears" and "sighs" "sent from hearts contrite" (*PL* 10.1086–91). Although Samson's seventh (558–76) and eighth (999–1002) declarations of sin show signs of despair and disorientation, they are only minor reversals, the first brought on by the transient "sense of Heav'n's desertion" (632), the second a dramatic irony significant in the main for the matter-of-factness with which Samson can now allude succinctly to his offenses, contrite confession having largely neutralized conviction's "deadly stings" (623). Hence the ninth and last stage in the hero's exorcism of guilt and sorrow requires only the catalytic intervention of a male complement to the Woman of Timna. When Harapha of Gath taunts Samson (1156–67) by cruelly inventorying the punishments he has (unjustly) endured, Samson finds on the contrary that "these evils I deserve and more, / Acknowledge them from God inflicted on me / Justly" (1169–71). But this is an almost trivial or at any rate a peremptory confession: it is as if Samson, having spread guilt thin by fully eight times rehearsing his known offense and God's own retributive justice, becomes impatient at reiterating a conviction by now self-evident (to everyone but Harapha). Anyway, regenerate Samson has more important things on his mind than crime and punishment: "[I] despair not of [God's] final pardon / Whose ear is ever open; and his eye / Gracious to re-admit the suppliant" (1171–73). This hard-won insight, no labor of a Sabbath day, echoes and confirms regenerate Adam's conviction that "if we pray him, will [God's] ear / Be open, and his heart to pity incline" (*PL* 10.1060–61). Both Samson and he are voicing an optimism altogether warranted, for both are (unwittingly) echoing God's promise in *Paradise Lost* 3 that

> To Prayer, repentance, and obedience due,
> Though but endeavor'd with sincere intent,
> *Mine ear shall not be slow, mine eye.*
> (191–93; emphasis mine)

At this juncture a fully revivified Samson has been readmitted to Naziriteship, and *Samson Agonistes* can proceed now rather more quickly than before to its climactic catastrophe. When Samson later declines to commit idolatry, a sin "which in [God's] jealousy / Shall never, *unrepented*, find forgiveness" (1375–76; emphasis mine), he knows whereof he speaks, for he has experienced, fully and deeply, the opposite process whereby *any* sin, however grievous, may become as if it were not. For the gift of sorrow unfeigned and humiliation meek that punctuates all nine of repentant Samson's laments, he owes thanks first to a loving God, whose prevenient grace descending has softened his stony heart, and second to the Woman of Timna, whom a provident God has sent to render him inexcusable:

> This well I knew, nor was at all surpris'd,
> But warn'd by oft experience: did not she
> Of *Timna* first betray me, and reveal
> The secret wrested from me in her height
> Of Nuptial love profest, carrying it straight
> To them who had corrupted her, my Spies,
> And Rivals?
> (381–87)

She did indeed, and no man ever owed more to a treacherous spouse: for her contribution to his first (felix) culpa Samson must therefore sing, "Timnae gratias!"

III

I began this chapter by citing epigraphically the concluding lines of *A Mask,* and I would like to return now to that point of departure. The poem contains Milton's first attempt to utilize the epic motif of celestial descent in anything like sustained fashion. The attendant Spirit who oversees its action descends from "the starry threshold of *Jove's* Court" in order to protect the virtuous (lines 1, 12–15)—specifically a young Lady and her two Brothers—from the wicked enchantments of Comus. The descent is arranged and accomplished preveniently (78–82) in order to verify the heroine's conviction that

> the Súpreme good, t' whom all things ill
> Are but as slavish officers of vengeance,
> Would send a glist'ring Guardian, if need were,
> To keep my life and honor unassail'd.
> (217–20)

The Lady's point is later reiterated by her Elder Brother (453–63), who complacently assures himself that his lost sister's virgin innocence will conduct her safely through the wild wood into which she has wandered. The Brother imagines her safe conduct in terms of the motif of celestial descent:

> So dear to Heav'n is Saintly chastity,
> That when a soul is found sincerely so,
> A thousand liveried Angels lackey her,
> Driving far off each thing of sin and guilt.
> (453–56)

In any realistic reckoning these sentiments are pure hyperbole; and indeed by the time the Elder Brother, having learned that his sister is the captive of Comus, sets off on a search-and-rescue operation, reality's dark dream has shrunken his optimistic mathematics and transformed his facile confidence into the more modest entreaty "some good angel bear a shield before us" (658). But although he relies less now on supernature than on his drawn sword to protect the Lady, in the fantasy world of *A Mask* it is only the Brother's arithmetic that turns out to have been exaggerated: his prayer for a good angel has been answered before its utterance—in the person of the attendant Spirit disguised as the shepherd Thyrsis. After assorted complications (designed primarily to enhance the impact of the poem as spectacle) the Lady is duly rescued, safe, sound, and quite virginal. By way of conclusion the attendant Spirit *"Epiloguizes,"* sententiously and magically, in propria persona:

> But now my task is smoothly done,
> I can fly, or I can run
> Quickly to the green earth's end,
> Where the bow'd welkin slow doth bend,
> And from thence can soar as soon
> To the corners of the Moon.
> (1012–17)

Consistent with the decorum of its genre, *A Mask* thus emphasizes the frankly contrived supernaturalism of its plot. Such is the firmly persuasive power of virtue in Milton's transcendental allegory that chastity can cause earthquakes (793–99), traverse the skies, and even summon God down to earth:

> Mortals that would follow me,
> Love virtue, she alone is free,
> She can teach ye how to climb
> Higher than the Sphery chime;
> Or if Virtue feeble were,
> Heav'n itself would stoop to her.
> (1018–23)

In his anxiety to certify virtue's ability to venture Neoplatonistically beyond the primum mobile, the attendant Spirit speaks of celestial descent only hypothetically (for "Virtue" most emphatically is *not* "feeble"), but his apodosis may be taken indicatively and unconditionally, for the Spirit's own role in *A Mask* has been literally to stoop from Heaven in Heaven's stead virtue to defend.

The author of *Paradise Lost* knew, on the other hand, that in our world such *dei ex machina* as the attendant Spirit are hard to come by:

that is why in his diffuse epic Milton reserves the notion of angelic descent for a time (*in illo tempore*) and a place (the fresh woods and pastures new of Paradise) in which such literal visitations might appear plausible. At the same time he immeasurably complicates the matter (compared to his practice in *A Mask*) by availing himself of certain motivational distinctions that he may have discovered in Virgil. Although Mercury descends in the 4th *Aeneid* ostensibly to hasten Aeneas's departure from Carthage, Virgil is also concerned with the god's role as *psychopompous*—guide to the underworld—a role that Hermes fulfills (for example) in the 24th *Odyssey*. As Thomas Greene has pointed out, "The chthonic associations of Mercury's staff [in the *Aeneid*] anticipate . . . the literal death of Dido, a death which his descent is to bring about. Mercury's mission is *actually* to send a soul to the Lower World."[72] We have seen that just this sort of distinction between apparent and actual motives is needed to come to terms with the mission of Raphael in *Paradise Lost:* allegedly conceived in pity but apparently executed in legalistic self-righteousness, the angel's descent turns out *in the event* actually to have been a restorative work of merciful supererogation. In *Samson Agonistes* such motivational bifurcation is still more pronounced: in the event (and only then) Samson's marriage to the Woman of Timna is seen to have been designed by a loving God less to slaughter Philistines than to hasten the hero's regeneration—even if to his dying day Samson never comprehends this truth. But then why *should* the Danite perfectly fathom God's "uncontrollable intent" (1754)? Like everyone else in the play, he frequently utters misspoken prophecies and essays erroneous projections of the divine will. To know more about why God urged him to marry the Timnite obviously does not concern Samson (since he no further knows); nor, more importantly, would such knowledge alter his known offense.

Samson Agonistes of course returns us to the fallen world of *A Mask;* moreover, it is generically a tragedy, and if we may believe the prefatory epistle, its author will have taken care in the "disposition of the fable" to observe standards of "verisimilitude and decorum," standards derived presumably from the Greek "Tragic Poets, the best rule to all who endeavor to write Tragedy." We can expect Milton assiduously to have avoided any overt use of the celestial descent motif in his play, for it is probable that he shared Aristotle's reservations about the appropriateness in tragedy of such a contrivance:

> it is obvious that the unravelling of the plot should arise from the circumstances of the plot itself, and not be brought about *ex machina*

---

72. *Descent from Heaven*, 82 (emphasis mine).

. . . . The *deus ex machina* should be used only for matters outside the play proper, either for things that happened before it and cannot be known by the human characters, or for things that are yet to come and that require to be foretold prophetically—for we allow to the gods the power to see all things. However, there should be nothing inexplicable about what happens. (*Poetics* 15)

In *Samson Agonistes* Milton is even more cautious than Aristotle about the *deus ex machina:* although God is everywhere present in the plot machinery, he and his providential instruments come and go on viewless wings; any and all miraculous celestial descents occur strictly offstage and are relegated to the distant past (23–29, 361). The poet is so concerned with exorcising the magical from his version of the Samson saga that he even demystifies the hero's hair, insisting that Samson's Herculean strength is circumfused throughout his body rather than somehow—God knows how—resident in his ample locks (1140–44).

But it is with regard to the Woman of Timna that Milton most skillfully makes a virtue of the verisimilitude enjoined upon him by the Aristotelian norms of tragic action. On the one hand, the regeneration of fallen Samson *must* proceed as a consequence of prevenient grace descending—Milton's theology demands as much. But on the other hand, there can be no Raphael to descend *ex machina* in violation of tragic decorum. As Irene Samuel has said (albeit to quite different effect), "Milton's is so distinctively the ethic of the will and reason freely choosing that a *deus ex machina* resolution of plot would be repugnant to him on theological and moral no less than on artistic grounds."[73] I quite agree. Samson must oft be warned of his sinful state by ordinary human means—so the extraordinary genius of Milton hits upon the quiet expedient of the Woman of Timna. Whereas a late redactor of Judges, embarrassed by the frankly sexual motivation of Samson's gentile marriage, added verse 14:4 (as a corrective scholium) to the preformed units between which it appears in the received text,[74] Milton goes the redactor one step better: in *Samson Agonistes* the Timnite becomes the indispensable *femina ex machina* when, in a master stroke of poetic compression, the poet calls upon her to do for Samson precisely what Raphael has done for Adam and Eve. In this way he can orchestrate the resolution of his tragedy's plot complications by relying on divine intervention (for only God can soften Samson's stony heart), but without forfeiting a scintilla of human probability (for there is no God but only a mere woman in the visible renovative machinery).

73. *"Samson Agonistes* as Tragedy," 242.
74. See *The Anchor Bible: Judges,* introduction, translation, and commentary by Robert G. Boling, 229–30 (n. 4).

Moreover, the substitution of the Woman of Timna for Raphael has the additional convenience of anticipating Milton's kenotic Christology. The following parody of a stanza from *Ode on the Morning of Christ's Nativity* may serve to illustrate the point:

> That glorious Form, that angel affable,
> And that far-beaming blaze of Majesty,
> Wherewith God planned at Heav'n's high Council-Table,
> To help our father admit sin's gravity,
> He laid aside; and Samson thus to free,
> Forsook to call on Raphael that Day,
> But choose instead a Timnite bride, though made of
>   mortal Clay.

The decision to substitute the Woman of Timna for Raphael is as much Milton's as it is God's, of course; and how felicitously our poet has chosen! Mary Ann Radzinowicz has noted that in *Samson Agonistes* (and, I would add, in *Paradise Lost* as well) "predestination is adjusted to liberty so that from the human point of view it will always appear that God improvises after the event."[75] The Timnite episode seems to be such an improvisation, for Milton's God *appears* to have sent the Woman of Timna for the stated purpose of harrying Philistines and only post hoc—after Samson has succumbed to Dalila—to have devised a second strategy wherein she hastens Samson's regeneration by convicting him of sin. In reality, however, the whole scenario has been part of that predestination by which, thanks to his prescience, a loving God can providentially arrange for his creatures' regeneration before they have sinned.

In the prefatory epistle to *Samson Agonistes* Milton observes that "Tragedy, as it was anciently compos'd, hath ever been held the gravest, moralest, and most profitable of all other poems." Doubtless he has in mind chapter 26 of the *Poetics*, in which Aristotle compares epic and tragedy in order to document the aesthetic superiority of the latter:

> Tragedy has everything that epic has. . . . Moreover, this form of imitation achieves its ends in shorter compass, and what is more compact gives more pleasure than what is extended over a long period. . . . Then there is less unity in the imitation of the epic poets, as is shown by the fact that any one work of this kind contains matter for several tragedies. . . . If, therefore, tragedy is superior to epic in all these respects, and also in fulfilling its artistic function, . . . then obviously, in achieving its ends better than epic, it must be the better form of art.

Although I hesitate to impose Aristotle's evaluative categories upon

75. *Toward "Samson Agonistes,"* 47.

Milton's poetry—for as I have argued, *Paradise Lost* is an epic with a tragic center, and as I have implied, *Samson Agonistes* extends the boundaries of tragedy into epic—still I am tempted to conclude, from the solid intricacy packed into its Timnite episode, that Milton's closet drama outdoes even his Old Testament epic in the matter of poetic excellence. At the very least, the tragedy climaxes and concludes the poet's lifelong preoccupation with making the Bible consistent with his profoundly rational theodicial concern to justify the ways of God to men.

Conclusion

Throughout this study I have sought to articulate two related themes central to the major poetry of John Milton: (1) his demonstration that Scripture is insufficient unto itself, and (2) the corollary hypothesis that he is the first great feminist in Western culture. Both issues seem to me to have been misunderstood or underestimated by many of the poet's commentators.

As to the first of them, the privileged position conferred on the Bible by those who subscribe to its literal inerrancy comprises, I believe, an insuperable obstacle to a just assessment of Milton's sometimes radical adjustments of the received text. A recent collection of apposite critical essays, *Milton and Scriptural Tradition: The Bible into Poetry*, illustrates how uncritical acquiescence to the authority of Scripture can impoverish one's approach both to it and to the reconstructive work of the blind bard. James H. Sims, coeditor of the collection, prefaces its nine essays by proposing that their authors share, at least implicitly,

> an understanding of "scriptural tradition" very much like Milton's own: "scriptural" excludes the apocryphal, the noncanonical, and "tradition" is limited to the interrelationships and literal meanings of the texts that comprise Scripture and to what can be reasonably inferred from those texts, taking into account the principle of the analogy of faith—that is, treating the Bible as one inspired book without internal contradictions, and, therefore, interpreting particular passages in the light of the clear tenor of the whole of scriptural teaching.[1]

To his credit, Sims is reluctant to straitjacket either Milton or his commentators "within such a narrow definition" (p. vii); and if one were to delete the phrase *without internal contradictions* from this editor's description of "scriptural tradition," the poet himself might find it compatible with his programmatic recasting of Genesis 1–3, I Timothy 2:11–15, and Judges 13–16. But if we may judge what Sims (and his coeditor, Leland Ryken) mean by "scriptural tradition" *operationally*, in

---

1. Preface, in James H. Sims and Leland Ryken, eds., *Milton and Scriptural Tradition: The Bible into Poetry*, vii.

terms of the essays comprising the volume, the tentativeness of the contributors' several approaches implies that, whether or not they agree in principle with the editors' exegetical conservatism, they have in fact (with respect to their contributions to *Milton and Scriptural Tradition* at any rate) found it possible to live comfortably with a Milton who "treat[s] the Bible as one inspired book without internal contradiction."

I do not, however, begrudge Sims, Ryken, and others their emphatically reductive point of view: a minimalist esthetic that produces impoverished readings of Milton and his sources has, after all, the negative virtue of avoiding the opposite extreme of misreading him as among the last and most vocal of Judeo-Christian misogynists. Far more damaging to the integrity of Milton's life and work are interpretations that persist, *whether intentionally or not*, in aligning the poet with an uninterrupted continuum of bigoted institutional male dominance extending, it is argued, from premonarchical Israel through seventeenth-century England and beyond.

I am less troubled than perhaps I should be by the strident denunciations of such militant anti-Miltonists as Katherine M. Rogers,[2] Marcia Landy[3] (who has been compellingly answered by Barbara K. Lewalski),[4] and Sandra Gilbert[5] (whose readings of *Paradise Lost* have been rebutted in a discriminating critique by Joan Malory Webber).[6] Critics such as these argue from clearly stated exegetical assumptions: their opposition to Milton is an open and answerable apparition. But how is one to approach the more formidable task of defending the blind bard's egalitarian gender ethic from those who inadvertently undermine it in the very act of trying to articulate it?

The question, as I hope to have demonstrated, is far from a quibble. It seems to me both striking and suggestive that the following female friends of Milton have, thanks to their under- or overestimation of prelapsarian Eve's innocence, added a certain plausibility to the charge that the poet is a misogynist: Diana Benet, Joan Bennett, Georgia Christopher, Cheryl Fresch, Diane McColley, Maureen Quilligan, and Stella Revard.[7] The work of these scholars, with its considerable

2. *The Troublesome Helpmate: A History of Misogyny in Literature,* passim; discussed above, Chapter Two.

3. "Kinship and the Role of Women in *Paradise Lost.*"

4. "Milton on Women—Yet Once More." (Landy responded to Lewalski's response in " 'A Free and Open Encounter': Milton and the Modern Reader.")

5. "Patriarchal Poetry and Woman Readers: Reflections on Milton's Bogey"; discussed above, Chapter Two.

6. "The Politics of Poetry: Feminism and *Paradise Lost.*"

7. Benet, "Abdiel and the Son in the Separation Scene," 130, 132–33; Bennett, " 'Go': Milton's Antinomianism and the Separation Scene in *Paradise Lost,* Book 9," 398–99; Christopher, *Milton and the Science of the Saints,* 151–59; Fresch, "Milton's Eve and the Problem of the Additions to the Command"; McColley, *Milton's Eve,* passim;

strengths and its sometimes damaging theodicial imprecisions, is recapitulated and indeed climaxed by the recent publications of Mary Nyquist, especially her essay "Reading the Fall: Discourse and Drama in *Paradise Lost*."

This often-admirable study is both traditional (it cites Calvin and Luther, among other Reformation exegetes, to situate *Paradise Lost* 9 as an essentially Protestant rendering of the fall as occurring in a number of well-defined dramatic stages) and innovative (it deploys distinctions, both intra- and intertextually, derived from such contemporary narratologists as Gerard Genette). But for all its elegance, the essay reasserts (whether intentionally or not I cannot say) the misogynistic anteriorizing of Eve's transgression espoused by Saint Augustine, Thomas Aquinas, Thomas Browne, and others. The first woman's lapse is said to occur in "causally related stages." Notwithstanding Milton's emphatic "yet sinless" (*PL* 9.659), a remark designed, as I have suggested,[8] to exonerate Eve with respect to her alleged softening of the biblical prohibition with the subjunctive "lest ye die" (663), Nyquist asserts that "readers . . . are to see that Eve's defense of the command is not as fervent or courageous as it should be"; it therefore marks "the first stage of her fall." Other (culpable) links include her "inwardly assenting to the tempter's lies," a charge reminiscent of Aquinas's misogynistic opinion that the unfallen intellect is incapable of being deceived; "her experience of desire for the forbidden fruit," which is, however, to confuse prelapsarian sinless deliberation with postlapsarian sinful choice; and her allegedly culpable soliloquy (9.745–79), which Nyquist matter-of-factly interprets as designed by Milton "simply" to inform us that "in the silent interim between her last speech [659–63] and it, *Eve has beyond doubt fallen*."[9]

The persistence of this and similar opinions, rooted in the institutional misogyny of I Timothy 2:11–15, in the work of some of Milton's most sophisticated and sympathetic contemporary critics adds, I hope, a certain relevance to the sort of exegesis I have been essaying. Whatever the limitations imposed on Milton by his sex and by the circumstances of his cultural milieu, the poet is clearly not a misogynist, and interpretations to the contrary should be assiduously eschewed. Only by doing so can we hope, in the legitimately urgent present climate of feminist revisionism, to move on to the more compelling question of whether the bold rewriting of the Bible that preoccupied Milton should in fact be countenanced at all. This man set

Quilligan, *Milton's Spenser: The Politics of Reading*, 228; and Revard, "Eve and the Doctrine of Responsibility in *Paradise Lost*," 76. All are discussed above in Chapter Two.

8. See pp. 76–84, 93–96.
9. "Reading the Fall," 216–18, 221.

about to rehabilitate Scripture by repudiating its misogynistic spirit even as he preserved its very letter ("The woman *was* deceived and became a transgressor"): but might he not have served culture better—served *us* better at any rate—by essaying a revisionist critique without its rehabilitative counterpart? I have no answer for this question, but the relevance of Milton's efforts to the gender-related cultural transformations presently underway in the West (the stake, roughly, of what E. D. Hirsch, Jr., calls *significance*) cannot be adjudicated until the fact of his major poems' sexual egalitarianism (the stake, roughly, of what Hirsch calls *meaning*)[10] is accepted by the interpretive community at large.

It has been the burden of the present argument to promote such acceptance.

10. *The Aims of Interpretation*, 1–16.

Works Cited

Allen, Don Cameron. "The Idea as Pattern: Despair and *Samson Ago-nistes*." Chap. 4 in *The Harmonious Vision: Studies in Milton's Poetry*. Baltimore: Johns Hopkins University Press, 1970.

Alter, Robert. *The Art of Biblical Narrative*. New York: Basic Books, 1981.

Anchor Bible, The. Genesis: Introduction, Translation and Notes. Translated by E. A. Speiser. Garden City, N.Y.: Doubleday, 1964.

———. *Judges*. Translated by Robert G. Boling. Garden City, N.Y.: Doubleday, 1975.

Ancient Near Eastern Texts Relating to the Old Testament. Edited by James B. Pritchard. Princeton: Princeton University Press, 1969.

Aquinas, Thomas. *Summa Theologica*. 60 vols. Translated by the Fathers of the English Dominican Province. New York: Blackfriars, 1964.

———. *Summa Theologica*. In *The "Summa Theologica" of St. Thomas Aquinas, Second Part of the Second Part, QQ. CXLI-CLXX*. New York: Benziger Brothers, 1921.

Aristotle. *Physics*. Translated by R. P. Hardie and R. K. Gaye. In *The Basic Works of Aristotle*, edited by Richard McKeon. New York: Random House, 1941.

———. *Poetics*. In *Aristotle, Horace, Longinus: Classical Literary Criticism*, translated by T. S. Dorsch. New York: Viking Penguin, 1965.

Augustine, Saint. *The City of God*. Translated by Marcus Dods. In *Great Books of the Western World*, general editor Robert M. Hutchins. Chicago: University of Chicago Press, 1971.

Barker, Arthur E. "Calm Regained through Passion Spent: The Con-clusions of the Miltonic Effort." In *The Prison and the Pinnacle*, edited by Balachandra Rajan, 3–48. Toronto: University of Toronto Press, 1973.

———. "*Paradise Lost*: The Relevance of Regeneration." In *"Paradise Lost": A Tercentenary Tribute*, edited by Balachandra Rajan, 48–78. Toronto: University of Toronto Press, 1969.

———. "Structural and Doctrinal Pattern in Milton's Later Poems." In *Essays in English Literature from the Renaissance to the Victorian Age Pre-*

sented to A. S. P. Woodhouse, edited by Millar MacLure and Frank W. Watt, 169–94. Toronto: University of Toronto Press, 1964.

Benet, Diana. "Abdiel and the Son in the Separation Scene." *Milton Studies* 18 (1983): 129–43.

Bennett, Joan S. " 'Go': Milton's Antinomianism and the Separation Scene in *Paradise Lost,* Book 9." *PMLA* 98 (1983): 388–404.

———. "Liberty Under the Law: The Chorus and the Meaning of *Samson Agonistes.*" *Milton Studies* 12 (1978): 141–63.

Berry, Boyd M. *Process of Speech: Puritan Religious Writing and "Paradise Lost."* Baltimore: Johns Hopkins University Press, 1976.

Blenkinsopp, J. "Structure and Style in Judges 13–16." *Journal of Biblical Literature* 82 (1963): 65–76.

Blessington, Francis C. *"Paradise Lost" and the Classical Epic.* London: Routledge & Kegan Paul, 1979.

Bloom, Harold. *A Map of Misreading.* New York: Oxford University Press, 1975.

Browne, Sir Thomas. *Pseudodoxia Epidemica.* In *The Works of Sir Thomas Browne,* edited by Geoffrey Keynes. 4 vols. Chicago: University of Chicago Press, 1964.

Burden, Dennis. *The Logical Epic: A Study of the Argument of "Paradise Lost."* Cambridge: Harvard University Press, 1967.

Calvin, John. *Commentaries upon Genesis.* Translated by J. King. Edinburgh: Calvin Translation Society, 1845.

Carey, John. Introduction to *Samson Agonistes.* In *The Poems of John Milton,* edited by John Carey and Alastair Fowler. London: Longman Group Limited, 1971.

Chambers, A. B. "The Falls of Adam and Eve in *Paradise Lost.*" In *New Essays on "Paradise Lost,"* edited by Thomas Kranidas, 118–30. Berkeley: University of California Press, 1971.

Christopher, Georgia B. "Adam and Eve in *Paradise Lost.*" *PMLA* 91 (1976): 115–17.

———. "Homeopathic Physic and Natural Renovation in *Samson Agonistes.*" *ELH* 37 (1970): 361–73.

———. *Milton and the Science of the Saints.* Princeton: Princeton University Press, 1982.

———. "The Verbal Gate to Paradise: Adam's 'Literary Experience' in Book X of *Paradise Lost.*" *PMLA* 90 (1975): 69–77.

Chrysostom, John. *Homily on Timothy,* xi. In *Homilies on the Epistles of Paul.* Oxford: John Henry Parker, 1843.

Comestor, Peter. *Historia Scholastica.* In *Patrologiae cursus completus . . . Series Latina,* edited by J.-P. Migne. 221 vols. Paris: Garnier, 1844–1864.

Crosman, Robert. *Reading "Paradise Lost."* Bloomington: Indiana University Press, 1980.

Daniels, E. F. "Milton's Fallen Angels—Self Corrupted or Seduced." *Notes and Queries* 205 (1960): 447–50.

Danielson, Dennis. *Milton's Good God: A Study in Literary Theodicy.* Cambridge: Cambridge University Press, 1982.

Dante Alighieri. *Paradiso.* Vol. 3 of *The Divine Comedy.* Translated by Mark Musa. New York: Viking Penguin, 1986.

Diekhoff, John. "Eve, the Devil, and *Areopagitica.*" *Modern Language Quarterly* 5 (1944): 429–34.

———. *Milton's "Paradise Lost": A Commentary on the Argument.* London: Routledge & Kegan Paul, 1946.

DiSalvo, Jackie. " 'The Lord's Battells': *Samson Agonistes* and the Puritan Revolution." *Milton Studies* 4 (1972): 39–62.

Donne, John. *The Complete Poetry of John Donne.* Edited by John T. Shawcross. Garden City, N.Y.: Doubleday Anchor, 1967.

———. "The Sunne Rising." In *Donne: Poetical Works,* edited by Herbert J. C. Grierson. 1929. Rpt. Oxford: Oxford University Press, 1971.

———. *The Sermons of John Donne.* 10 vols. Edited by George R. Potter and Evelyn M. Simpson. Berkeley: University of California Press, 1955.

Evans, J. M. *"Paradise Lost" and the Genesis Tradition.* Oxford: Clarendon Press, 1968.

Fish, Stanley E. "Question and Answer in *Samson Agonistes.*" *The Critical Quarterly* 11 (1969): 237–64.

———. *Surprised by Sin: The Reader in "Paradise Lost."* London: Macmillan & Co., 1967.

Fletcher, Harris F. *The Use of the Bible in Milton's Prose.* Urbana: University of Illinois Press, 1929.

Fresch, Cheryl. "Milton's Eve and the Problem of the Additions to the Command." *Milton Quarterly* 12 (1978): 83–90.

Frye, Roland M. *Milton's Imagery and the Visual Arts: Iconographic Tradition in the Epic Poems.* Princeton: Princeton University Press, 1978.

Gagen, Jean. "Adam, the Serpent, and Satan: Recognition and Restoration." *Milton Quarterly* 17 (1983): 116–21.

Gallagher, Philip J. "Beyond the Oedipus Complex." *Milton Quarterly* 18 (1984): 84–92.

———. "Creation in Genesis and in *Paradise Lost.*" *Milton Studies* 20 (1984): 163–204.

———. "Milton's Bogey." *PMLA* 94 (1979): 319–21.

———. "More Theirs by Being His: Teaching Milton to Undergraduates." *Milton Quarterly* 11 (1977): 4–9.

————. "On Reading Joseph Wittreich: A Review Essay." *Milton Quarterly* 21 (1987): 108–13.

————. "*Paradise Lost* and the Greek Theogony." *English Literary Renaissance* 9 (1979): 121–48.

————. " 'Real or Allegoric': The Ontology of Sin and Death in *Paradise Lost*." *English Literary Renaissance* 6 (1976): 317–35.

————. Review of Timothy J. O'Keeffe, *Milton and the Pauline Tradition*. In *Milton Quarterly* 16 (1982): 99–101.

————. "The Role of Raphael in *Samson Agonistes*." *Milton Studies* 18 (1983): 255–94.

————. "*Summa contra Pastorem et Lectorem*." *Milton Quarterly* 19 (1985): 53–60.

Gilbert, Allan H. *On the Composition of "Paradise Lost": A Study of the Ordering and Insertion of Material*. Chapel Hill: University of North Carolina Press, 1947.

Gilbert, Sandra. "Patriarchal Poetry and Women Readers: Reflections on Milton's Bogey." *PMLA* 93 (1978): 368–82.

Greene, Thomas. *The Descent from Heaven: A Study in Epic Continuity*. New Haven: Yale University Press, 1963.

Guillory, John. *Poetic Authority: Spenser, Milton, and Literary History*. New York: Columbia University Press, 1983.

Hamlet, Desmond. *One Greater Man: Justice and Damnation in "Paradise Lost*." Lewisburg, Pa.: Bucknell University Press, 1976.

Häublein, Ernst. "Milton's Paraphrase of Genesis: A Stylistic Reading of *Paradise Lost*, Book VII." *Milton Studies* 7 (1975): 101–25.

Herbert, George. "Sinnes round." In *The Works of George Herbert*, edited by F. E. Hutchinson. 1941. Rpt. Oxford: Clarendon Press, 1972.

Hesiod. *Hesiod: "Theogony*." Edited by M. L. West. Oxford: Oxford University Press, 1966.

————. *Theogony*. In *Hesiod*, translated by Richmond Lattimore, 119–86. Ann Arbor: University of Michigan Press, 1959.

————. *The Works and Days*. In *Hesiod*, translated by Richmond Lattimore, 15–117. Ann Arbor: University of Michigan Press, 1959.

Hill, John S. "Vocation and Spiritual Renovation in *Samson Agonistes*." *Milton Studies* 2 (1970): 149–74.

Hirsch, E. D., Jr. *The Aims of Interpretation*. Chicago: University of Chicago Press, 1976.

Hobbes, Thomas. *Of Liberty and Necessity*. London, 1654.

Hodge, A. A. *A Commentary on the Confession of Faith*. Philadelphia: Presbyterian Board of Publication, 1913.

Homer. *Odyssey*. Translated by Albert Cook. New York: W. W. Norton, 1967.

Hyman, Lawrence W. "The 'true experience' of *Samson Agonistes*." *Milton Quarterly* 13 (1979): 90–95.

Interpreter's Bible, The. 12 vols. Edited by George Arthur Buttrick et al. New York: Abingdon-Cokesbury Press, 1951–1957.

Jackson, Thomas. *A Treatise on the Primeval Estate of the First Man.* In *Works.* 12 vols. Oxford: Oxford University Press, 1844.

Kerrigan, William. *The Prophetic Milton.* Charlottesville: University of Virginia Press, 1974.

———. *The Sacred Complex: On the Psychogenesis of "Paradise Lost."* Cambridge: Harvard University Press, 1983.

Krouse, F. Michael. *Milton's Samson and the Christian Tradition.* Princeton: Princeton University Press, 1949.

Labriola, Albert C. "Divine Urgency as a Motive for Conduct in *Samson Agonistes*." *Philological Quarterly* 50 (1971): 99–107.

———. " 'Thy Humiliation Shall Exalt': The Christology of *Paradise Lost*." *Milton Studies* 15 (1981): 29–42.

Landy, Marcia. " 'A Free and Open Encounter': Milton and the Modern Reader." *Milton Studies* 9 (1976): 3–36.

———. "Kinship and the Role of Women in *Paradise Lost*." *Milton Studies* 4 (1972): 3–18.

Lawrence, Henry. *An History of Angells.* London, 1650.

Lawry, Jon S. *The Shadow of Heaven: Matter and Stance in Milton's Poetry.* Ithaca, N.Y.: Cornell University Press, 1968.

Lewalski, Barbara. "Milton on Women—Yet Once More." *Milton Studies* 6 (1974): 3–20.

Lewis, C. S. *A Preface to "Paradise Lost."* New York: Oxford University Press, 1961.

Lieb, Michael. "*Paradise Lost* and the Myth of Prohibition." *Milton Studies* 7 (1975): 233–65.

Lloyd-Jones, Hugh. *The Justice of Zeus.* Berkeley: University of California Press, 1971.

Low, Anthony. *The Blaze of Noon: A Reading of "Samson Agonistes."* New York: Columbia University Press, 1974.

Marvell, Andrew. "Upon the Hill and Grove at Bill-borow." In *The Poems and Letters of Andrew Marvell,* 3d ed. Edited by H. M. Margoliouth. Oxford: Clarendon Press, 1971.

McColley, Diane Kelsey. *Milton's Eve.* Urbana: University of Illinois Press, 1983.

Milton, John. *The Complete Prose Works of John Milton.* 8 vols. General editor, Don M. Wolfe. New Haven: Yale University Press, 1953–1982.

———. *John Milton: Complete Poems and Major Prose.* Edited by Merritt Y. Hughes. New York: Odyssey Press, 1957.

———. *John Milton: "Paradise Lost."* Edited by Alastair Fowler. London: Longman Group Limited, 1971.

———. *The Poems of John Milton.* Edited by John Carey and Alastair Fowler. London: Longman Group Limited, 1971.

Nyquist, Mary. "Reading the Fall: Discourse and Drama in *Paradise Lost.*" *English Literary Renaissance* 14 (1984): 199–229.

Perkins, William. *The Whole Treatise on the Cases of Conscience.* In *Workes,* translated by Thomas Pickering. Cambridge, 1618.

———. *Two Treatises.* Cambridge, 1597.

Pierce, Thomas. *The Divine Philanthropie Defended.* 2d series. London, 1657.

Quilligan, Maureen. *Milton's Spenser: The Politics of Reading.* Ithaca, N.Y.: Cornell University Press, 1983.

Radzinowicz, Mary Ann. *Toward "Samson Agonistes": The Growth of Milton's Mind.* Princeton: Princeton University Press, 1978.

Rajan, Balachandra. " 'To Which Is Added *Samson Agonistes*—.' " In *The Prison and the Pinnacle,* edited by Balachandra Rajan, 82–110. Toronto: University of Toronto Press, 1973.

Reichert, John. "Against His Better Knowledge: A Case for Adam." *ELH* 48 (1981): 83–109.

Revard, Stella P. "Eve and the Doctrine of Responsibility in *Paradise Lost.*" *PMLA* 88 (1973): 69–78.

Reynolds, Henry. *Mythomystes.* 1632? Rpt. in Edward Tayler, editor. *Literary Criticism of Seventeenth-Century England.* New York: Knopf, 1967.

Rogers, Katherine M. *The Troublesome Helpmate: A History of Misogyny in Literature.* Seattle: University of Washington Press, 1966.

Said, Edward. *Beginnings: Intention and Method.* New York: Basic Books, 1975.

Samuel, Irene. "*Paradise Lost* as Mimesis." In *Approaches to "Paradise Lost,"* edited by C. A. Patrides, 15–29. Toronto: University of Toronto Press, 1968.

———. "The Regaining of Paradise." In *The Prison and the Pinnacle,* edited by Balachandra Rajan, 111–34. Toronto: University of Toronto Press, 1973.

———. "*Samson Agonistes* as Tragedy." In *Calm of Mind: Tercentenary Essays on "Paradise Regained" and "Samson Agonistes" in Honor of John S. Diekhoff,* edited by Joseph Anthony Wittreich, Jr., 235–57. Cleveland: Case Western Reserve Press, 1971.

Seigel, Catharine F. "The Reconciliation in Book X of *Paradise Lost.*" *Modern Language Review* 68 (1973): 260–63.

Sherry, Beverley. "Not by Bread Alone: The Communication of Adam and Raphael." *Milton Quarterly* 13 (1979): 111–14.

Sims, James H. *The Bible in Milton's Epics.* Gainesville: University of Florida Press, 1962.

Sims, James H., and Leland Ryken, eds. *Milton and Scriptural Tradition: The Bible into Poetry.* Columbia: University of Missouri Press, 1984.

Sirluck, Ernest. "Milton Revises the *Faerie Queene.*" *Modern Philology* 48 (1950): 90–96.

Slights, Camille. *The Casuistical Tradition in Shakespeare, Donne, Herbert, and Milton.* Princeton: Princeton University Press, 1981.

———. "A Hero of Conscience: *Samson Agonistes* and Casuistry." *PMLA* 90 (1975): 395–413.

Sophocles. *Oedipus Tyrannos.* Translated and edited by Luci Berkowitz and Theodore F. Brunner. New York: W. W. Norton, 1970.

Speiser, E. A. See *Anchor Bible.*

Spenser, Edmund. *The Faerie Queene.* In *Spenser: Poetical Works,* edited by J. C. Smith and E. De Selincourt. 1912. Rpt. London: Oxford University Press, 1965.

Steadman, John M. " 'Faithful Champion': The Theological Basis of Milton's Hero of Faith." *Anglia* 77 (1959): 12–28.

Stein, Arnold. *Heroic Knowledge.* Minneapolis: University of Minnesota Press, 1957.

Stollman, Samuel S. "Milton's Dichotomy of 'Judaism' and 'Hebraism.' " *PMLA* 89 (1974): 105–12.

———. "Milton's Samson and the Jewish Tradition." *Milton Studies* 3 (1971): 185–200.

Summers, Joseph. *The Muse's Method: An Introduction to "Paradise Lost."* 1962. Rpt. New York: W. W. Norton, 1968.

Svendson, Kester. *Milton and Science.* Cambridge: Harvard University Press, 1957.

Tayler, Edward. "Milton's *Samson:* The Form of a Christian Tragedy." *English Literary Renaissance* 3 (1973): 306–21.

Tertullian. *On the Apparel of Women.* In vol. 4 of *The Ante-Nicene Fathers: Translations of the Writings of the Fathers down to A.D. 325,* edited by Alexander Roberts and James Donaldson. Buffalo, 1884–1886.

Ulreich, John C., Jr. " 'This Great Deliverer': *Samson Agonistes* as Parable." *Milton Quarterly* 13 (1979): 79–84.

Webber, Joan Malory. "The Politics of Poetry: Feminism and *Paradise Lost.*" *Milton Studies* 14 (1980): 3–24.

West, M. L. See *Hesiod: "Theogony."*

Whiting, George W. "*Samson Agonistes* and the Geneva Bible." Chap. 7 in *Milton and This Pendant World.* Austin: University of Texas Press, 1958.

Willey, Basil. *The Seventeenth Century Background.* 1934. Rpt. Garden City, N.Y.: Doubleday, 1953.

Williams, Arnold. *The Common Expositor: An Account of the Commentaries on Genesis, 1527–1633.* Chapel Hill: University of North Carolina Press, 1948.

Wittreich, Joseph Anthony, Jr. *Interpreting Samson Agonistes.* Princeton: Princeton University Press, 1986.

————. *Visionary Poetics: Milton's Tradition and His Legacy.* San Marino, Calif.: Huntington Library, 1979.

Yates, John. *A Modell of Divinitie, Catechistically Composed.* London, 1623.

Index

Abdiel, 64–66, 87–93, 117; deceived, 91; defiance paradigm of sinless temptation, 55; exposes deceit, 117; not deceived, 64

Adam: compared to Samson, 134–35, 159–62, 164; created first, 14; falls undeceived, 68, 96–100, 120; greater transgressor, 100–124; misogyny of, 127, 148–49; naming, 35, 37–40; penitent, 124, 127–28; redemption of, 125–30, 148; self-deception of, 99–100, 107, 126–27, 148–49; uxoriousness of, 72, 98, 100, 122

Adam and Eve: reconciliation of, 125–30; separation scene, 62–74, 107

Agrippa, Henricus Cornelius, 100

Alcuin, 111

Alter, Robert, 34–35, 38, 48

Aquinas, St. Thomas, 7, 74–76, 78–79, 81, 83, 89, 90, 106–10, 113–14, 116, 123, 129, 173; on Adam's sin, 113; on Eve's sin, 78–79, 95, 106–7, 113–14; on Lucifer's fall, 89–90; on I Timothy, 106–7, 109

Aristotle, 53, 55, 144; in relation to *Samson Agonistes*, 134–35, 157, 163, 167–69

Augustine, St., 7, 72, 75–76, 78, 83–84, 103, 105–7, 109, 114, 118–19, 123–24, 129, 173; on Adam's sin, 102, 105; on Eve's sin, 60, 95; on I Timothy, 75, 102, 105–6, 119

Barker, Arthur E., 133, 140

Beelzebub, 87, 117

Belial, 4–6

Benet, Diana, 64, 172

Bennett, Joan S., 64, 172

Bible: 2 Corinthians 6:15, 4; 2 Cor. 11:13, 97; 2 Cor. 11:14, 52; Deuteronomy 4:2, 1; Deut. 6:16, 150; Ephesians 5:14, 3; Eph. 5:31–32, 41; Exodus 22:5 and 23:24, 152; Genesis 1–3, 6, 171–72; Gen. 1:1–5, 9–14; Gen. 1:11–13, 14–17; Gen. 1:14–19, 9–14; Gen. 1:20–25a, 14–17; Gen. 1:24–25, 17–26; Gen. 1:26–29, 26–33; Gen. 1:31–2:3, 44–46; Gen. 2:5–6, 14–17; Gen. 2:7–9a, 26–33; Gen. 2:15–17, 31–33; Gen. 2:16–17, 26–31; Gen. 2:18–25, 33–44; Gen. 2:19a, 14–17; Gen. 3:1a, 17–26; Gen. 3:4–5, 79; Gen. 3:6, 110; Gen. 3:12, 112; Gen. 3:13, 96, 111, 123; Gen. 3:14–15, 125–27; Gen. 3:17, 110–11; Gen. 3:22, 118; Gen. 19:1–11, 4; Hebrews 11:1–32, 152; James 1:15, 86; John 18:38, 81; Judges 13–16, 151, 153–56, 171–72; Judges 19:16–30, 4; Luke 12:47–48, 113; Matthew 5:28, 92; Numbers 6:1–21, 151; I Peter 5:8, 52; Proverbs 8:27, 11; Revelation 12:10–13, 141; Rev. 19:17, 53; Rev. 20:10, 3; Romans 5:12, 105, 118; I Samuel 2:12–25, 4; I Timothy 2:11–15, 7, 52, 74–75, 96–97, 100, 102, 105–7, 109, 113–16, 120–23, 126, 128–29, 171–73

Blenkinsopp, J.: on *Samson Agonistes*, 151–52

Blessington, Francis C.: on classical prototypes of celestial descent, 139–40

Browne, Sir Thomas, 7, 49–50, 55–61, 63, 79, 108, 111–12, 115–17, 129; on Adam's sin, 108–10, 112–13, 120; on Eve's sin, 50, 56–58, 78–80, 82, 100, 111–12, 116; misogyny of, 50, 56–58, 78, 83, 92, 109–14, 173; *Pseudodoxia Epidemica*, 49, 55, 111; on I Timothy 2:11–15, 109, 120

Burton, Robert, 52

Calvin, John, 7, 122, 124, 129, 143, 173; on the fall, 118–19; on I Timothy, 118–19

Carey, John: on unregenerate Samson, 136